THE PHOTOSHOP AND PAINTER ARTIST TABLET BOOK

Creative Techniques in Digital Painting

Using Wacom and the iPad

Cher Threinen-Pendarvis

Peachpit Press

The Photoshop and Painter Artist Tablet Book, Second Edition

Cher Threinen-Pendarvis
www.pendarvis-studios.com

Peachpit Press
www.peachpit.com

To report errors, please send a note to errata@peachpit.com

Peachpit Press is a division of Pearson Education.

Peachpit Press editor: Karyn Johnson
Cover design: Mimi Heft
Cover illustration: Cher Threinen-Pendarvis
Book design, art direction, and layout: Cher Threinen-Pendarvis
Technical Editor: Jennifer Lynn
Copyeditor: Jennifer Lynn
Proofreader: Linda Seifert
Indexer: Joy Dean Lee
Production and prepress manager: Jonathan Parker
Production editor: Tracey Croom

This book was set using the Minion and Helvetica families. It was written and composed in
Adobe InDesign CS3. Final output was computer to plate at Courier Kendallville, Kendallville, Indiana.

ISBN-13: 978-0-321-90335-8
ISBN-10:   0-321-90355-8

Printed and bound in the United States of America.

To our Creator,
from whom all inspiration comes.
To my husband, Steven,
for his friendship and love.
To my mother, Wanda, my father, Claude,
and my brother, Larry.
— Cher Threinen-Pendarvis

Acknowledgments

The Photoshop and Painter Artist Tablet Book, Second Edition would not have been possible without a great deal of help from some extraordinary people and sources. This book was in progress for a year—and it was a wonderful journey.

Heartfelt thanks go to my special friend and colleague Linnea Dayton, who brainstormed with me during the first edition book development process. My warmest thanks also go to my longtime artist friend Bert Monroy, for writing such a wonderful foreword for the book.

A special thank you goes to the talented designer John Odam, for his inspiration and friendship. John designed the clever sidebar icons and also gave helpful critiques of the early book cover designs. Warmest thanks go to my gifted photographer friend Melinda Holden for her beautiful photographs of my studio and location painting.

I'd like to thank my co-workers "behind the scenes" on The Photoshop and Painter Artist Tablet Book team. I'm grateful to Jennifer Lynn for her helpful technical reads and copy editing. Warmest thanks go to Linda Seifert for her detailed proofreading, Joy Dean Lee for her careful indexing, and production manager Jonathan Parker for his thorough production and prepress expertise.

Sincere thanks go to my friends and colleagues at Peachpit Press. The inspiration for this book came to me several years ago. A special thank you goes to Nancy Ruenzel for understanding my vision and for her support of the book. My warmest thanks go to Karyn Johnson for her advice through the development of the project and to the rest of the publishing team for their support. Thank you very much, Peachpit, for giving me the opportunity to write this book.

My special thank you goes to Ted Nace and Linnea Dayton for giving me the opportunity to publish my first book, The Painter Wow! Book, twenty years ago.

A big thank you goes to the wonderful folks at Wacom for their incredible pressure-sensitive tablets that help us artists unlock the creative power of Painter and Photoshop. Sincere thanks goes to Hope Hadduck for her support of the project and to Douglas Little and Don Varga for their support. Special thanks go to Darren Higgins for his stunning photographs of the Wacom tablet and pen that are shown in Chapter 3. A warm thank you also goes to the Wacom folks that I've enjoyed working alongside at the trade shows and conferences—Peter Deitrich, Weston Maggio, and the rest of the Wacom team.

My warmest thanks go to the brilliant creators of Painter—Mark Zimmer, Tom Hedges, and John Derry—for creating such an incredible program.

My sincere thank you goes to Stephen Bolt and Andy Church, the User Interface Designer and Product Manager for Painter, and to Tanya Lux, the Senior Product Marketing Manager, for their support. I'm also grateful to Project Manager Lee Genereau and the Painter development team: Christopher Tremblay, Vladmir Makarov, Caroline Suave, Pascal Becheiraz, Alex Piasko, Andrew Carmichael, Rina Fougere, Ruby Quesnel, Melanie Becker, and the rest of the team.

My special thanks go to the great people at Adobe—Tom and John Knoll, Mark Hamburg, Chris Cox, and to Jerry Harris (PixelPaint co-creator and creator of the Brush engine in Photoshop), and to the rest of the team for creating such an awesome program. Sincere thanks go to the other people at Adobe who were supportive of this book.

My warm thank you goes to Dan Steinhardt and all of the folks at Epson for their scanner and color printers that were helpful for testing printmaking techniques.

Thank you to all of our inspiring artist friends, colleagues, and family: Carol Benioff; Mary, Bob, and Brittany Envall; Ken and Robert Goldman; Rick and Joelle Geist; Drew and Susannah Bandish; David Lucas; Dr. Walter Munk and family; David Murline and family; Glenn and Heidi Hening; Glenn Sakamoto; Jamie Welsh Watson; Dirk and Maria Brandts; Bruce and Morgan Cowan; Jon, Rosa and Sydney Wegener; Michele Jacquin and Jim; Janine Reese Packett; Annie Wynhausen; Mark Snovell; Thomas Threinen and family; Linnea and Paul Dayton; Jack and Jill Davis; Bert Monroy and Zosia; Sharon Steuer and Jeff; Mark and Mary Zimmer; John, Pam, and Logan Derry; Chelsea Sammel and Peter; Kathy Hamon; Claude Szwimer; Jean-Luc Touillon; Lynda Weinman, Bruce, and Jaimie; Tanya Staples and Matt; Rick and Alice Champagne; Katrin Eismann and John; Pedro Meyer; Renata and Mario Spiazzi; Richard and Rita Cefalu; Mike and Susan Hickey; Valentine Ching Jr. and family; Jan Sunn Carrea and family; John Clark; Bud Scelsa; Larry and Michaelanne Gephart; Stevie, Betsy and Amber Lis; Jeff Ching; Tom and Jenny Wolverton; Eric and Amy Huffman; Marshall Myrman; Marcus and Lori Hale; Julie Roulette and Dane Perlee; Mike, Pam, April, and Kai Casey; and other friends and family. I love you all.

My sincere thank you goes to my inspiring art professors, Professor Daryl Groover, Dr. Paul Lingren, and Dr. Jean Swiggett. Thank you for encouraging my work.

My heartfelt thanks goes to our Pendarvis and Stanhope families for their support and love. Special thanks goes to our grand-nephew Brady and grand-niece Brooke who loaned me their colorful wooden trains so that I could use them for reference when painting *The Three Trains* illustration for Chapter 10. Warm thanks goes to our nieces Paige and Bryn, grand-niece Morgan and grand-nephew Jake, whose colorful artwork decorates our kitchen and brings us smiles. A warm acknowledgment goes to Jenna Klein and Armand Barolotti, two very talented young friends. You have a wonderful life ahead of you.

A heartfelt thank you to these special "co-workers:" to my husband, Steve, for his loving encouragement and patience; and to our cats, Sable and Marika, the close companions who keep me company in the studio. (Sable and Marika provided me with [sometimes] welcome interruptions that caused me to take breaks, by volleying their toy mouse onto my desk so we could play fetch.) Warmest thanks go to my brother Larry Stanhope, my aunt and uncle Natalie and John Stanhope, my cousins Cathy and Naomi, my sister-in-law Joy Young and dear friends Lisa Baker, Susan Bugbee, Elaine Chadwick, Skip Frye, Libby Goodman, Don Jolley, Linda King, Julie Klein, Elizabeth Meyer, Anna Trent Moore, Mary Mills, and Andrea Siedsma, who shared sincere encouragement and prayers. Thanks for checking in with me while I worked and for the fun lunch breaks that we shared in the water at our favorite surf spots.

Finally, I would like to thank all the other family, friends, and colleagues who have been so patient and understanding during the development of this book.

About the Author and Artist

Hand-working a digital print of Path to Water, North *using soft pastel*

An award-winning artist and author, Cher Threinen-Pendarvis has always worked with traditional art tools. A native Californian, her artwork is a reflection of the inspiring travels she has made with her family around the Pacific Rim—Hawaii, the Philippines, Japan, and China, to name a few. Her mother, Wanda, was also an artist, and their times of sitting together and drawing on location was especially inspiring to Cher as she developed her interest in plein-air painting. Painting on location has also brought her closer to her community in San Diego, where she has lived most of her life, because of her volunteer efforts to help protect the Sunset Cliffs Natural Park—a place she often paints.

A pioneer in digital art, Cher has created illustrations using the Macintosh computer for more than two decades. (Some of her early drawings with a mouse can be seen in the gallery at the back of the book.) She has been widely recognized for her mastery of Painter, Photoshop, and the Wacom pressure-sensitive tablet, and has used

Borrego, a traditional watercolor painted in plein air on Arches cold-pressed watercolor paper

Agaves on the Edge, Summer, painted using the Artists' Oils medium in Painter IX using location sketches for reference

these electronic tools since they were first released. Exercising her passion for Painter's artist tools, Cher has worked as a consultant and demo-artist for the developers of Painter. Her artwork has been exhibited worldwide, and her articles and art have been published in many books and periodicals. Cher holds a BFA with Highest Honors and Distinction in Art specializing in painting and printmaking, and she is a member of the San Diego Museum of Art Artist Guild and the Point Loma Artists Association. She has taught Painter and Photoshop workshops around the world, and is principal of the consulting firm Cher Threinen Design. Cher is author of all 10 editions of the highly-praised volume of techniques and inspiration, *The Painter Wow! Book*.

To learn more about Cher, please visit her Web site at www.pendarvis-studios.com.

Foreword

The computer, in one way or another, touches every facet of our daily lives. Most households today have a computer. Usually it is used to perform the basic functions of today's technology-driven society: email, access to the Internet, work and, of course, games. The computer also puts at your disposal the tools that allow you to be creative.

Whether we admit it or not, we all possess a left side to our brain. We all share a creative side. Some take advantage and pursue that calling in the form of photography, whether it's taking photos with a simple point-and-shoot camera or with a truckload of expensive equipment.

If painting is one's pursuit, the media choices can range from a simple pencil to a collection of the finest oil paints. The computer has opened enormous opportunities, with new tools that once we could only dream about. From an endless collection of paintbrushes to a piece of chalk in any possible color, every tool for the photographer and painter is available when you need them, at the touch of a button. All without the need for toxic darkroom chemicals or paint thinners or the smell that goes with them. Did I mention no clean-up afterwards?

For traditionally trained painters and photo retouchers, technology, like the Wacom pressure-sensitive tablet, has reached a point where the very tool that is held by the hand to interact with the computer looks and feels like a pen. Devices such as the Wacom Cintiq now let you work directly on the screen as if you were standing before an easel and canvas. Yes, there is a learning curve. All this great stuff, but how do you use it?

Standing in the computer graphics books section of a bookstore makes you feel like you're standing in front of a haystack faced with the task of finding a needle. If you happened to pick up this book, then you can stop searching. Let me tell you what sets this book apart from the rest. One of the things that make this book so crucial for tackling that learning curve is the level of detail that Cher has gone into to help you master these tools. Most important is how she makes it easy to understand what is being taught.

Cher Threinen-Pendarvis is an artist who I have had the pleasure of calling my friend since the computer screen measured only nine inches and offered pixels that were either black or white. I have seen her talent and vision evolve through many years of dedication and exploration of graphics software and digital tools.

Many companies that produce graphics software and hardware have commissioned her to demonstrate the features of their products. Cher's vast experience, coupled with her amazing talent for teaching, has produced a book that will be of tremendous help to you for mastering these digital tools. The many illustrations throughout the book clearly demonstrate the point being made and are beautiful to look at. It's great just to have in your collection.

Many do have a talent but never had any training. Others might not have great talent but enjoy playing. In either case, a little education can make a vast difference in the end result. That's where this book comes in.

Cher comes from a traditional background with training in the fundamentals of art. Composition and shading are terms that rarely enter the vocabulary of the average person, yet are so vital to the creation of a piece of artwork—these are the subjects she lives with.

What she is doing with this book is filling in those educational gaps that the average computer user is hampered by. Cher is an educator. But that is not the whole story. She makes each project a personal experience. She starts with the inspiration. What she sees and feels about her subjects. The steps she takes in preparing for the task ahead. She then takes you on a detailed journey to the finished product.

If you have ever attended any of her seminars or heard her speak at a trade show, you know how eloquently she can dispense information. She has a soothing voice, yet it conveys the excitement she feels about the digital medium. I see her as a female Bob Ross painting "Happy Trees" while eliminating the stress of everyday life.

Somehow she has managed to transfer the patience and understanding she demonstrates as a teacher onto the words in this book.

As an expert in both Photoshop and Painter, Cher shows you the processes for effects from within either program or a combination of the two. She guides you through the nuances achieved by the use of pressure-sensitive tablets. Then she teaches you how to take your concepts beyond the obvious—to that realm where creativity takes on a life of its own.

As I mentioned earlier, there are bountiful illustrations throughout the book that take you clearly through the processes she is explaining. This book is the art class you never took and wish you had. It might not make you a Michelangelo, but it will give you an understanding of the basics of art. It will give you the confidence to take your doodles to the next level.

Painting on a computer with a tablet can seem complex, but Cher brings it down to a manageable level so you can use them to let your creative juices run wild.

I have no doubt you will refer to this book over and over again, not just for the techniques but also for inspiration.

Bert Monroy
Berkeley, California, 2013

Contents

Introduction

Early artists used charcoal from their cooking fires to decorate the walls of their cave homes. Inspired by a cave painting I saw in the Dordogne valley in France, I drew this sketch using an Intuos tablet and Charcoal brushes in Painter.

I was inspired to write this book because I have enjoyed using digital art tools for more than two decades, and I am amazed by how the tools have matured and become more sensitive and user-friendly. One of the main inspirations for the book comes from the new form of creativity that the tablet and stylus give to artists. Without them, we could not enjoy painting sensitive brushwork in Photoshop and Painter—two programs that are continuously maturing with each release. Although this book has been written for those readers using Painter X3 and Photoshop CS6 and earlier versions, the lessons are all presented in a way that can be applied to future releases of the software.

Who This Book Is For. I have written this book for artists, illustrators, photographers, and designers of all levels who want to tap the creative power of using a tablet with Photoshop and Painter and develop their own style of painting with these applications. Whether you are an experienced artist or are just beginning to dabble and are nervous about your artistic skills, the computer can help you reach new freedom and confidence. If you are an experienced artist, you can paint from life using the eye-to-hand coordination that you developed as an artist. If you don't feel confident drawing from scratch, this book offers exercises that will give you practice. Painting using a computer is more forgiving

than most conventional media because you can draw or assemble a composition and save multiple versions as you work. You can try new approaches to your composition, undo without ruining your work, and open a previously saved version and begin again from that point. So much is possible with the computer.

Drawing using a good quality tablet and cordless stylus is completely free and natural whether you draw from life, from memory, or use a reference. The art tools and hardware have become so good in recent years that you can work with the new tools and become immersed in the creative process in much the same way that you can using traditional tools.

Conch Shell Study shows the sensitive shading that is possible using an Intuos tablet and pastel presets in Photoshop

Using oil brushes and texture-sensitive pastel brushes in Painter, I painted Downstream Path, Summer, *shown here as a detail.*

The Artist's Digital Tools. Painter, Photoshop, the stylus and tablet, and the iPad and its apps are new "mark-making" tools in a long ancestral line of art tools. Early artists drew scenes of their daily life on the walls of their cave homes using charcoal

 Drawn by hand. To keep your hand-to-eye coordination in practice, it's a good idea to keep a sketchbook with you at all times. This is also useful for recording details that inspire you and for making notes. You might also enjoy using your iPad, or laptop, tablet, and pen, for sketching. In Chapter 1 you'll find information about setting up for drawing on location.

from their cooking fires and paint made from clay and natural tints on the surfaces of stones. Later, many kinds of wet paint media (such as oil-based paint) and dry media (such as pencils and pastels) were invented. With the invention of photography, artists were able to develop a keener eye as they captured their visions with a camera. And for centuries, artists have found printmaking processes like etching and intaglio to be important for their craft.

Today, think of your stylus and the brushes in Painter and Photoshop, and the iPad and its art tools as a new kind of pencil, a new kind of charcoal, a new kind of watercolor paint, a new oil paint, and more!

Photoshop is an essential tool for illustrators and artists who want to do retouching, compositing, color correction, painting, and more. If you draw and paint, Painter is an

 Digital to conventional. A study painted on the computer can also be used as a reference for artwork done with conventional tools. My husband, Steve, is a surfboard builder. We often draw studies on the computer, make large prints, and then use them as references when painting on surfboards using acrylic paint. I have also used my digital studies as references for traditional art on paper or canvas, painted using conventional media.

This detail of Punta San Antonio, Spring *features brushwork that enhances the center of interest.*

essential tool because of the realism of its natural media brushes, textures, its unique special effects, and the tactile feel of its paint media. The portability between the two programs has become very good, and they complement one another. The tablet and stylus are really the bridge between your expressive hand and the computer. They give you the freedom to produce pressure-sensitive brushwork in Painter and Photoshop. The iPad and its art tools allow you to sketch freely in your studio or on location. When used together, these tools are capable of making your artwork reflect your creative intent.

Approach. This book is not a replacement for the documentation that ships with the tablet, Photoshop, Painter, or the iPad and its apps, and it doesn't cover every function of these products. Instead, it focuses on features related to drawing and painting such as sketching with the iPad; assembling brushes and paint in Photoshop and Painter; choosing brushes that change their brushstroke shape,

opacity, or texture based on hand movement; and customizing brushes to work better with a tablet and pen.

The *Photoshop and Painter Artist Tablet Book* covers composition, line, tone and form, creative use of color, and more. In the early chapters of this book, you'll have an opportunity to express yourself using different approaches to drawing (such as contour

Using photography creatively with painting. Artists such as Leonardo da Vinci and Jan Vermeer were known to use the camera obscura and other similar devices to help them sketch out proportions quickly in their compositions. In the nineteenth century, Eugene Delacroix, Edgar Degas, Thomas Eakins, and others used the camera as a reference source. Contemporary artists have used the technique of projecting a slide on their canvas as they lay out their compositions.

A photograph can be an aid and an inspiration, but try not to fall into the practice of copying the entire photograph. Instead, I suggest pulling elements from the photograph that you want in your composition. To create a great image, you need to carefully study your subject and pay attention to elements such as highlight and shadow, form, and modeling. In Chapters 10, 13, and 14, I'll show you how to use a photo for reference and how to incorporate several elements into a composition.

If you are a photographer who wants to add brushwork to your images, the exercises in Chapters 5–8 will be helpful to you. These chapters will help you practice good methods of visualizing your subject and hand-to-eye coordination, and your ability to render line and form will improve. As you work, you'll gain practice in how to see the forms and how to paint brushstrokes that will reveal the forms. If you want to paint over your photos, you'll learn techniques for thinking about your subject and its forms and modeling them. This experience will be evident in your work.

and gesture) using your stylus and tablet with Painter and Photoshop. Following the exercises on linear drawing, you'll find projects that will give you practice with modeling form, using value and tone. Then you'll discover projects that will help you improve your compositions, for instance, by enhancing the focal point in a painting, by simulating canvas and paper, using mixed media, and more.

 Record the light of the moment. Because light changes so quickly when you're painting on location, you can record the light as it was at that moment by shooting a digital photo and then use the photo as a reference to help remember the lighting in your scene when you get back to your studio. However, in my opinion, the digital photo will not replace the experience of creating elements for your painting on location. I recommend taking the time to at least do a composition drawing and make color notes while on location.

The projects in the book are presented with color illustrations that are my own creations. You may prefer different subject matter or work in a different style, but these illustrations are intended to show you how to apply the techniques to use in your own work. I hope you enjoy the artwork, creative thought processes, and techniques in this book.

Color and value. Will your colored painting hold up in black and white? When I painted this pastel painting in color, I massed the darker shapes together toward the right side and in the foreground as part of the composition design. To make sure I achieved a full range of tones—from the darkest values in the shadows to accents of white in the highlights—I squinted my eyes to blur the image, visually reducing it to dark and light shapes. Then I added deeper values and brighter highlights where needed. Notice how the composition holds up when converted to black and white.

Path to Water, North *was begun on location (using a laptop, Wacom tablet, and Painter) at Sunset Cliffs Natural Park in San Diego, California. It was painted with the Pastel and Chalk brushes in Painter.*

How to Use This Book

An overview and artist statement are located facing the featured art on the opening spreads.

So that you can read through the development of an art project without getting bogged down with too many technical details, I designed *The Photoshop and Painter Artist Tablet Book* using a modular approach.

Each chapter begins with an overview of what you'll learn in the chapter. The chapter overview is followed by an artist statement about the drawing or painting projects. The artist statement is identified by an artist palette. Throughout the chapters you'll also find more artist statements and tips identified by the artist palette.

After the overview page at the beginning of each project, you'll find an Artist's Materials box that contains the tools that you'll use in the project. Right above the Artist's Materials box, you'll see sample brushstrokes that will let you know how the brushes listed in the Artist's Materials box will perform using your stylus and paint. To make it easy to identify which application you'll be using for a project, each Artist's Materials box is color-coded—a lavender-purple for Photoshop and a teal-green for Painter.

Throughout the book you'll find helpful Learn More About boxes that will help you find more information about the topics being discussed. When you encounter an orange asterisk after a term or at the end of a sentence, check the Learn More About box on the spread for an entry related to the term or concept discussed in the text.

Sprinkled throughout the book, you'll find four kinds of sidebars. The sidebars are identified by an artist palette (as described earlier), a hand with a stylus, an eye, and a paint can. The artist palette (shown earlier) identifies a conceptual tip from the artist-author, the hand with a stylus denotes a sidebar about the tablet and pen, the hand and the iPad identifies a sidebar related to the iPad, the eye identifies a sidebar about Photoshop, and the paint can shows a Painter-related sidebar. In a few places, I've used the stylus icon and the eye or the paint can icon to identify a combined tip that has information about the tablet and Photoshop or Painter. In a few cases I've combined a tip that has information about Photoshop and Painter using the eye and the paint can icons.

Where possible, I've separated technical information into mini-technique sidebars identified by a technique head,

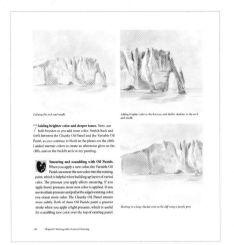

The Artist's Materials boxes are color-coded for Painter and Photoshop.

The Learn More About boxes tell you where you will find more information about a topic.

The artist's tips are identified by artist palette icons.

such as "Embossing Texture on an Image" on page 198 in Chapter 12. These sidebars are also identified by the warm gold background used on the small sidebars. In several places you'll find tips within a gold-colored sidebar spread that are set off with a white background like the PC/Mac tip below.

Zooming and panning. Use the Zoom Tool (or Magnifier) to zoom in to see areas of detail. When the Brush tool is chosen, you can temporarily switch to the Zoom Tool (or Magnifier) by pressing Ctrl/Cmd-Spacebar. To zoom out, press Ctrl/Cmd-Alt/Option-Spacebar. To pan around a magnified image while painting, you can press the Spacebar to temporarily switch to the Grabber Hand.

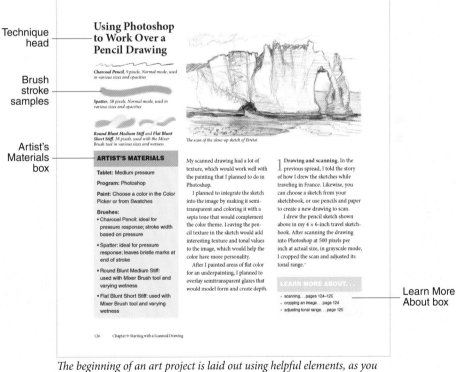

The beginning of an art project is laid out using helpful elements, as you can see here in this page from Chapter 9.

At work in the studio

1

The Digital Art Studio

Here you'll find suggestions for hardware and software and for setting up your studio, whether it's your own studio or *en plein air* (on location). This chapter also covers making the transition from traditional color theory to digital color tools. Finally, it offers information about pixels, resolution, and desktop fine art printmaking in the studio.

 Your studio is where you come to be creative, so you want it to reflect your personality, with surrounding objects and art that inspire you. My studio has an area with computer equipment for digital work and an area with an easel where I can use conventional art materials. Art decorates the walls, and there are sea shells, flowers, and photos from my travels, in addition to colorful pottery.

The hardware and software tools have matured to a point that artists are able to use them more intuitively and naturally. Tablets have become more sensitive and easy to use. To make the sensation of drawing on the computer more natural, the stylus has nibs that give you more sensation. For instance, one nib gives the feeling of pencil on paper, and the other nib is spring-loaded, giving the feeling of pushing on a traditional brush with stiff bristles. The iPad and apps such as Brushes and Art Studio are fun for sketching on location. The programs Painter and Photoshop have become more intuitive to use, and they can sense more nuances of your hand as you draw.

With the digital tools available today, you can become immersed in the painting process more completely, into the line, form, and color of your composition, rather than focusing on the technology when painting on the computer. Think of your digital tools as a new kind of pencil, a new pastel, a new watercolor, and a new kind of oil paint.

CP

Setting Up the Digital Art Studio

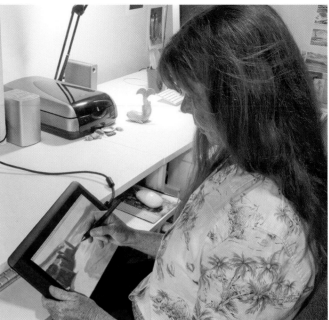

Working directly on a Cintiq interactive display

First of all, a digital artist's studio is not complete without Painter, Photoshop, and a great-quality pressure-sensitive tablet. And advances with the iPad and its art applications make the iPad a fun, useful addition.

Photoshop and Painter and Wacom tablets perform well on both Macintosh and Windows platforms. My first computer was a Mac, and I enjoy the easy-to-use operating system. Today I use Mac computers for painting and illustration. The processor speed is important, as are the amount of RAM and the speed of the hard disk.

Photoshop and Painter are "RAM-hungry" applications, so plan to buy lots of RAM for your computer. (My systems have at least 4GB of RAM.)

The display you choose is very important, both for the care of your eyes and for the quality of your images. Buy the highest-quality display that you can afford. (You'll need a minimum of 20 inches and a video card that will support millions of colors.) My studio has 24-inch flat panel Apple high-definition displays.

If you want to use scans in your art, you'll want to invest in a high-quality scanner. My choice is the Epson Perfection V750-M Pro. It features 4800 × 9600 dpi resolution and 48-bit color depth, and it can be used to scan reflective art or transparencies.*

If you'd like to shoot digital photos to use for reference or to use in your art, I recommend a digital SLR, such as the Canon EOS 6D or Nikon D7100.

It's a good idea to invest in a large external hard drive that you can use to safely back up your files. A CD/DVD burner is also useful for transferring files and for keeping archives of your work.

To create the paintings described in the book projects, I used Wacom Intuos tablets* and a Cintiq. The Cintiq is a pressure-sensitive display that allows you to work directly on screen. The Cintiq 13HD, 22HD, and 24HD sense 2,048 pressure levels.

In addition to my conventional sketchbooks, the iPad* is wonderful for sketching in the studio and on location, and it's an excellent presentation tool for showing your artwork.

In the studio with the Intuos and iMac

I use an iPad 3 with Retina display for sketching.

Finally, my studio has two inkjet printers: an Epson Artisan 1430 (for office work and small projects up to 13 inches) and an Epson Stylus Pro 4800 for 17-inch-wide fine art prints.*

Also, it's wise to invest in a large, stable desk and a comfortable chair that has arm rests and good lower-back support. (My studio has two 40 × 60-inch desks.)

LEARN MORE ABOUT. . .

★ working with a scanner. . . pages 124–125
★ Intuos tablet. . . pages 44–45
★ iPad. . . pages 4, 10–41
★ inkjet printers. . . page 9

PHOTOGRAPHS: MELINDA HOLDEN

Sketching on location using an iPad in the shade of an umbrella

Shading the screen with an umbrella while painting with an Intuos tablet and laptop

Setting up for painting on location. If you want to enjoy sketching outside with an iPad or laptop, these tips are for you. The light from the screen won't compete with natural sunlight. Plan to find a shady spot to set up or bring an umbrella that you can use to shield the screen. (A hood is also available for some displays.) I set up on a blanket, but you might want to use a folding chair. Two of my favorite times to paint are in the early morning or late afternoon because the shadows are the longest, which contributes to an interesting composition. The photos above show me sketching on a morning that had a soft cloud cover. The gray morning light did not produce long shadows, but it did offer other opportunities, such as the soft gradations in the sky and water and the interesting colors and forms of the cliffs.

Using multiple pens. For more spontaneity while painting, try using two pens when painting in Painter. You can set your Airbrush stylus to be a Digital Airbrush dipped in a color—for instance, blue—and set your grip pen to be the Square Soft Pastel dipped in a second color— green. You can now switch brushes and color quickly by picking up your other pen. If you're using two of the same kind of pen, it's a good idea to label each one so that you can identify them easily. To get started using two pens, use your first pen to choose a brush variant and color, and make a stroke. Then use your second stylus to choose a new brush and color, and make a stroke. Now when you switch back and forth, the pens will automatically help choose the brush and color.

The quick location sketch created on the iPad using Brushes

The quick location sketch created in Painter using the Intuos

Sketching on the go. You can enjoy the freedom of using a portable digital painting studio for working on location. Two favorite tools are a MacBook and an Intuos tablet. The Intuos tablet supports 2,048 levels of pressure, plus tilt, angle, direction, and rotation, making the sketching experience very natural.

The iPad is fun for location work because it is a more compact unit that is easy to carry. At this time, the iPad doesn't support true pressure sensitivity, but brushmarks can be varied with the speed at which you draw. (A stylus that simulates pressure sensitivity such as the Pogo Connect* can be used.) The iPad allows you to work directly on-screen with your fingers or a stylus made for the iPad. You can create fresh, bold drawings with applications such as Brushes and Art Studio.

I painted the image on the above left with the iPad and Brushes and the image on the right with the Pastel brushes in Painter. Because the light changes quickly when painting on location, I worked fast, laying in broad areas of color. For the iPad study using Brushes, I sketched in a similar way to the project on pages 14–15. For the Painter sketch, I enjoyed sketching with a Square Soft Pastel and Tapered Pastel. For more texture, I scumbled* using the Square Grainy Pastel. (These techniques are described

PHOTOGRAPH: MELINDA HOLDEN

Sketching on location using my iPad3, in the shade of an umbrella

throughout this book.) You'll notice a difference in the texture in the two images. For instance, the image on the left that was painted with the iPad has a bolder look, with less subtle texture. The painting on the right shows more delicate paper grain, and the brushstrokes have more sensitive variation from thick to thin.

 Optional nibs. Optional stroke nibs are available for the Wacom Grip Pen: a spring-loaded nib that adds tension that feels like a stiff brush and a felt nib for additional friction between the pen and tablet, much like conventional pencil on paper.

The Power of Color

For Mendocino Point, *I used dabs of complementary colors in the shadows.*

"Light, that first phenomenon of the world, reveals to us the spirit and living soul of the world through colors." Painter and color theorist Johannes Itten's observation inspires us to think about how color affects not only the appearance of what we see, but also our emotional response to the subject.

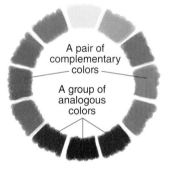

A pigment-based color wheel with 12 colors

A pair of complementary colors

A group of analogous colors

Today's color tools are so good that you can make an intuitive transition between traditional color theory and the digital color tools, while enhancing your own personal expression. In this section, we'll take familiar traditional terms and have fun applying them using the digital color tools in Painter and Photoshop.

Hue. The hue is the predominant spectral color, such as yellow or blue-green. Hue indicates a color's position on the color wheel or spectrum and tells us the color's temperature.

Saturation. Also known as *intensity* or *chroma*, saturation indicates a color's purity or strength.

Value. A color's lightness or darkness is its luminance or value.

Tint. You can create a tint of a color (lightening it, or increasing its value) by mixing it with white or a lighter color; or in the case of transparent washes, you can dilute the color with a clear medium like water.

Shade. You can mix a shade of a color (darkening it, or decreasing its value) by adding a darker color. To use a tonalist approach, you might want to add dark gray or black. I carefully observe the shadows when I'm painting; and often build the shadows by adding dabs of a darker complementary color to them. See "Color Inspiration and Interpretation" on page 193 for more information.

A blue color at full saturation (top), and a tint and a shade of the color in Painter

A blue color at full saturation (top), and a tint and a shade of the color in Photoshop

Tints, shades, and saturation in Painter. To choose a hue in Painter from the Color panel, click in the Hue Ring. To create a tint of the color, move the little circle higher in the Saturation/Value triangle in the Color panel. To create a shade of a color, move the little circle lower in the Saturation/Value triangle.

To adjust the saturation of the color, move to the right in the Saturation/Value triangle to increase saturation or move to the left to decrease it.

Tints, shades, and saturation in Photoshop. You can choose a hue from the Color panel or the Color Picker. I've used the Color Picker here because it's more intuitive to select a hue and then make a tint or shade of the color. Click on the Foreground Color in the Toolbox to open the Color Picker and choose a hue in the vertical Color slider. To choose a tint, click higher in the large Color field and click lower to choose a shade.

To adjust the saturation of a color in Photoshop, move to the right in the Color field to increase the saturation or move to the left to decrease it.

 "Traditional" digital color mixes. With the Mixer, it's intuitive to apply paint (such as the blue color shown on the right of the Mixer pad) and then mix tints and shades using colors from the color wells or the Color panel.

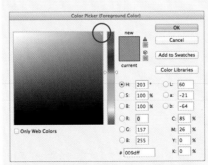

The Color panel in Painter. The color is shown at full saturation.

The Color Picker in Photoshop. The color is shown at full saturation.

Using the Mix Color tool in Painter's Mixer panel to create tints and shades

Pixels and Image Resolution

Peppers study, painted using Painter

Images created in Photoshop and Painter are pixel based. Pixels are square elements arranged in a grid that builds the image file. The resolution of an image is determined by the number of pixels per inch (ppi).

Resolution is a term that describes the number of pixels, or the amount of data in a bitmap (raster) image file. Illustrations created in programs like Adobe Illustrator or Corel Draw are vector based. Vector-based images consist of mathematical instructions that describe vectors, rather than pixels. Vector graphics are scalable and transformable, without loss of quality. Pixel-based images, on the other hand, are resolution dependent, which means that quality can suffer if the image resolution is too low for the size and method of printing that is used.

How will the image be used? Before beginning an illustration, it's a good idea to plan ahead: How will you

Vector images are comprised of mathematically described paths.

present your image? Will it appear in a book or magazine that is printed using an offset press? Will it be printed on an inkjet printer at a fine art service bureau? Will you print your image on your own studio inkjet? Take this planning into account when you are starting a new file or when you are scanning images (or shooting digital photos) that you will use to create a composite illustration.

Resolution for offset printing. This book was printed using a four-color commercial offset printing process. I created the images at their final dimensions at a resolution of 300 pixels per inch. To be printed on an

offset press, the square pixels are converted into a grid of round dots for half tones. The (half tone) line screen used for this book is 150 lpi (lines per inch).

To figure out how large a file you should start with, you need to know the line screen. Typical line-screen resolutions are 56 lpi (screen printing), 85 lpi (newspaper), 133 lpi, 150 lpi, and 200 lpi (magazines and books). If your line screen is 150 lpi, it's recommended that you multiply the line-screen number (150) by two. Two is a conservative factor to use,

The New dialog box in Photoshop showing the dimensions and the resolution

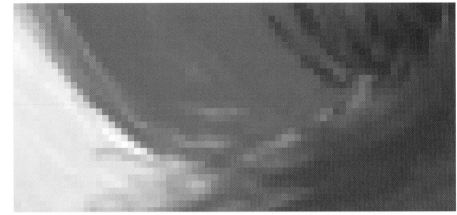

Peppers *study; detail shown at 300%*

A 1600% enlargement of a portion of the peppers image showing the grid of pixels

and this would create an image resolution of 300 ppi.

Resolution for inkjet printing.
When creating an image file to print on my Epson 2200, I set up the file at its final dimensions (for instance, 20 × 16 inches), with a resolution between 150–300 ppi. I've not noticed improvement in quality with settings higher than 200 pixels per inch.

Prior to creating an image file that will be printed at a fine art service bureau, speak with your service bureau representative to find out the equipment requirements. Service bureaus use equipment from different manufacturers—for instance, Iris, Epson, Hewlett-Packard, and Roland. The printing equipment might

require different resolutions, and some might require that you convert your RGB file to CMYK color mode (such as the Iris, for instance).*

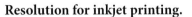 **Resizing, resampling, and interpolation.** The illustrations below show the Image Size dialog box in Photoshop (Image > Image Size). Painter has a similar dialog box (Canvas > Resize). The dialog box on the left is set up to resize an image. Resizing changes the physical dimensions of a file, without changing the number of pixels in the file. Resampling, however, uses a process called *interpolation* to increase or decrease the number of pixels in the file. Resampling can cause softness and artifacts in a file. It's recommended not to resample "up" more than 10%. Resampling down is less harmful to the file, but some sharpening might be needed. When you're using interpolation, Photoshop and Painter remap pixels to enlarge or reduce the size of the image. If you enlarge the image, new pixels are manufactured. Pixels are discarded when you resample to a smaller size.

LEARN MORE ABOUT. . .

* inkjet printing. . . page 9
* color modes. . . page 202

Image Size			Image Size		
Pixel Dimensions: 20.6M		OK	Pixel Dimensions: 5.15M (was 20.6M)		OK
Width: 2400 pixels		Cancel	Width: 1200 Pixels		Cancel
Height: 3000 pixels		Auto...	Height: 1500 Pixels		Auto...
Document Size:			Document Size:		
Width: 8 Inches			Width: 4 Inches		
Height: 10 Inches			Height: 5 Inches		
Resolution: 300 Pixels/Inch			Resolution: 300 Pixels/Inch		
☐ Scale Styles			☐ Scale Styles		
☑ Constrain Proportions			☑ Constrain Proportions		
☐ Resample Image:			☑ Resample Image:		
Bicubic Automatic			Bicubic Automatic		

Resizing an image (left) and resampling (right)

Fine Art Printmaking in the Studio

I made an artist proof of Along Tomales Bay *on an Stylus Pro 4800*

Many affordable alternatives are available for artists who want to proof their images or make fine art prints in their own studio using archival inks and papers.

Today's desktop inkjet printers deliver beautiful color prints. The Epson printers (the Stylus Pro 4800 and the Stylus Pro 3880, for instance) are good printers not only for pulling test prints before sending images to a fine art service bureau, but also for use in experimental fine art printmaking.

The Epson Stylus Pro 3880 ships with a nine-color Epson Ultra Chrome K3 inkset, and it produces water-resistant prints, especially when used with Epson's Enhanced Matte or Somerset Velvet for Epson paper. If you'd like to experiment on them by applying pastel or acrylic paint, these prints will accept the media without smearing or running.

Many traditional art papers are now manufactured for digital printmaking—for instance, Arches, Crane Museo, Somerset, Concorde Rag, and Hahnemuehle's German Etching papers, which are available from Cone Editions' Ink Jet Mall or Digital Art Supplies. Also, new canvases are available for use with inkjet printers. For instance, check out the artist-grade canvases available from Digital Art Supplies, located on the web at www.digitalartsupplies.com.

 Larger format prints. If you're looking for a large format printer, the Epson 3880 is an excellent choice. It is a desktop nine-color inkjet printer that uses the Epson UltraChrome pigmented inks. It handles media from 17 inches wide and can handle heavier substrates, up to cardboard 1.5 mm thick.

Henry Wilhelm has done important research regarding the longevity of different ink and substrate combinations. A comparison of longevity with the different inks and papers is available through Wilhelm Imaging Research, Inc., on the web at www. wilhelm-research.com.

You can find more information on these topics in the "Printmaking and Archival Concerns" chapter of *The Painter Wow! Book.*

 Fine art print studios. You can order large exhibition-quality prints from a digital printmaking studio such as Cone Editions Press or Trillium Press. In the Appendix in the back of this book, you'll find a selective list of printmakers that trusted colleagues and I have worked with.

Think of the iPad as your mobile digital sketchbook

2
Sketching on the iPad

In the first part of this chapter, you'll find an overview of my favorite art applications and styli for the iPad. These beginning and intermediate level projects cover sketching and studies that can be finalized in Photoshop and Painter. The chapter includes short projects featuring Brushes, ArtStudio, Sketchbook, Procreate, Adobe Ideas, and Adobe Photoshop Touch.

 Think of the iPad as a digital sketchbook that you can take anywhere. An overview of the projects in this chapter follows: With Brushes, I painted a plein air sketch of the Cliffs park near our home. It is a study for the painting that is used on the cover of this book. A second Brushes project incorporates loose sketching from life. In the following projects with ArtStudio, I sketched a pencil portrait of a friend and painted color studies with dry and wet paint. For another piece, I used Sketchbook Express to make a pencil sketch of a lizard who lives nearby and later added color washes to the drawing in Sketchbook Pro. Whenever possible, I enjoy sketching from life on my iPad. The next project shows a quick figure study in Procreate using its Pencil and Pastel brushes. While relaxing one Sunday afternoon, I sketched from my imagination using Adobe Ideas. As I enjoyed the expressive nature of the Brush tool, playful drawings of dolphins emerged. The Adobe Ideas projects show the drawings and how to color them. Inspired by my love of Hawaii, its people, and its culture, I designed a collage sketch using Adobe Photoshop Touch that is featured in the final project in this chapter and in Chapter 14. The Photoshop Touch sketch is imported into Adobe Photoshop and Painter for finishing.

CP

Favorite iPad Painting Tools

Using the Wet Paintbrush in ArtStudio, I sketched Bird of Paradise.

There are many sketching and painting applications, and several styli choices for the iPad. Here are some of my favorites.

SKETCHING APPS FOR THE IPAD

Brushes. Two of my favorite features of Brushes 3 are the simplicity of its interface and the efficient controls for making custom brushes. Brushes 3 by Taptrix, Inc. offers two tools, the Brush and Eraser. You can choose from a selection of brush presets, and adjust the brush size. After choosing a brush and a color, you can easily finger paint or draw with a stylus on the screen. Using the brush settings, you can create your own brush presets. It's also possible to import photos from the Camera Roll. The free version provides one layer for painting. The $2.99 upgrade for Brushes 3 allows you to use up to 10 layers and also offers layer effects. Brushes 3 also allows you to record the sketching process and you can play back the process of your drawing. It's easy to export your drawing to the Camera Roll, Photo Library, and more.

ArtStudio. A full-featured painting application, Lucky Clan's ArtStudio features a versatile array of brushes. One of my favorites is the Wet Paint Brush, which allows you to apply paint and blend. You can make adjustments to a brush and save your custom brush as a favorite. ArtStudio also boasts a Smudge tool that is very helpful for blending tones and colors. After choosing a brush and a color, you can paint with your finger or draw onscreen with a stylus. It's also possible to import photos from the Camera Roll and edit them using selections and effects. Exporting files from ArtStudio is easy; just choose Export from the File menu and Export your image as a JPEG, PNG, or PSD file to your photos, email, and more.

Procreate. A full-featured program, Procreate offers an intuitive interface and quick performance. Easily accessible sliders allow you to adjust the size of your brush and opacity as you work. The color picker, layer options, and quick zoom functionality are easy to use. My favorite features are its variety of responsive brush tools and its ability to blend or smudge paint which is lacking in some other apps. When you're ready, you can export the image to your Photo Library, email, and more

Sketchbook. Autodesk's SketchBook offers a good variety of drawing tools, including pencils, pens, and markers, with an intuitive interface. A few favorite features are its drawing tools—especially the Pencils—and the ease of working with layers and transparency.

Using pencils and brushes in Sketchbook Pro, I drew Fence Lizard, *shown here as a detail.*

In Sketchbook Express, files can be exported to your Photo Library, Facebook, Twitter, or to a printer. The Pro version also allows sharing via email, Flicker, Dropbox, and more. With a stylus, you can create quick sketches or more involved studies.

Adobe Ideas. Adobe Ideas shines as a versatile vector application for inking sketches and drawings. I appreciate its efficient interface and the quickness of the tools. Adobe Ideas boasts several drawing tools: the pencil, brush, marker, and pen. Other tools include the eraser, paint bucket, colors, and layers. Additionally, images from the photo library can be imported into Adobe Ideas, and you can also access the onboard camera. After creating your image, it can be imported into Adobe Illustrator as a vector file.

Adobe Photoshop Touch. I appreciate the ease with which you can create sketches with photo imagery, layers, and special effects on your iPad with Adobe Photoshop Touch. Then you can open the file in Adobe Photoshop and complete your vision.

IPAD STYLUS IDEAS

Some artists enjoy finger painting on their iPad and achieve good results. I usually use a stylus because more precision can be achieved. However, more pressure is required to draw a stroke with a stylus, as the tip of the stylus needs to compress a bit. Here are a few styli that work well for me.

Wacom Bamboo Solo. Wacom offers three Bamboo styli for the iPad: the Solo, Duo, and Pocket versions. I prefer the Solo and recommend it for sketching. The Wacom Bamboo Solo has a good weight and feel.

Nomadbrush Flex. From Nomadbrush, the Flex paintbrush stylus features a synthetic brush tip with a smooth touch. I like the fluid control and natural feeling that the brush tip gives while sketching.

Pogo Connect. From Ten One Design, the Pogo Connect uses Bluetooth to simulate pressure sensitivity with compatible applications. The button on the side acts as an "Undo" button in many apps. The stylus requires a AAA battery. To set up the stylus, down-load the free pairing app and connect. Each app has its own simple method of connecting with the stylus , usually found in iPad "Settings" or preferences within the app. I found the simulated pressure sensitivity exciting, but it was challenging to achieve consistently. This stylus requires more pressure applied to display a brushstroke.

Using Brushes 3 for a Quick Color Sketch

Try out a variety of brushes.

The composition sketch drawn in dark gray

Brushes 3 overview. Brushes has two basic tools, the Brush and Eraser. When you launch Brushes; the Gallery page appears. To create a new file, tap the + icon. A new empty image is created. In the painting file, a toolbar along the bottom of the screen allows you to access tools, from left to right: the Color Well, Brush, Eraser Settings, Size slider, Undo, Redo, Effects, and Layers icons.

Brushes records your process as you sketch. You can replay a painting by choosing its thumbnail in the Gallery, opening the file, and tapping the play icon.

To export an image from Brushes, tap the Sharing icon. You can save the file to your photos, email it, share to Facebook, and more.

1 **Trying out brushes and drawing a sketch.** The color study featured in this project is a plein air sketch for a painting that I created in Painter with a Wacom tablet. To begin, create a new image file. Tap the Color Well to open the Color panel and choose a color. Tap the Brush Settings icon to open the Brush Settings panel; then choose a brush preset.

Experiment by making marks with a variety of the brush presets.

For a brush that draws textured marks similar to charcoal or pastel, I chose the third preset down from the top, and I chose a dark gray color. Make practice marks to get a feel for the brush. (You can tap the Undo icon to remove your practice marks.) When you're comfortable with the brush, draw a loose sketch.

Choosing a dark gray in the Color panel

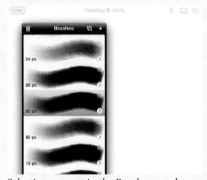

Selecting a preset in the Brushes panel

Using varied blues to paint the sky and water

Laying in base colors on the hills and plants

The finished rough color study

2 Painting with color. This color study is drawn on location. The composition, shapes, and color notes are important inspiration for a painting that I later created in Painter at my studio. The loose study shows the general composition, movement, color, and lighting.

When you're satisfied with your sketch, choose a warm blue color for the sky. Using the Size slider, increase the size of your brush and then loosely paint color onto the sky. For the feeling of clouds, use curved strokes. For the water, choose a cooler blue, and paint with more horizontal strokes.

3 Adding texture and details. Take time to examine your study. Does the composition need refinement?

For more drama in the sketch and to enhance its focal point, I added touches of light purple to the sky. Then, to balance the color, I carried it into the foreground by painting small, loose strokes of purple onto the shaded areas of the foreground plants. I changed the shape and size of the two plants in the midground, and painted ochre and gold on the hill to separate the two plants. To finish, I added short, energetic strokes of light green to the sunlit areas of the plants.

This study is used as inspiration for a painting created with Painter later in the book. To export your study from Brushes, press the Share icon and add it to your photos or save it as a JPEG and email it to yourself.

Good work! You have completed this project. On the next spread, we will work with Pencils in Brushes.

 Sampling color from the image in Brushes. Position your finger or stylus over the color you want to sample; then tap and hold. The Eyedropper tool will appear showing the updated color in its ring and in the color swatch and color picker.

Sampling color using the Eyedropper

Making a Pencil and Sketching in Brushes 3

The thicker strokes on the top are drawn with the default brush. The thinner strokes are drawn with the custom pencil.

1 Setting up for sketching. We will explore brushes, sketch, and make a pencil. Begin by opening a new image. Tap the Color Well to open the Color panel and choose a dark gray. Tap the Brush Settings icon to open the Brushes panel, and then choose the third preset from the top. The Brush panel should look like the illustration to the right. Make practice marks to get a feel for the brush.

Now let's make a pencil. Make a copy of the brush so you can create your own brush, and preserve the original. To make a copy, tap the square icon with the + (plus) a copy appears. Select the copy and click the tiny arrow to the right of the brush preset to open its settings.

First we'll change the tip. The brush tips are located in the scrolling menu at the top. Change the shape from square to round. Adjust the sliders as follows: Increase Hardness to 100; increase Intensity to 56; set Dynamic Angle at 39; set Dynamic Weight at 63; and reduce Dynamic Intensity to 8.

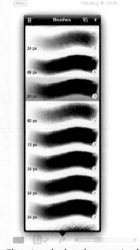
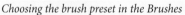

Choosing the brush preset in the Brushes

The default settings for the brush preset

Quick sketches of Marika and Sable drawn from observation using the new custom pencil

When you're finished making adjustments, click the Brushes button to return to the Brushes presets. You will see your new brush in the list. Make practice marks with your new pencil. If you'd like to make more adjustments, open the preset settings again and adjust the sliders.

2 **Sketching with the pencil.** Now that you're comfortable with the pencil, draw loose, expressive sketches. The lines will vary thickness with the speed that you draw them. Start out with a lighter gray, and build up to a darker tone. I sketched our cats, Marika and Sable. For the quick sketches shown above, I varied the size of the pencil from about 5–8 pixels using the Size slider.

Good work! You have completed the mini-projects with Brushes. In the next project, we will work with ArtStudio.

The settings for the custom pencil

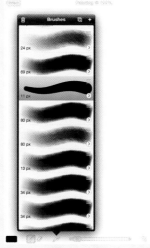

The new custom pencil in the Brushes panel

Sketching a Pencil Portrait Using ArtStudio

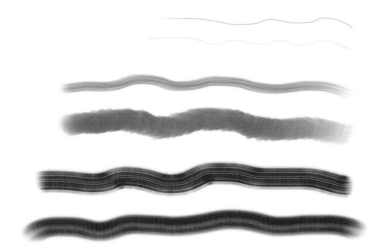

ArtStudio overview. When you launch ArtStudio, by default a new, blank image opens. The interface is well organized: there's the top menu, right toolbar and left toolbar, with mark-making tools on the left and color swatches on the right. The left and right toolbars are scrollable. Drag to scroll and reveal more tools and colors. The bottom toolbar features Favorite Brushes, Layers, Brush Size, Brush Opacity and Undo / Redo. To choose a drawing tool, tap a tool icon, such as the Pencil. To choose a color, tap the top color swatch; the Color Editor panel opens. In the panel, tap a swatch to choose it, or tap and drag to choose a color in the light and saturation field (the large square). You can also mix a new color using the sliders.

ArtStudio features the Pencil, Wet Paint Brush, Paint Brush, Spray Paint, Dots, Eraser, Smudge, Bucket Fill, Gradient, Text, Clone, Heal, Dodge / Burn and Eyedropper tools. Tapping twice on the Pencil icon brings up the Pencil settings window, in which you can choose a different tip, and edit the Blur, Size, Opacity, and more. Each tool has its own settings window.

Painting brushstrokes with the Pencil, Wet Paint Brush, and Paint Brush

1 Exploring drawing tools. For this project, we will explore brushes and sketch a portrait. Begin by opening a new file. Tap the color icon to open the Color Editor and choose a color. (I chose a dark gray.) Tap the Pencil icon to choose it. Draw a wavy line using 100% opacity; then reduce the opacity to about 70% and make a second stroke. For the sketch, we will use the Pencil at reduced opacity. Now tap the Wet Paint Brush to choose it. Choose a bright red color. Explore making strokes with the Wet Paint Brush. Access the Wet Paint Brush settings by double-tapping the tool. Experiment with the different tips. Next, choose a rusty brown. Tap the Paint Brush tool to choose it, and practice making brushstrokes.

Choosing a dark gray in the Color Editor

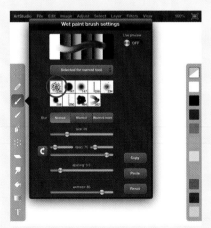

The Wet Paint Brush settings. The top left tip is selected.

The rough sketch with light pencil

Sketching shapes and forms

The final portrait sketch

2 Sketching a portrait with pencil. For a look of creamy traditional paper, I filled the background layer with a light brown. Mix a light color in the Color Editor and then choose Edit > Fill Layer. For this portrait drawing, I began by sketching from life. Find a friend to sit for you or use a photo for reference. Position your model near a window, showing a straight-on view or a three-quarter view with natural light coming from one side. If no window is available, a lamp with a soft light will do.

Before you begin, carefully study the form of the head. Imagine the head as a three-dimensional oval in space. Imagine the eyes as three-dimensional balls that sit in the sockets. Study the negative space around the head to help define the edges of the face. Study the proportions, for instance the horizontal distance between the eyes and the

vertical distances of the forehead, then from the eyes to the tip of the nose and to the lips and chin.

Begin by using a low-opacity pencil to sketch an oval for the basic head shape. Draw loosely. Starting with a low-opacity gray, slowly build up to darker tones as you go. I varied the size of the pencil from about 8–15 pixels using the Size slider, and varied the opacity from 50–80% over the course of the drawing.

For a fresh, expressive look, all the pencil strokes are hatched, not smudged or blended. I used a combination of "sketchy line" style* and contour drawing,* along with subtle cross-hatching* for modeling forms.

LEARN MORE ABOUT. . .

* "sketchy line" style. . . page 89
* contour drawing . . page 89
* cross-hatching. . . page 116

3 Refining the drawing. When you're ready to refine your drawing, zoom in to an area such as the eyes (pinch the screen outward with two fingers to zoom), and sketch the details. I wanted this portrait drawing to be fresh and loose, so I did not draw tight, constrained details.

Zoom back out and take a careful look at your drawing. Would your drawing benefit from having a few lines along the edge of the face strengthened? Would you like to add shading on the planes of the face?

For a subtle, expressive look and added dimension, I used subtle contour lines in conjunction with cross-hatching. This is most noticeable along the left side of the face. To finish, I added a few darker strokes on the hair, lips, and eyes.

Painting a Color Study Using ArtStudio

These strokes were painted with four painting tools (left to right), Wet Paint Brush, Paint Brush, Paint Brush with Smudge, and Dots.

The loose brush sketch

1 Conceiving the project and trying out brushes. For this project, the objective is to create a landscape with bold, flat areas of color. You will begin by sketching in color with a brush, then lay in flat areas of color over the sketch. You can work from a reference, paint from your imagination, or sketch from observation, in plein air. Your reference could be a traditional sketch you have drawn or a photograph. For the *Mountain View* study, an inspiration was a previously painted plein air study, and I also painted from my imagination.

Explore making different kinds of brushstrokes using the Wet Paint Brush and Paint Brush. The Smudge tool allows you to push and pull color. With the Dots brush, you can add texture to your artwork.

The Wet Paint Brush is a round brush that paints brushstrokes like an oval brush with a bristly tip. In Wet Paint Brush settings, its default Wetness value is 85%. The Wetness allows you to lay down a new color over existing paint and subtly blend the two colors. The Paint Brush performs like a flat brush, and it is useful for laying down color quickly.

2 Choosing color and sketching. To begin, choose File > New to open a new image, and choose a color that will coordinate well with the color theme you plan to use. (I chose a light blue.) To edit the color, tap the blue color swatch to choose it; then tap the top color swatch to open the Color Editor. Lighten the blue by moving the cursor to the left in the color field. When you've chosen your color, tap outside the Color Editor to close it. Now tap the Paint Brush to choose it. Using the Paint Brush at 100% opacity, draw a loose, expressive sketch.

Choosing a light blue using the Color Editor. The Paint Brush is chosen in the left toolbar.

Painting base colors on the sky and mountains in the background

Painting brighter areas of color on the mid-ground hills

Painting color over color to refine shapes and linear accents in the landscape

3 Laying in base colors. When your sketch is as you like it, begin to lay in broad areas of color. Use the Paint Brush to brush color areas on to your painting. Don't focus on details at this stage but on creating interesting color shapes. As you work, you can change the size of your brush using the Brush Size slider near the bottom of your screen. Colors with less saturation and contrast will recede, whereas bolder colors with saturation and contrast will come forward. For the distant hills, I mixed a medium-toned gray green.

Mixing a gray green in the Color Editor. The New Color and Current Color are also shown in the Color icon on the right toolbar.

4 Painting color over color. As you paint, enhance your composition by adding more color areas. I worked from the background to the foreground, working in brighter colors and more contrast, as I refined the composition.

The Paint Brush is a flat brush that paints a stroke with fairly even thickness, with a bristled, square tip. By painting over the trailing edge of a brushstroke, you can achieve the look of a tapered stroke, as I did in the illustrations showing the background mountains, above.

 Saving your own colors. Using the Color Editor in ArtStudio, you can mix a color and save the new color into a color swatch. Choose a new color. Drag and drop your new color onto a square in the Color Editor.

Dragging a new color onto a color square in the Color Editor

 Swapping colors. In ArtStudio, to swap Color 1 and Color 2, double-tap on the Colors icon in the right toolbar. (The Colors icon shows color 1 and color 2 in a diagonally split color square.)

Blocking in color on the mid-ground and foreground

5 Refining the composition. A natural hand-drawn look is important to the style of *Mountain View.* In this step you will analyze your composition and then add final details and texture.

Step back and take a careful look at your composition. Does your eye meander, traveling from the background to the foreground in an interesting way? Are the shapes and colors that you have painted pleasing to your eye? At this point, I decided to make changes to the hills and foliage on the right side of my study. I repainted the large, dark green area, adding an area of lighter green. And I also painted more areas of darker green so the dark green foliage shapes would echo one another and step forward in the composition.

You can use the Smudge tool to pull and blend color. The Smudge tool is located in the left toolbar. Here, I used it to finesse the two light orange brushstrokes in the center of the painting. Position the tool over the area you want to refine, and pull

In this detail, you can see the base color on the hills and lake.

I used the Smudge tool to smudge and "pull" the orange paint into a tapered linear accent.

The completed Mountain View *study with texture accents*

in the direction you want the stroke to taper.

ArtStudio has preset brushes that allow you to add interesting touches of texture. To complete the piece, I

For the texture on the foreground sand and on the darker water, I used the Dots tool.

used the Dots tool (located in the left toolbar) to paint interesting textures onto the foreground sand and to add a shimmery look to the blue water.

Good work! You've completed this project. In the next project, we will work with the Wet Paint Brush in ArtStudio.

 Making a soft, streaky Paint Brush. The Paint Brush in ArtStudio applies color and can paint beautiful streaky strokes with a careful touch. To make a softer, streaky brush, tap the Paint Brush to open its Settings. By default, the top footprint is chosen. For a softer, expressive streaky stroke, try the fourth choice from the left.

Saving a new brush in ArtStudio. You can save a customized brush as a Favorite in ArtStudio by tapping the Heart icon to open the Favorite Brushes list, choosing Add, and then naming your new brush. The new brush will appear in Favorites.

Painting with Wet Paint in ArtStudio

The expressive pencil sketch

Painting directly over the sketch

1 **Starting with a pencil sketch.**
For this project, we will create a painterly color study, beginning with a sketch. You can work from a reference, or sketch from observation, as I did. Choose a simple subject with good lighting (such as a flower with leaves). We will begin by making a pencil sketch, and then block in color directly over the drawing.

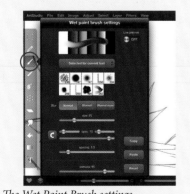

The Wet Paint Brush settings

Take a good look at your subject, and observe its linear aspects, its movement, and its forms. The negative space—the space around the subject—is important to viewing and painting the subject. For my study, I chose a Bird of Paradise plant and sketched from observation.

When you're ready to begin drawing, create a new file. Choose the Pencil tool in the left toolbar and size it to about 12 pixels. Choose a color. (I chose a medium gray.) Begin by sketching lightly, and slowly build a descriptive pencil sketch.

2 **Painting the background.** When your sketch is ready, choose the Wet Paint Brush in the left toolbar. The Wet Paint Brush is a round brush that paints brushstrokes similar to a traditional oval brush with a bristly tip. The Wetness feature in this brush allows you to apply new wet paint that blends with the existing paint on your image.

In the case of my subject, the background was dark without many details, and the subject was lit by the sunlight. Beginning with the space around your subject, enjoy applying paint with the smeary brush. Paint the background simply, so the focus will be on the center of interest. I painted varied dark blues and greens for my background.

Laying in more color and modeling forms

The completed color study of the Bird of Paradise

3 **Modeling the forms and adding details**. When your background is roughed in, begin painting your subject. Lay in the base colors first; then add touches of deeper color for the shadows and lighter colors for the highlights. Let your brushstrokes follow the forms.

When the basic colors and forms are laid in, take a careful look at your composition. What areas need to be refined? Does the center of interest need a brighter highlight or more saturated color? Zoom in on your image to finesse details. In areas with the brightest sunlight, I brightened highlights along the edges of the flower petals using a small Wet Paint Brush. Then I mixed a more saturated blue-purple in the Color Editor, and applied it to the rounded base of the Bird of Paradise flower. Using multiple bands of color, I subtly modeled the base of the flower and the leaves. The reflected light under the blue and purple flower base was interesting, and I painted it using a small Wet Paint Brush.

To finish, add painterly touches to the edges of your background using the Wet Paint Brush. Choose white in the Color Editor, and loosely paint back in to the edges of your image. Using the smeary Wet Paint Brush, I worked back and forth with white, dark blue, and dark green for the look of flickering rays of light shining along the top edges of the study.

Congratulations! You have completed the projects with ArtStudio. In the next section we will work with Sketchbook.

 Making a Wet Paint Brush blender. The Wet Paint Brush in ArtStudio applies color and can blend color with a careful touch. By default, the Wetness is set to 85% in Wet Paint Brush Settings. To smear and pull color while applying less new color, try increasing the Wetness settings.

Drawing With Sketchbook Express

Sketchbook overview. Sketchbook features a streamlined interface. The toolbar along the top of the screen includes the Gallery, New Sketch, Info, Undo, Redo, Brush Editor, Draw Style, Symmetry Mode, Text, Layer Transform, and Layer Editor icons.

To choose a drawing tool, tap the Brush icon to open the Editor. The Editor is divided into two areas: the Brush Editor and Color Editor. To choose a Hue, tap or drag in the Hue Ring; to adjust the saturation and value, tap or drag in the Saturation and Luminance diamond. The previous and current color are visible in the Previous and Current Color Selection icon. You can also mix a new color using the sliders. In the Brush Editor you can choose brushes and also edit their attributes.

Sketchbook Express features a selection of Pencils, Brushes, Pens, Markers, Erasers, and more. With Sketchbook Express, you can work with up to three layers. Sketchbook Pro boasts more brushes, layers, and other options.

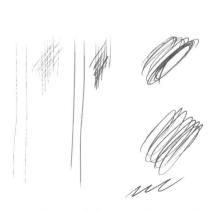

Strokes drawn with the #1 Pencil, #2 Pencil, and #3 Pencil

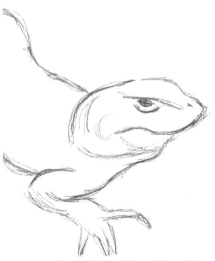

Starting to sketch the lizard using the #2 Pencil

1 **Trying out brushes.** Create a new image file. Tap the Brush icon to open the Editor and in the Color Editor, choose a dark gray. In the Brush Editor, tap the Pencil icon to choose it, and then choose a tip by tapping it. For a fine, grainy line, choose the #1 Pencil tip. For thicker lines, use the 2, 3, and 4 choices. Make practice marks to get a feel for the pencils.

Tap the Brush icon to open the Brush Editor. The Pencil tool with the #2 tip and a gray color are chosen.

2 **Sketching with the pencil.** Choose a subject for your sketch. I chose to sketch a Western Fence Lizard that lives nearby. You can work from observation or use a photo for reference. Study your reference carefully. For this project, I used a combination of "sketchy line" style,* along with cross-hatching* for modeling forms* and the cast shadow.

When you are comfortable with the pencils, begin sketching your subject. Start out with the #2 tip, and build up to a darker tone with the #3. The lines will vary in thickness with the speed that you draw them. Using the Brush Properties Puck, you

LEARN MORE ABOUT. . .

* "sketchy line" style. . . page 89
* cross-hatching. . . page 116
* modeling forms. . . pages 96, 111

Using the #3 Pencil to build up darker lines for emphasis

The completed sketch of the Western Fence Lizard, with the skin pattern and the cast shadow

can adjust the Size and Opacity of a brush. To access the Brush Properties Puck, tap the tiny circle icon near the bottom of the screen. In the Puck, drag upward to increase brush size and downward to decrease it. For Opacity, drag to the left to increase opacity and to the right to decrease it. While sketching, I varied the size of the pencil by dragging in the Puck.

The Brush Properties Puck is enabled in Sketchbook Express.

3 **Refining, adding details and texture.** When the proportions of your subject are roughed in, take a careful look at your drawing. Are there lines that need strengthening? Will hints of texture, and a bit more contrast improve your sketch?

Each Western Fence Lizard has subtly different colored patterns in its scales. After studying the lizard sketch, I decided to add a touch of patterning to her back. Using a #1 Pencil tip, I lightly sketched the pattern, letting my strokes follow the direction of the forms. Then, to give her presence in space, I sketched a cast shadow using a #2 Pencil tip and cross-hatching.

4 **Exporting a sketch.** When you are satisfied with your sketch, you can export your sketch from Sketchbook Express as a JPEG to your Photo Library. In the Gallery window, tap once on the sketch you want to export. A blue border will appear when it is selected. Tap the Export icon (the flower with the arrow) at the bottom of the screen. Select Photo Library, and in the Export window, choose the image orientation.

Good work! You've completed this sketch with Sketchbook Express. In the next project, we will use Sketchbook Pro to add color to a drawing.

Coloring a Drawing with Sketchbook Pro

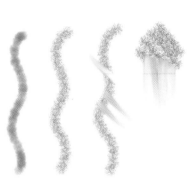

Painting transparent strokes with the brushes

The background is painted with light washes.

1 **Trying out brushes.** In this project, you will use Sketchbook Pro to color a drawing with transparent washes of color. First, make a new image and practice with brushes. Tap the Brush icon to open the Editor. The Editor is divided into two sections, the Color Editor and the Brush Editor. In the Color Editor, choose a color. In the Brush Editor, scroll to the fourth page of brushes and then choose the brush in the top center by tapping it. Make practice strokes. Now choose the brush to its right and paint. With these two brushes, you can simulate a watercolor look. Experiment with varying the opacity. The opacity and size can be changed in the Brush Editor or using the Brush Properties Puck, as in Sketchbook Express.

Next, choose the Smudge tool and experiment with smearing brushstrokes that you have painted.

2 **Painting the background.** You can open the sketch that you drew in Sketchbook Express (as I did) or draw a new pencil sketch in Sketchbook Pro. My sketch was exported to the Photo Library on my iPad. To import a sketch, in the Gallery window, tap the Import icon (the flower with the plus) at the bottom of the screen. Select the image you want to import. The image will appear in a new file.

Now, add a new layer for your colored brushwork. Tap the Layer

Simulating pressure. To date, there is no true pressure-sensitivity with the iPad. Most apps use velocity to simulate pressure-sensitivity, which can seem counterintuitive to those accustomed to using a Wacom pressure-sensitive tablet. With practice, sensitive, natural-looking line drawings can be achieved.

Access the side toolbars by tapping the small dot near the bottom of the screen. Scroll the toolbars to reveal more options.

The fourth page of the Brush Editor with the top center brush chosen.

Painting the body of the lizard

The completed quick sketch, with colored washes

Editor icon and when the window appears, tap the + icon to add a transparent layer. The active layer will have a blue border.

For a watercolor look, in the Brush Editor, scroll to the fourth panel of brushes and then choose the brush in the top center. Reduce its opacity to about 80%. I used this brush, with varied brown, gold, and gray colors to paint the background. To smooth areas of the background, I used the Smudge tool.

3 **Painting the lizard.** When your background is as you like it, add a new layer to your image for the subject coloring. To paint the subject, I used the textured brush to the right of the tip used in Step 2. This brush can paint a watercolor look and has texture reminiscent of handmade paper. Using varied browns, I painted the lizard's head and body. As I do

with traditional watercolor, I left the highlights as untouched white paper. As you work, let your strokes follow the shapes of the forms. To finish, I used the Smudge tool to blend a few areas on the back of the reptile.

Congratulations! You've finished the Sketchbook projects. In the next lesson, we will paint a study using Procreate.

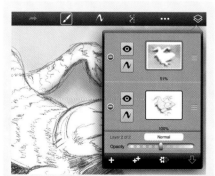

The background layer is active in the Layer Editor.

The fourth page of the Brush Editor with the textured brush chosen.

The fourth page of the Brush Editor with the Smudge brush chosen.

Making a Quick Color Study Using Procreate

Procreate overview. Procreate is a full-featured application with brushes and paint, layers, selections, special effects, and more. The brushes in Procreate simulate realistic paint application and smudging and can incorporate grain.

The interface is well organized: there's a top menu and right toolbar, with mark-making tools, layers, and color tools on the top. Adjustments to brushes (such as size and opacity) can be made on the right toolbar. You'll find the Undo and Redo icons in the right toolbar. To paint, tap the Brush icon to open the Brushes window. The Brushes window features tools for sketching, inking, painting, airbrushing, and more. The painting capabilities are versatile; for instance, the Paint, Smudge, and Eraser tools can use the same brush presets. To choose a color, tap the color icon; the Color panel opens. In the panel, tap a swatch to choose it, or tap and drag to choose a color in the light and saturation field (the large square).

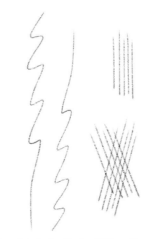

Strokes sketched with the 6B Pencil

Strokes sketched with the Soft Pastel

1 **Exploring brushes.** In this project we will focus on sketching on the canvas and on layers. To begin, we'll choose a color and try out the brushes that I used to paint my piece.

When you launch Procreate, by default the Gallery opens. Create a new file by tapping the + (plus) icon in the upper right of the Gallery window. In the New window, choose a resolution, and a new file will open. To choose a color, tap the

Color swatch in the upper right of the screen. Tap and drag in the saturation and brightness color field, or drag in the hue slider to pick a color. (I chose a brownish-gray.) Next, tap the Brush icon to open the Brush panel and tap to select the 6B Pencil. Have fun making practice marks with the 6B Pencil. Open the Brush panel and tap to select the Soft Pastel preset, and then make practice marks with this brush.

Choosing a color in the Color panel. Additional tools are located in the top and right toolbars.

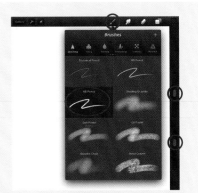

The 6B Pencil preset is selected in the Brush panel. The Size and Opacity sliders are located on the right.

The loose pencil sketch

Laying in color with the Soft Pastel

Brushing in general color areas

2 Making a sketch. You can sketch from life as I did, draw from the imagination, or use a reference photo. For my subject I drew a live model in the "sketchy line"* style. Begin by choosing the 6B Pencil in the Brush panel. The size and opacity of the brush can be adjusted using sliders on the right toolbar. To adjust the size, tap the Size slider and drag up to increase the size; drag down to decrease the size. (As I worked, I varied the brush size from 30–50%.) The Opacity slider is located below the Size slider, and operates in the same fashion. As you draw with the 6B Pencil, the strokes taper from thick to thin based on the speed that you draw.

LEARN MORE ABOUT. . .

* "sketchy line" style. . . page 89
* modeling forms. . . page 111

3 Laying in color with pastel. This study is meant to be a quick, loose sketch, showing general forms,* color, and lighting. In this step you will paint the base colors and values. For this study I used cool colors for the background and warmer colors for the foreground and figure. Darker values are used in the background and foreground with lighter values on the subject (figure). The center of interest in the

The pencil sketch is drawn on Layer 1. Layer 2 is selected and ready for color.

composition is the figure and the warm, pastel colors and light values on her skin help to bring the viewer's eye to the center of interest.

When you are satisfied with your sketch, open the Color panel and choose a deep gray-blue color for the background. Add a new layer for the color. Tap the Layers icon to open the Layers panel and tap the + (plus) icon to make a new layer. This layer will be named Layer 2 by default. You will notice in the Layers panel that your pencil sketch is on Layer 1. Procreate automatically generates a layer above the canvas when you open a new file. Tap once on Layer 2 to select it.

Using the Soft Pastel brush, loosely paint color onto the background behind the figure. For the feeling of a flat surface, as in a wall, make loose vertical strokes. For the seat, choose a warm gray-brown similar

The in-progress study with soft, grainy color

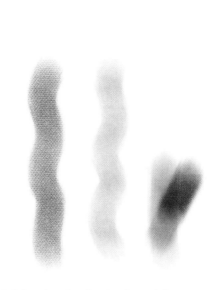

Soft Pastel strokes showing the varied texture

The finer texture can be seen on the arm.

to the color used for the pencil drawing. Rough in the shapes for the seat using loose horizontal and angled strokes. You can vary the size of the Soft Pastel as you work using the Size slider. After the general shapes for the background and seat, I used a light, neutral brown to begin painting the skin.

4 **Varying the texture.** The Soft Pastel paints with a rich grainy texture. Procreate allows you to adjust the scale of the texture using the Grain Behavior window. For my piece, I began by using the default Grain Behavior Scale setting, 253%. Then, for a more subtle look (for instance, on the skin), I decreased the texture size to 128%. The varied texture adds interest to the study.

To adjust the texture, tap the Brush icon to open the Brush panel and tap twice on the Soft Pastel to open its settings window. From the small row of icons at the bottom of this window, choose the Grain icon by tapping it. In the Grain window, reduce the size of the grain by

moving the Scale slider to the left. I used the subtle texture setting to paint the figure and lighter areas on the background wall.

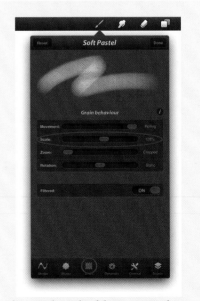

Adjusting the scale of the texture in the Grain Behavior window

The brighter rose color added to the skin

The completed quick color study

5 Painting the figure and adding final touches. Carefully observe the forms and values on the figure, and gradually build up color, value, and texture. To build up color subtly as you work, you can vary the opacity of the Soft Pastel using the Opacity slider.

Step back and carefully examine your piece. Would your study benefit from brighter highlights in a few areas and deeper tones in the shadow areas? Would a bit of brighter color enhance your subject? On my piece, the colors were fairly neutral, and the lighting was soft. I strengthened a few of the lines in the sketch by drawing with the 6B Pencil and a dark gray-brown. Then, using the Soft Pastel with dark browns and blues, I painted a few darker shadows on the drapery. For a warmer feeling on my subject, I painted warm pastel browns, light oranges, and rosy pinks onto the skin. Then I added

 Versatile brushes. Procreate offers versatile brushes. For instance, the Paint, Smudge, and Eraser tools can use the same brush presets.

a few strokes of brighter rose to the shadow on the arm, leg, and side. To blend a few areas, I used the Smudge tool with the Soft Pastel preset.

To finish, I brightened highlights on the shoulder, arm, and knee.

Good work! You have completed the color study project with Procreate. In the next project, we will work with Adobe Ideas.

Sketching with Adobe Ideas

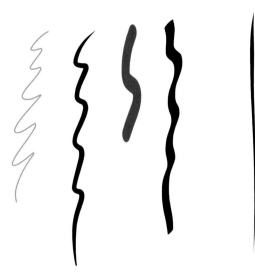

Pencil, Brush, Marker, and Pen strokes

A variety of strokes drawn with the Brush tool

Adobe Ideas Overview. A versatile vector application for inking sketches and drawings, the drawing and coloring tools in Adobe Ideas are the Pencil, Brush, Marker, Pen, Eraser, and Paint Bucket. Layers provide flexibility. Images from the photo library can be imported into Adobe Ideas and you can also access the iPad camera. Images created in Adobe Ideas can be imported into Adobe Illustrator or Photoshop as a vector file.

1 **Exploring the drawing tools.** In this project we will focus on getting acquainted with Adobe Ideas and sketching. To begin, we will choose a color and try out the drawing tools. Of the drawing tools, the Brush and Pen are my favorites

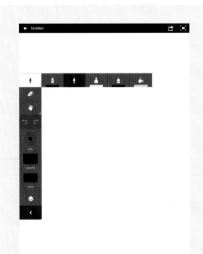

The Adobe Ideas interface with the mark-making and coloring tools menu open

because you can sketch expressive thick-to-thin lines with them.

When you launch Adobe Ideas, by default the Gallery opens. You can create a new file by tapping the + (plus) icon near the bottom of the Gallery window. After tapping the + (plus) icon once, an empty new image appears. You will see a menu along the top of the screen and a toolbar on the left side. Tap once on the Pencil icon to reveal the set of mark-making and coloring tools: the Pencil, Brush, Marker, Pen, and Paint Bucket. In the Toolbar, you will also find the Eraser, Undo and Redo, Size, Opacity, Color, and Layers icons.

Have fun making expressive marks while trying out the drawing tools.

Dolphin Play *was drawn with the Brush tool in Adobe Ideas.*

2 **Sketching with the Brush tool.** The Brush is my favorite drawing tool in Adobe Ideas. Drawing from my imagination, I used the

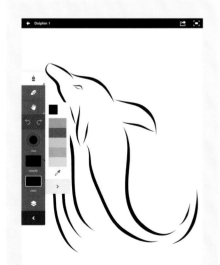

The open Color panel

Brush tool to create these whimsical sketches of dolphins. The Brush tool allows you to draw with expressive thick-to-thin lines, and the strokes vary in thickness based on the speed that you draw them. As you draw, Adobe Ideas applies smoothing to the vector strokes.

For this series of sketches, I used the Brush tool and black color. Choose the Brush tool in the toolbar and then tap the Color icon to choose black for the color. Practice drawing smooth graceful curves with the Brush tool. You can adjust the width of the brush by tapping

the Size icon in the toolbar, and dragging up to increase the size and down to decrease the size. While making these drawings, I sized the Brush to 15–20 pixels.

Good work! You have completed this project with Adobe Ideas. In the next project, we will use Adobe Ideas to color the drawing.

Coloring with Adobe Ideas

A detail of the black-and-white sketch

Using the Paint Bucket, tap on a line or shape to color it

1 **Getting started with color.** For this project, you can draw directly in color or add color to a drawing as I did. For my piece, I colored a copy of the black-and-white sketch of dolphins made in Adobe Ideas.

To begin, open the Gallery in Adobe Ideas and make a duplicate of a black-and-white drawing, so you don't accidentally replace it. Tap the Duplicate Files icon in the upper right of your screen to open the Duplicate Files window, and then select the image you want to copy. When the image is active, a check mark will appear on the image. Tap the Duplicate button to make the copy. The copy will appear in the gallery; tap the image to open it.

2 **Filling lines with color and creating a theme.** Adobe Ideas makes it fun to color vector art made in the application. I colored the *Dolphin Play* sketch using the Paint Bucket tool. Begin by choosing the Paint Bucket tool. In the Toolbar, tap

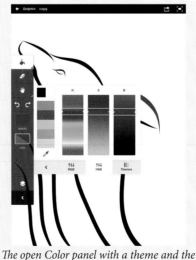

The open Color panel with a theme and the HSB color sliders.

the Brush icon to open the menu, and tap to select the Paint Bucket. The Paint Bucket remembers the most recent color used. Now choose a color in the Color panel. In the toolbar, tap the Color icon to open the Color panel with its swatches and eyedropper. To fully open the panel with the color sliders, click the small arrow under the eyedropper. The open Color panel offers a theme of

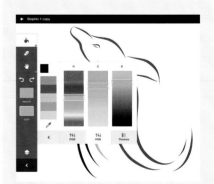

Using the Color panel and the HSB sliders to mix a tropical turquoise

The second dolphin is colored with a bright red-orange.

Dolphin Play in whimsical color

colors, an eyedropper, and RGB (red, green, blue) sliders, and HSB (hue, saturation and brightness) sliders. The eyedropper is useful for sampling color directly from the image. In the toolbar, tap the Brush icon to open the menu, and tap to select the Paint Bucket. Using the Paint Bucket, you can color a vector line or shape, by tapping once on it with the Paint Bucket tool. Pinch to zoom in to your image, and then tap on a shape with the Paint bucket tool to edit its color. Repeat this process to fill the shapes that you desire.

A theme is a collection of colors that you save to use in your work. To create a theme from the colors in your drawing, open the Color panel and tap Themes. Another window opens with available space. Tap the + (plus) icon. Adobe Ideas generates a theme using the colors in your image. Tap on Save to save your colors. The colors appear in Themes in the Color panel.

Colors in an existing theme can edited. Mix a new color. In the toolbar, tap and hold on the color icon; you will see an outline appear. Drag and drop the new color on to a space on the color theme column. Your new color will appear in the theme. Continue to add colors as desired.

Congratulations! You have completed the projects with Adobe Ideas. In the next project, we will create a collage sketch using Adobe Photoshop Touch.

 Making a color background fill. To make a background fill in Adobe Ideas, begin by adding a new layer for the fill. Next, use a drawing tool (such as the Brush or Pen) to sketch a continuous line around the perimeter of your image. You can then fill the area with color using the Paint Bucket tool. After making your colored background, open the Layers panel, tap on the small icon to the right of the layer name, and drag to reposition the layer with the fill.

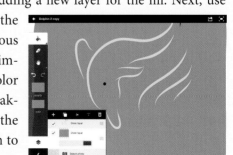

The filled layer is positioned below the line sketch.

Making a Collage Sketch with Adobe Photoshop Touch

A detail of the in-progress collage. The layer with the palm trees is set to a transparent blend mode.

Adobe Photoshop Touch overview. With Adobe Photoshop Touch you can edit and apply effects to your photos. I appreciate the ease with which you can create sketches using photo imagery, layers, and special effects on your iPad with Adobe Photoshop Touch. The sketch created in this project can be exported as a PSD file and opened in Photoshop for finishing touches. This *Live Aloha* collage sketch is used with a project in Chapter 14 that incorporates Photoshop and Painter.

1 **Getting started.** For this project we will get acquainted with Adobe Photoshop Touch by making a collage sketch using a variety of imagery. I titled my collage *Live Aloha* as we love Hawaii and the genuine Aloha we have experienced there.

To begin, launch Adobe Photoshop Touch; the Gallery window appears. Press the + (plus) icon to open a new file. I like the easy-to-use interface.

The Adobe Photoshop Touch interface with its top menu, vertical menu on the left with tools, and the Layers panel on the lower right.

The menu along the top contains several icons with which you can access features and effects. The menu along the top of the efficient interface contains icons with which you can access menus with features and effects: the Back Arrow (to save a file to the gallery), Picture + (import picture), Pencil (edit functions such as cut and copy), Selection (selection operations such as Select Pixels, Inverse, and Feather), the Transform tool icon, Adjustments icon, *fx* icon (creative filter effects for your photos), *&* icon (miscellaneous commands such as Crop, Image Size, Rotate, and more), and the Full Screen Mode icon. A toolbar on the left side of the screen contains selection tools, the Brush tool, Rubber Stamp, Eraser, and the Blur tool. Tool options are nested with some of the tools.

The morning photo with brightly colored sky

The high-contrast photo of palm trees

2 **Composing with images.** My love of Hawaii, its people, and culture inspired me to create a Hawaiian theme incorporating photos shot when visiting the islands.

You can build a collage using your own photos. With the new file open, import a photo for the background. To import a picture, tap the Picture + icon and then browse to locate the image. (I chose an image with a brightly colored sky.) Tap to select

the desired image then tap the Add button near the bottom of the screen. When the image appears, tap the blue check mark to place it in the image. To adjust the position or size of the image, use Transform. Press the Transform icon. In transform mode, you will see handles on the sides of the image. Press and drag on a handle to edit the size of the image.

Next, for a look similar to mine, choose a high-contrast image that

will add interest to the top and sides of your image. I chose a photo of palm trees. Press the Picture + icon, and then browse to locate your photo. Press the Add button to import it. As you did with the first photo, when the image appears, tap the check mark to place it in the image.

To color the high-contrast photo of the palm trees, I experimented with blend modes that are available in the Layers panel. The Layers panel

The background photo is imported into the collage file.

Using the Transform function to scale the photo to cover the background

The second photo imported is a high-contrast image.

The palm trees layer is placed and then colored using a transparent blend mode

The transparent Overlay blend mode works well with a silhouette image.

The photo of Steve surfing has beautiful lighting.

and layer stack are located in the lower right of your screen. In your image, tap once on the topmost layer to select it. A white border will appear around the selected layer. Press the Layers icon to open the Layers panel. To set the Blend mode, press the arrow to open the menu, and then choose a new blend mode. A live preview allows you to easily experiment with the different Blend mode looks. (After previewing them, I settled on Overlay.) When you have

Setting the blend mode for the palm tree layer to Overlay in the Layers panel

made your choice, tap on the image outside the panel to accept the choice and to close the panel.

The surfer and the title "Live Aloha" are the focal point of my collage. Next, I imported a photo of Steve surfing. Import your third image by tapping the Picture + icon and navigating to locate your image. Choose an image that will make a nice focal point for your collage. I chose this photo of Steve for his graceful style, the lighting, and the clear, tropical water. When you place your photo, you will see handles along its edges. Press the check mark to accept the import.

In this project, I used the Transform tool to reposition the photo and scale it. With the layer selected, tap the Transform icon (with the four arrows) at the top of the screen. You will see handles appear along

the edges of the active photo. Press and drag to reposition the photo. To scale it, drag on a corner handle. When you are satisfied with the position and size, accept it by tapping the blue check mark icon on the panel at the bottom of the screen.

Next, press the surfer layer thumbnail to select it, and drag it below the palm trees layer in the layer stack. The Overlay mode applied to the palm tree layer above will alter the color of the underlying layers.

Using the Transform tool to scale the photo of the surfer

The oval selection on the surfer layer

The finished Live Aloha collage sketch

3 **Editing with a selection.** Next, I used a selection to give the surfer photo an oval shape. The selection tools are located in the vertical toolbar. Press and hold the Marquee Selection tool to reveal and choose the Circle Selection tool. With the layer active, press and drag a selection around the areas that you want to keep. For a smooth transition along the edge, feather

the selection. From the Select menu, choose Feather, and in the panel at the bottom of the screen, set the Feather to 2 pixels. To accept, press the blue check mark. Next, reverse the selection to preserve the surfer and delete the remainder of the layer contents. Open the Select menu and choose Inverse. To remove the contents of the inverted selection, in the top menu press the Pencil icon to access the Edit menu and select Clear from menu.

4 **Adding a title.** As a final step, add a title to the collage. On the top menu, tap the & icon, to open its menu. Press the Text icon and a text layer appears on your image. To edit it, tap the small word "TEXT" on the panel at the bottom of your screen, and a keyboard appears. Type your title; I typed "Live Aloha." To edit the font style, tap the styled type on the panel to open the font menu. (I chose Brush Script Std Medium.) When you are finished editing your text, tap the check mark to accept the changes. To scale or reposition the title, use the Transform tool as you did with the subject photo in Step 2. Now, take a good look at your design to check the interplay of the objects.

Good work! You have completed a creative collage using Adobe Photoshop Touch. This project completes the chapter.

The oval selection on the surfer layer, with the open Select menu. Note that the surfer layer is under the palm trees layer in the layer stack order.

Using the Transform tool to scale and position the title on the image.

Art materials in the studio

3
PHOTOSHOP, PAINTER, AND TABLET BASICS FOR ARTISTS

Here you'll find instructions for setting up your drawing tablet, drawing and navigating with the tablet and stylus, customizing your workspace, and more. Both Painter and Photoshop have brushes, color tools, layers, blend modes, and methods for isolating portions of images, but each program has its own strengths. In the individual sections that are devoted to Photoshop and Painter, you'll find definitions of terms and some comparisons between the two programs.

 The Wacom Intuos tablet and stylus provide the freedom to paint with a cordless pen and communicate the expressive nuances of hand and wrist movements to the computer through programs like Painter and Photoshop. Without a fine-quality tablet and stylus, I could not create the paintings that you see in this book. I choose to use the Intuos line of tablets because they allow sensitivity that other tablets do not, such as higher levels of pressure sensitivity, tilt, bearing, and other movements. Without this complex sensitivity, the brushes in Painter and Photoshop would not perform the way you see them pictured in the illustrations that demonstrate the brushstrokes. I'm amazed at how good Photoshop is with compositing, color correction, and painting. Painter continues to delight me with its incredible variety of realistic natural media brushes and textures, that I enjoy using with my paintings. Together with the tablet, these two programs make up the perfect work environment for a fine artist or an illustrator.

Introduction

This chapter is not meant to cover everything basic about the tools used in this book—it focuses on favorite features of the hardware and software that are useful for artists who want to paint.

Photoshop and Painter overlap in some areas of functionality, and they both have unique strengths. Both programs have brushes and features for working with color, layers, and selections. *Layers* are elements that hover above the image background, providing a great deal of flexibility in composing artwork. A *selection* is an area of the image that has been isolated so that changes can be made to the contents only, or to protect the area from change. You'll find more information on these topics later in this chapter and in the projects that follow.

Portability. The portability between Photoshop and Painter has improved. You can now move files with layers, layer masks, and alpha channels between the programs with the layers intact—if you remember a few basic rules. To take a Photoshop file into Painter, save your working Photoshop file in Photoshop format to preserve the native effects and functions such as layer styles and adjustment layers. Then make a copy of your working file with the layers converted to pixel-based layers, and save it in Photoshop format for opening in Painter. When working in Painter, always save your working Painter file in RIFF format (Painter's native format). RIFF format preserves Painter's native brush effects such as "wet" Watercolor paint, thick Impasto paint, special effects layers, and other native effects. If you'd like to take a Painter file into Photoshop,

save a copy of the file in Photoshop format with any special layers (such as adjustment layers or layer styles) converted to default (pixel-based) layers. Chapter 14 demonstrates working between Photoshop and Painter.

The Intuos tablet. Without a quality tablet, I could not have created the beautiful paintings in Painter and Photoshop that you'll see in the projects and gallery later in this book. You will not achieve the full performance of the brushes with just the software and a mouse. The Intuos tablets feature 2,048 levels of pressure, and they sense subtle variations in your wrist and arm movements—such as tilt and bearing—that other tablets do not. The Intuos5 offers a resolution of 5,080 lines per inch, which allows for greater accuracy while navigating and drawing.

Anatomy of a
Tablet and Stylus

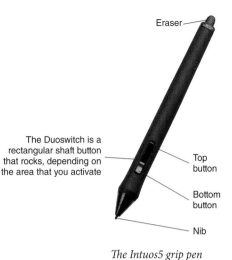

Eraser

The Duoswitch is a
rectangular shaft button
that rocks, depending on
the area that you activate

Top
button

Bottom
button

Nib

The Intuos5 grip pen

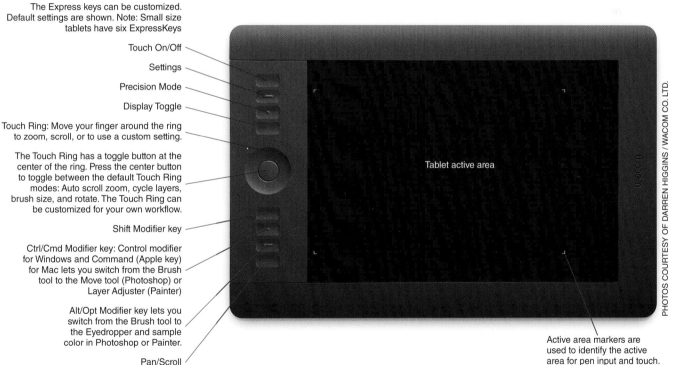

The Express keys can be customized.
Default settings are shown. Note: Small size
tablets have six ExpressKeys

Touch On/Off

Settings

Precision Mode

Display Toggle

Touch Ring: Move your finger around the ring
to zoom, scroll, or to use a custom setting.

The Touch Ring has a toggle button at the
center of the ring. Press the center button
to toggle between the default Touch Ring
modes: Auto scroll zoom, cycle layers,
brush size, and rotate. The Touch Ring can
be customized for your own workflow.

Shift Modifier key

Ctrl/Cmd Modifier key: Control modifier
for Windows and Command (Apple key)
for Mac lets you switch from the Brush
tool to the Move tool (Photoshop) or
Layer Adjuster (Painter)

Alt/Opt Modifier key lets you
switch from the Brush tool to
the Eyedropper and sample
color in Photoshop or Painter.

Pan/Scroll

Tablet active area

Active area markers are
used to identify the active
area for pen input and touch.

PHOTOS COURTESY OF DARREN HIGGINS / WACOM CO. LTD.

The illustrations above show the Intuos5 tablet and Intuos5 grip pen. If you learn to use the ExpressKeys while painting, you can eliminate the use of your keyboard during most painting tasks. The illustration above shows the ExpressKeys and Touch Ring. You can modify the tablet preferences to customize the keys. If you have an earlier Intuos tablet, the shaft buttons on the stylus operate the same as the Intuos5.

Getting Started with Your Tablet

Sitting up straight while painting, with the arms of the chair adjusted to match the table

PHOTOGRAPH: MELINDA HOLDEN

GETTING COMFORTABLE WITH YOUR TABLET

The photograph above shows me using my tablet at my desk. I recommend choosing a chair that has an adjustable back and arms because working on the computer requires a lot of sitting. (When working on the computer, remember to get up and take breaks to stretch.) Notice how I have the arms of the chair adjusted to match the height of the pull-out shelf on my desk. Then I adjusted the chair height so that I could align the arms of the chair with the pull-out on the desk. This setup keeps my arms supported and relaxed while working. If I'm making wide, expressive strokes on a large tablet, I lower the chair arms so that I can sweep broadly with my hand. If I'm doing a lot of typing, I place my keyboard on the tablet. When I'm painting, the keyboard is on the table above the tablet, as shown in the photo.

It helps to sit up straight when you're painting. You'll have more energy. It's so easy to get lost in your art and slump in the chair. Other times, I place my tablet in my lap when I want to relax and draw. I find that this position feels similar to sketching with my conventional sketchbook on my lap.

In addition to helping you draw more expressively on the computer, you can use your stylus as a useful, comfortable pointing device when you need to choose a command from a menu or to move a panel around on the screen. It feels more natural in your hand than a mouse. Spreading your hand and pushing a mouse for hours can lead to wrist problems. I prefer to use my stylus for drawing and some of the pointing tasks because it keeps my hand from getting overworked.

 Keeping a safe distance. If you want to take a break from drawing, or if you need to use your mouse, move your stylus off the tablet surface so that the tablet will not sense it. (The stylus will become active when it is approximately 6mm or .25 inches from the tablet surface.)

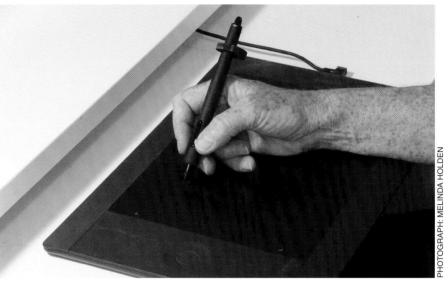

Photo of the artist's hand in a comfortable position for drawing

DRAWING AND NAVIGATING WITH THE STYLUS

Follow the manufacturer's directions for connecting the tablet to your computer and for installing the tablet software. The top left of the tablet is orientated to the top left of your display.

Navigating using Pen mode. By default, your tablet will be set up in Pen mode, which is the mode you'll want to use for drawing. With Pen mode, the cursor will jump to wherever you move it on the screen using absolute positioning, which means that every point on your tablet corresponds to exactly one point on the screen. If you'd like to choose a color, lift the stylus up from the tablet and point to a new color in the Color panel (touch once on it). Lift up the pen and touch it back onto your image where you want to paint. Then press and draw across the tablet to make a brushstroke. To move a panel onscreen, first point to the item to select it and then drag it to move it.

Making brushstrokes in Photoshop. To draw in Photoshop, choose the Brush tool in the Tools panel. A brush will automatically be chosen, but if you'd like to use another brush, open the Brush Preset Picker on the Options bar and select a brush preset.

Making brushstrokes in Painter. To draw in Painter, choose the Brush tool in the Toolbox. A brush will automatically be available, but if you'd like to use another one, choose a brush category (such as the Pencils) by clicking the small triangle on the Brush Selector to open the Brush Library, then choose a brush category (such as Pencils) and a variant (such as the 2B Pencil variant of Pencils).

Hold your stylus in your hand comfortably, similar to how you would hold a pencil or conventional pen. (You can hover the pen over the tablet to reposition the cursor if needed.) Touch your stylus to your tablet and press down, keeping your pen in contact with the tablet as you complete the first brushstroke. Lift up to start another brushstroke.

To achieve the brushstrokes you'd like to paint, you might have to press harder with your stylus on the tablet than you're accustomed to pressing down on a pencil when you're drawing on paper.

Using a Tapered Pastel brush in Painter, I drew these brushstrokes. I used a default Medium Tip Feel setting for the top stroke and my favorite medium-soft setting for the bottom stroke.

CHOOSING YOUR SETTINGS FOR YOUR STYLUS

Taking a look at important settings. After you have connected your tablet to your computer and have installed the software, you can open the tablet application and begin learning about the settings. The driver dialog box has been redesigned for the new Intuos5 tablet. If you have an earlier tablet, the settings are similar (for instance, the Intuos4). If you have already begun to use your tablet and want to follow this exercise, I recommend resetting the tablet application to its global defaults by clicking the Reset Tab to Default button.

Adjusting the Tip Feel tab. In my opinion, the Tip Feel tab is the most important window because its settings affect how Photoshop and Painter interpret the pressure that you apply to the tablet. The Tip Feel controls the hardness or softness of the pressure curve. The harder the pressure curve, the firmer you'll have to press on the tablet to make a brushstroke appear on your screen, and the less variation in the stroke. With a softer curve, you'll

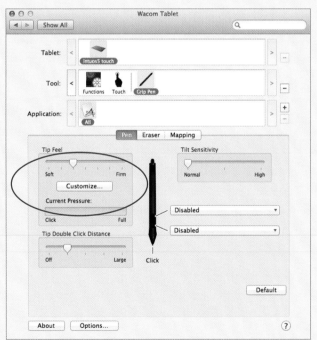

Customizing the Tip Feel controls under the Pen tab in the Intuos5 driver window

I drew the top Tapered Pastel brushstroke using the firmest Tip Feel setting, and it required that I press very firmly to make a mark. I drew the bottom stroke using the softest setting using very light pressure.

be able to draw by applying much less pressure. As you can see by looking at the illustration above, if you choose a setting that is too hard or too soft, you'll lose the delicate, expressive control you need. When you experiment with the range of Tip Feel settings in the Wacom Tablet window, you might find out that you prefer different settings for Photoshop and Painter, as I do. In the projects that follow later in this book, you'll notice suggested tablet settings listed in the Artist's Materials boxes. To learn about customizing the buttons on the stylus for expressive sketching, turn to the next page.

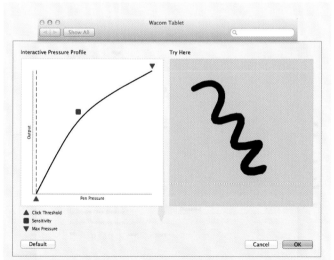

The Customize window (for the Intuos5) displays an Interactive Pressure Profile for the stroke, and it allows you to draw a test stroke.

 Customizing settings for applications. You can set up specific preferences for your favorite application. First, launch the programs for which you want to arrange settings. In the Wacom Tablet window, click on the tool you want to customize (I chose the Grip Pen icon) and then click the small plus to the right of the Applications field. The Select Application window will appear. Make a choice from the list of applications, and click OK. Back in the Wacom Tablet window, click on the application you want to arrange, and then adjust the settings. (I clicked on the Adobe Photoshop CS6 icon and on the Pen tab and adjusted the Tip Feel for a harder pressure curve. Then, because I like a softer pressure curve with Painter's brushes, I clicked on the Corel Painter icon and adjusted the Tip Feel settings for this program.)

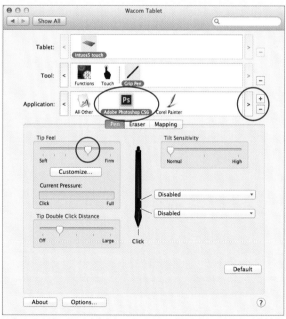

Adjusting the Tip Feel settings to a harder pressure curve for Photoshop

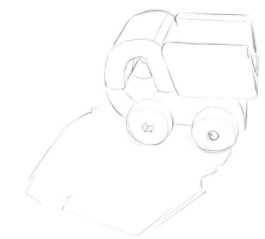

Quick sketch drawn in Painter with the Cover Pencil

Coloring the sketch with loose brushstrokes of pastel and chalk

Customizing the buttons on the stylus for expressive sketching. Next, configure the tool buttons on the pen (for all applications). Click the Pen tab. For the top button on the stylus, leave the button set to Erase. While doing expressive sketching, I often roll the stylus in my hand, which makes it easy to accidentally push one of the buttons while holding the stylus. For the exercises and projects in Chapters 3–7, I recommend setting the two

shaft buttons to Disabled (or Ignored) because an artist holds this area of the pen while drawing. For more methodical work such as painting subtle, graduated values, you can set the shaft buttons to help you to sample color while you're painting. The tablet is automatically mapped to fit the screen on the computer where it is installed, as shown below.

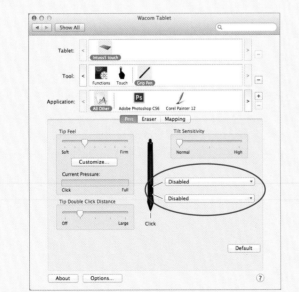

The Duoswitch controls under the Pen tab are set to Disabled, and are ready for quick sketching.

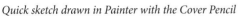

The Mapping tab showing the Mode set to Pen, Screen, and Tablet areas set to Full

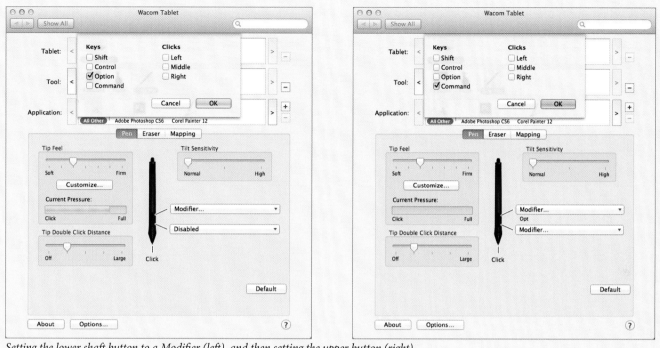

Setting the lower shaft button to a Modifier (left), and then setting the upper button (right)

CUSTOMIZING THE STYLUS BUTTONS

Setting the Duoswitch pen shaft buttons to sample color. When doing quick sketching, I prefer to set my stylus buttons to Disabled (or Ignored) so that I don't accidentally press them if I am rolling the pen in my hand. For doing more sustained work, it's helpful to set up the buttons so that you can sample color on-the-fly in Photoshop and Painter by toggling from the Brush tool to the Eyedropper tool. In the Wacom window, click on the Pen tab; then click the pop-up menu for the upper shaft button, and choose Alt (PC) or Option (Mac). Click OK.

Setting a pen shaft button to help adjust a layer. You can set up the second shaft button to temporarily switch from the Brush tool to the Move tool in Photoshop or to the Layer Adjuster in Painter. In the Pen tab, click on the lower shaft button pop-up menu, and choose Control (PC users) or Command (Mac). If you do more compositing work with layers in Photoshop and more of your painting in Painter, it's a good idea to set up your tablet preferences to reflect how you use the pen in each program. You might want to program your pen Duoswitch to use the modifiers for Photoshop (to quickly reposition a layer on your

image) and then set the Duoswitch to be disabled in Painter while you're painting.

 A helpful eraser. It's a good idea to leave the button on the top end of the stylus set to function as an Eraser (its default setting) so that you can turn your pen upside down and erase on-the-fly.

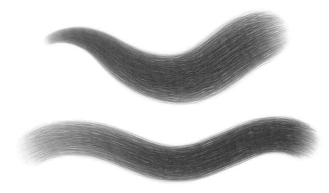

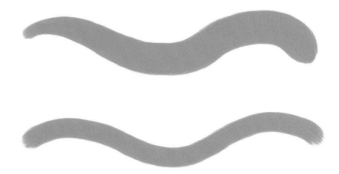

Brushstrokes painted in Painter using the Thick Acrylic Round. Top: varied pressure; bottom: pressure controlled by the Pressure Hold key.

Strokes painted in Photoshop using the Gouache brush from Chapter 10. Top: varied pressure; bottom: pressure controlled using the custom Pressure Hold key.

Setting a button to control pressure. You can set a button on your pen so that you can retain a particular amount of pressure on-the-fly while you are drawing a brushstroke. In the Wacom window, choose the Pen tab. Select a key you want to program, click its pop-up menu, and choose Pressure Hold. After setting up your Pressure Hold key, try making some brushstrokes in each program.

Begin making a stroke, and then press the key to retain the pressure you were applying at that moment. To draw a thinner stroke on-the-fly without changing your brush size, press the key and then begin painting the stroke.

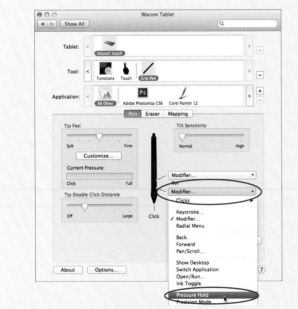

Setting up the Pressure Hold option in the Pen settings window

Changing the size of a brush using tablet keys. You can set the tablet keys on an Intuos5 to the bracket keys, which are a shortcut in Photoshop and Painter for changing brush size. (Press the left bracket key [to reduce the size. To increase its size, use the right bracket].) In the Wacom window, click on Functions, and then click ExpressKeys. When the window appears, choose a key and select Keystroke from its pop-up menu. When the Keystroke menu appears, type [and click OK. To set a key to increase the brush size, use the] key and follow the same process as before.

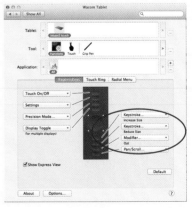

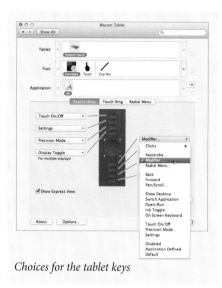

Choices for the tablet keys

Pressing a tablet key to sample color while painting

PHOTOGRAPH: MELINDA HOLDEN

CUSTOMIZING BUTTONS ON AN INTUOS5 TABLET

Setting up for your non-dominant hand. When you installed your Intuos5 tablet, you were asked to choose an orientation for a right- or left-handed user. The orientation that you choose determines the tablet's default settings. You can easily change the orientation and set up your tablet for right or left-handed users. The ExpressKey and Touch Ring settings automatically reconfigure when you change

The Orientation options menu in the Mapping window.

the handedness setting. Open the Wacom control panel, click the Pen icon and then select Mapping. For instance, I paint with my right hand. While I'm drawing, I can use my non-dominant hand on the buttons on the left side of the tablet.

For instance, the second key from the bottom by default is set to Alt/ Option. While painting with a brush in Painter or Photoshop, I can press this key to toggle from the brush to the Eyedropper to sample color from my image as I work.

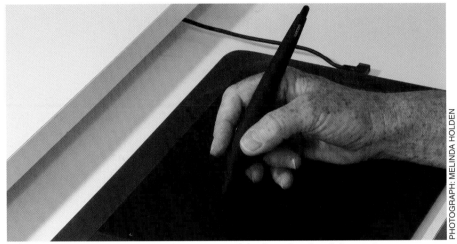

Using the stylus wheel on the airbrush pen to control the flow of media while painting

Airbrush Hard Round strokes (from left to right), button near to forward, midway, and all the way back

USING THE AIRBRUSH STYLUS

A special Wacom stylus. The Wacom Intuos Airbrush* stylus has a fingerwheel that provides additional control over the application of paint. You can operate the wheel independently of the pressure, tilt, or angle you apply to the stylus. Hold the stylus comfortably in your hand, and touch it to your tablet. Use your index finger to roll the wheel forward to reduce the flow of paint and backward to increase the flow of paint. In addition, both Photoshop and Painter have settings that take advantage of the fingerwheel. Many of the presets in Photoshop and the brush variants in Painter can be set to take advantage of the Airbrush stylus controls.

Adjusting size with the stylus wheel in Photoshop. You can set the Hard Round so that the stylus wheel controls the width of the stroke. Enable the Airbrush Style Build Up Effects button in the Options bar. In the Brush panel's Shape Dynamics window, set the Size Jitter Control pop-up menu to Stylus Wheel.

The Hard Round and the Shape Dynamics pane of the Brush panel

LEARN MORE ABOUT. . .

* Airbrushes. . . pages 55, 82, 83

Airbrush Soft Round strokes, from left to right: button near to forward, midway, and all the way back

Digital Airbrush strokes, from left to right: button near to forward, midway, and all the way back

Fine Spray Airbrush strokes, from left to right: button near to forward, midway, and all the way back

Adjusting flow with the stylus wheel in Photoshop. You can set the Soft Round so the stylus wheel controls the amount of media applied. Enable the Airbrush Style Build Up Effects button in the Options bar. In the Brush panel Transfer window, under Flow Jitter, set the pop-up menu to Stylus Wheel.

Adjusting size with the stylus wheel in Painter. You can set the Digital Airbrush (and other Airbrushes in Painter) so that the stylus wheel controls the stroke width. In the Size panel of Brush Controls, set the Size Expression pop-up menu to Wheel and the Min Size to about 20%.

Adjusting media flow with the stylus wheel in Painter. You can set the Fine Spray, Coarse Spray, and a few other Airbrushes so that the stylus wheel controls the amount of media applied. In the Airbrush panel of the Brush Controls, set the Expression pop-up menu to Wheel.

The Soft Round and the Transfer pane of the Brush panel

The Digital Airbrush in Painter and the Size panel of Brush Controls

The Fine Spray Airbrush in Painter and the Airbrush panel of Brush Controls

Round Blunt strokes, without rotation (left) and with rotation (right)

Round Soft Pastel strokes, from left to right: the default brush stroke and with Color Expression set to Rotation (right)

USING THE ART PEN STYLUS

Full rotation with the Art Pen. In your hand, the Art Pen has the feel of a traditional marker and it comes with chiseled and pointed nibs made of plastic or felt. In addition to pressure and tilt, the Wacom Art Pen stylus senses rotation from 0–360°. Many of the brush presets in Photoshop and the brush variants in Painter can be set to take advantage of the added dimension of rotation. As you try out these concepts, smoothly roll the Art Pen stylus in your fingers as you pull the brushstrokes.

LEARN MORE ABOUT. . .

* Mixer Brush tool. . . pages 132–134, 169

Adding rotation to a brush preset in Photoshop. You can set the Round Blunt preset so that the rotation controls the movement of bristles during a stroke. Choose the Mixer Brush tool* and the Round Blunt preset. In the Brush panel's Shape Dynamics window, set the Angle Jitter Control pop-up menu to Rotation.

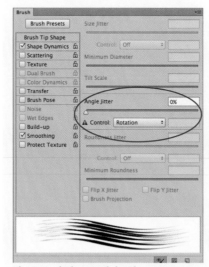

The Round Blunt and the Shape Dynamics pane of the Brush panel

Varying color using rotation in Painter. For varied color in grainy brushstrokes, you can set the Soft Round Pastel variant of Pastels so that the stylus rotation varies the color as you paint. In the Color panel, choose a Main Color (I chose a blue-purple) and an Additional Color (I chose a dark pink). In the Color Expression panel of Brush Controls, set the Expression pop-up menu to Rotation. I also varied the color subtly by setting the Color Jitter to 4%. Smoothly roll the stylus in your fingers as you pull the brushstroke, and you will see the color change.

The Round Soft Pastel in Painter and the Color Expression panel of the Brush Controls

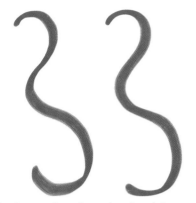

Flat Opaque Gouache strokes, from left to right: the default brush stroke and with Angle set Rotation (right)

Scattered Leaves strokes, from left to right: the default brush stroke and with Count Jitter set to Rotation (right)

Impressionist strokes, from left to right: the default brush stroke and with Stroke Jitter set to Rotation (right)

Varying angle using rotation in Painter. The Flat Opaque Gouache variant of Gouache can be set to vary the angle of the brush using rotation. In the Angle panel of Brush Controls, set the Expression pop-up menu to Rotation. Smoothly roll the stylus in your fingers as you pull the brush-stroke, and you will see the contours of the stroke subtly change. The default brush has Angle Expression set to Bearing, which works well for a standard stylus such as the Grip Pen.

Varying Scatter using rotation with a brush preset in Photoshop. You can set the Scattered Leaves preset so that the rotation controls the scatter of the marks during a stroke. Choose the Brush tool and the Scattered Leaves preset. In the Brush panel's Scatter window, set the Count Jitter Control pop-up menu to Rotation.

Varying Stroke Jitter using rotation in Painter. The Impressionist variant of Artists can be set to vary the randomness of the brush marks using rotation. In the Stroke Jitter panel of Brush Controls, set the Expression pop-up menu to Rotation. Increase the Stroke Jitter to 2.00. Smoothly roll the stylus in your fingers as you pull the brushstroke, and you will see the Impressionist brush marks vary as you paint.

Impressionist brush in Painter and the Stroke Jitter panel of the Brush Controls

The Flat Opaque Gouache in Painter and the Angle panel of Brush Controls

The Scattered Leaves brush in Photoshop and the Scattering pane of the Brush panel

Photoshop Basics for Painters

Rather than focus on the nuances of every tool in Photoshop, this section focuses on the basics of Photoshop with painters in mind. Here, you'll find information and tips about brushes and tools that take advantage of the tablet. This section includes an overview of the interface, information about the Brush panels and Color panels, helpful tips for painters, and ideas for customizing your Photoshop workspace.

Let's begin with an overview of the Photoshop interface. By default, the Tools panel displays 20 tools. When you see an arrow in the lower right of a tool's field, click and hold, and the tools that are nested underneath the top tool will pop out.

The Options bar is a context-sensitive panel at the top of the Photoshop screen that shows the settings for the current tool. In the upper right of the Options bar, you'll notice a docking area where you can store often-used panels.

 Hide and show. Press the Tab key to hide or show the Toolbox and all of the panels that are open.

PHOTOSHOP'S TOOLBOX

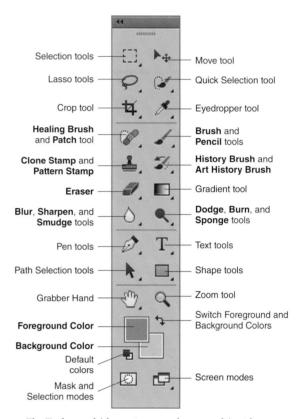

The Tools panel (shown in two-column mode) with an emphasis on the painting, toning, and focus tools that have controls that you can set up for a tablet

The pen offers more control than the mouse when using Photoshop. I painted these two brushstrokes with the Hard Round 19 pixels preset from Photoshop's default brushes. I painted the red brushstroke with a stylus and tablet and the blue brushstroke using a mouse.

THE PHOTOSHOP PAINTING WORKSPACE

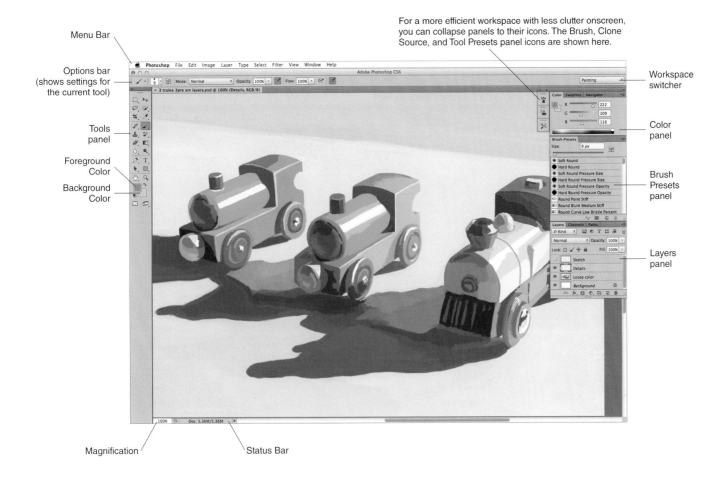

Menu Bar

Options bar (shows settings for the current tool)

Tools panel

Foreground Color

Background Color

For a more efficient workspace with less clutter onscreen, you can collapse panels to their icons. The Brush, Clone Source, and Tool Presets panel icons are shown here.

Workspace switcher

Color panel

Brush Presets panel

Layers panel

Magnification

Status Bar

When you first launch Photoshop, the Essentials (or Default) workspace is loaded. To switch to the Painting workspace, go to the Window menu and choose Workspace, Painting. The names of workspaces also appear in the workspace switcher in the Options bar. In the Painting workspace, three panel groups are docked on the right. The Color panel displays sliders that you can adjust to mix color, or you can choose color by clicking in the Color Bar at the bottom of the panel. With the Brush Presets panel you can quickly switch between brushes. Next, the Layers panel allows you to store and manage elements that float above your image background.

The magnification of the document is displayed in the lower-left corner of the Photoshop window (100% magnification displays your image with the most accuracy). The Status Bar lets you view the Document size, Scratch sizes, Timing information, and Efficiency information.

For The Three Engines, *I created swatches to store my colors and then painted on layers.*

Helpful panels. The Layers panel lets you organize the floating elements in your illustrations. For flexibility, you can paint individual elements on their own layers if you like and then hide or show them or move them around. I tend to create an underpainting on its own layer and then add refined values and details on their own layers, as shown in *The Three Engines.* The computer provides flexibility that suits each artist's own workflow.

With the Color panel, you can choose color. Click in the Color Bar to choose a color, or use the sliders. If you have a series of illustrations with the same color theme, the Swatches panel is a useful place to store the colors.

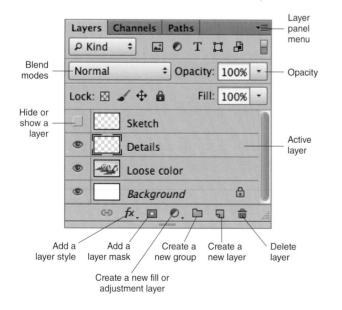

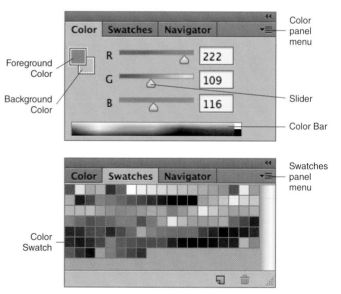

When painting Sunrise, *I used blending modes and reduced opacities for delicate color mixes.*

The Brush and Brush Presets panels. With the Brush panel, you can choose a preset brush or create your own custom brush. You can use the brush presets with the Brush, Pencil, and Mixer Brush tools; The History Brush and Art History Brush tools; the Clone Stamp and Pattern Stamp tools; the Dodge, Burn, and Sponge tools; and the Blur, Sharpen, and Smudge tools. On the left of the panel, under Brush Tip Shape, are the names of windows where more controls are located. You'll learn about them in the section "Customizing Brushes," later in the chapter.

The Brush Presets panel allows you to choose a brush quickly and size it. Other options include access to the Brush Presets panel menu, with which you can load and use additional brush collections, reset brushes, save brushes, and more. Buttons at the bottom of the panel offer additional useful options, such as Create New Brush.

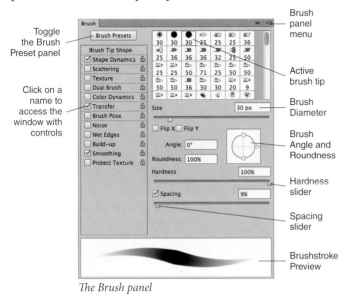

The Brush panel

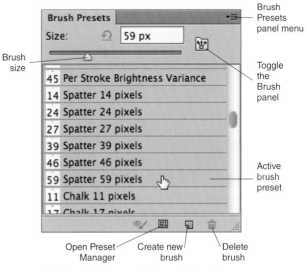

The Brush Preset panel, shown in list view

Brushstroke painted with the default Spatter 59 pixels preset

The shape of the brushstroke changes based on the pressure you apply.

CUSTOMIZING BRUSHES

You can modify a default brush preset to change its stroke width and opacity based on the pressure you apply to the stylus. To try out the brush settings, begin by choosing the Brush tool in the Tools panel and opening the Brush and Brush Presets panels. (Window > Brush).

 A helpful view. To set up the Brush Presets window with a list view for easier access to the brush presets, choose Small List from the Brush Presets panel menu.

Choosing a brush and painting a stroke. In the Brush panel, click Brush Presets to open the presets panel, scroll down the list to find the Spatter 59 pixels preset. Use your stylus to paint a squiggly brushstroke. You'll see an opaque stroke with some stray bristle hairs.

Setting the brush to change its stroke width. Back in the Brush panel, click on Shape Dynamics. In this window, set the Size Jitter Control pop-up menu to Pen Pressure. Make another squiggly stroke, and you'll see the thickness vary based on the pressure that you apply.

Choosing Small List view

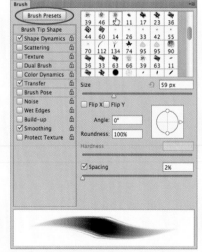

The Brush panel with dab and stroke previews for the Spatter 59 preset

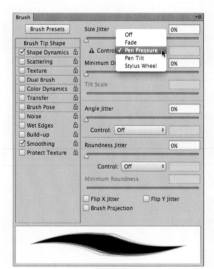

The Shape Dynamics window

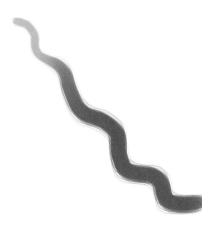

The shape and the opacity of the brushstroke change based on the pressure you apply.

Strokes of a second color demonstrate the varied opacity and the mixing of color.

The sky in the Porte d'Aval *study were painted with a custom Round Blunt Medium Stiff.*

Setting the brush to change its opacity. In the Brush panel, click on Transfer and set the Opacity Jitter Control pop-up menu to Pen Pressure. Make another stroke using varied pressure, and you'll see the opacity vary based on the pressure you use. Save the Brush preset.＊

Trying out the brush with more colors. For this exercise, make sure that the paint Mode menu in the Application bar is set to Normal. Now that you have a brush that will change opacity and stroke width based on pressure, paint a few more brushstrokes using different colors. You'll be able to create the look of semitransparent washes with delicate color mixes. By varying the pressure on your stylus, you can achieve a broad range from translucent to opaque.

You'll find examples of variations of this brush used in the projects in Chapters 9, 11, and 12. In the *Porte d'Aval* study, I painted clouds using the Mixer Brush tool＊ and a custom Round Blunt Medium Stiff preset. You can also achieve different transparent paint looks using various blend modes, such as Multiply, Soft Light, Overlay, and Color Burn.

The controls described in this section are used to create many of the custom brushes that are described in the projects later in this book.

The Transfer window

The Mode menu in the Options bar

LEARN MORE ABOUT. . .

＊ saving a brush preset. . . pages 61, 99
＊ Mixer Brush tool. . . pages 132–134, 169

More control. All of the Control pop-up menus in the Brush panel can be set to Off, Fade, Pen Pressure, Pen Tilt, or Stylus Wheel. (The Stylus Wheel operates with the airbrush pen fingerwheel.)＊

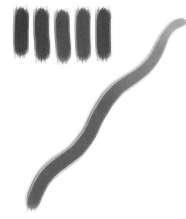

Brushstroke painted using firm pressure

Brushstroke painted using varied lighter pressure and short strokes painted using firm pressure

More dynamic color. You can paint with multiple colors by enabling Color Dynamics. Choose a foreground and a background color that are different in the Toolbox. In the Brush Presets panel, choose the custom Spatter preset that you made on the preceding page. In the Brush panel, click on Color Dynamics. Set the Control pop-up menu to Pen Pressure; then set the Foreground/ Background Color Jitter slider to about 10%. Using firm pressure on your stylus, make a squiggly brushstroke. Make another brushstroke using varied light-to-heavy pressure.

Next, make a few short strokes using heavy pressure. You will notice a varied mixture of the two colors cycle through the brushstrokes. Experiment with the other settings. Hue Jitter, Saturation Jitter, Brightness Jitter, and Purity provide more interesting color opportunities.

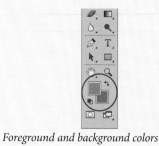

Foreground and background colors

The Color Dynamics window in the Brush panel

 Multiple undos. The History panel allows you to click back in history states and can function as a multiple undo alternative.

 Saving a new brush library. To avoid losing custom brushes when you reset Photoshop to defaults or do a reinstall, it's a good idea to save your custom brushes into your own library. To save a new brush library, choose Save Brushes from the pop-out menu on the Brush Presets panel. Name your new brush library. To have it appear in the list of brush libraries at the bottom of the Brush Presets panel in Photoshop, save it into the Brushes folder within the Presets folder in the Adobe Photoshop application folder.

Saving your files. When working in Photoshop, save your files in Photoshop format for the best performance and to preserve the program's native layers and effects, such as adjustment layers.

This is a workspace that I often use while painting.

Choosing a Brush Tool preset

CUSTOMIZING YOUR PHOTOSHOP WORKSPACE

A custom workspace. Close the panels that you won't need while painting and save your own panel layout by choosing Window > Workspace > New Workspace.

Docking panels. The panels are designed to snap together to help you keep your workspace tidy. You can create your own combinations of panels, for instance. Try dragging the Color panel into the Layers panel group.

 Smoother curves. When building custom brushes, make sure Smoothing is enabled in the Brush panel. Smoothing helps create smoother curves in your brushstrokes and is most noticeable when you're painting quickly with a stylus.

Preferred Painting Cursors. You can set the painting cursors to display the shape of the brush tip at the size it's being used. Choose File > Photoshop Preferences > Display and Cursors. Set the Painting Cursors to Full Size Brush Tip for most uses. When you're working with a tiny brush (just a few pixels), it can be difficult to see the tiny brush if you are not viewing using a high magnification. Then it's helpful to temporarily switch the painting cursor back to Standard.

Set Painting Cursors to Full Size Brush Tip.

Helpful Tool Presets. You can save your favorite brush presets as Tool Presets, located in the upper-left corner of the Options bar. Choose the Brush tool, and select a brush preset from the Brush Presets panel that you'd like to save into the tool presets. Click the small arrow to the right of the brush to open the Tool Preset Picker, and then click the gear button to open its pop-up menu. Choose New Tool Preset, and then name and save your preset. It's helpful to save tool presets for the Eraser and other tools, as well.

Click the gear button to open the menu.

Painter Basics for Artists

Instead of describing the details of every tool in Painter, this section focuses on the basics of Painter for artists who use a tablet. You'll find an overview of the interface, information about the Color panels, Brush Selector, Brush Library panel and Brush Controls panels, helpful tips for painters, and ideas for customizing your Painter workspace.

Let's begin with an overview of the Painter interface. The default Toolbox displays 21 tools. When you see an arrow in the lower right of a tool's field, click and hold, and the tools that are nested underneath the top tool will pop out. The Property Bar is a context-sensitive panel at the top of the screen that shows the settings for the current tool. All of Painter's brushes are designed to work their best with a tablet. The brushes can express the nuances of your hand, including subtle movement—pressure, tilt, bearing angle (direction), and more.

 Saving your files. Save your working Painter files in RIFF format (Painter's native format) for the best performance and to preserve the program's native layers and effects, such as the "wet paint" and "impasto" paint.

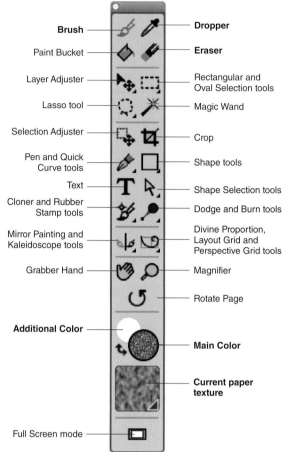

Brush	Dropper
Paint Bucket	Eraser
Layer Adjuster	Rectangular and Oval Selection tools
Lasso tool	Magic Wand
Selection Adjuster	Crop
Pen and Quick Curve tools	Shape tools
Text	Shape Selection tools
Cloner and Rubber Stamp tools	Dodge and Burn tools
Mirror Painting and Kaleidoscope tools	Divine Proportion, Layout Grid and Perspective Grid tools
Grabber Hand	Magnifier
	Rotate Page
Additional Color	Main Color
	Current paper texture
Full Screen mode	

The Toolbox with an emphasis on the painting, toning, and focus tools with controls that you can set up for a tablet

 The pen offers more expression than the mouse when using Painter. I painted these brushstrokes with the Round Camelhair variant of Oils in Painter. I drew the turquoise brushstroke with a stylus and tablet and the purple stroke using a mouse.

THE PAINTER WORKSPACE

The Brush Selector is where you choose Brush Categories and Brush Variants

The Property Bar shows settings for the current tool

Advanced Brush Controls

Brush Search

Menu Bar

Toolbox

Media selectors Patterns, Gradients, Nozzles, Weaves, and Looks

Navigator panel

Color panel

Layers panel

Document window

Panel groups are docked on the right when you first launch Painter. The topmost is the Navigator panel. The Navigator allows navigation while zoomed in, and shows the file size, magnification level, drawing modes and other helpful options. (100% magnification will display your image with the most accuracy.) The second panel grouping is related to color. The Color panel displays a Hue Ring and Saturation/Value triangle that you can adjust to mix color. Nested with the Color panel are the Mixer and Color Sets. With the Mixer, you can mix paint, just as you would on a traditional artist palette. Color Sets are useful for storing colors that you want to use again. The third panel group includes the Layers and Channels panels. The Layers panel allows you to store and manage elements that float above your image background. You can use the Channels panel to store your masks (alpha channels).

 Hide and show. Press the Tab key to hide or show the Toolbox and all of the panels that are open.

Detail of Quiet Moment, *described in Chapter 11*

Using the Mix Color tool in the Mixer to make a new color

Helpful panels. Use the Color panel to choose color. Click in the Hue Ring to select a hue and mix tints and shades of the color using the Saturation/Value triangle. The Mixer panel lets you mix color similar to how you would mix paint on a conventional artist's palette, whereas the Color Sets panel is a useful place to store your colors.

With the Layers panel, you can organize the elements in your paintings. Layers give you the flexibility to paint elements on their own layers, hide them, show them, and reposition them. As shown with the Layers panel below, often I like to colored washes on one layer, with the foreground washes and a drawing on layers above.

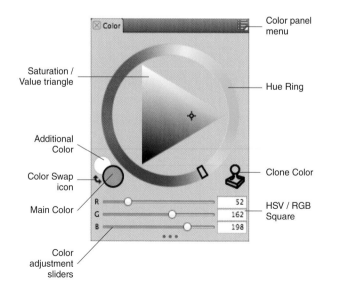

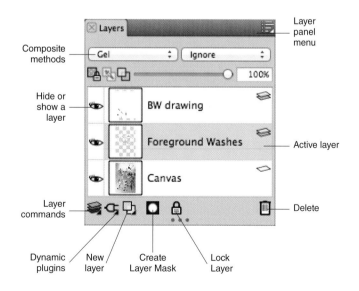

The Porte d'Aval Cliffs and Beach at Etretat *in progress with Oil Pastels*

Downstream Path, Summer *in progress with Oils, Impasto, and Pastel*

The Brush Selector and Brush Library. Painter ships with hundreds of exciting brushes. Use the Brush Selector and Brush Library to choose brush categories and brush variants.

To open the Brush Library, click the small triangle on the Brush Selector. It's easier to choose among the many brush categories using List View. To view the brush categories in List view, open the Brush Library, click the button in the upper right to open the pop-out menu and choose Category Display > Categories as List.

To choose a new brush category, click on a name in the list. You can display the Brush Variant menu using the List view (shown here) or Stroke view. Click on a variant name to choose a brush. The triangle to the right of the Brush Variant icon opens a pop-up menu that allows you to choose a variant—in my case, the Chunky Oil Pastel.

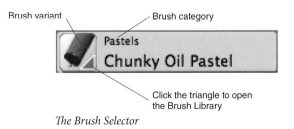

The Brush Selector

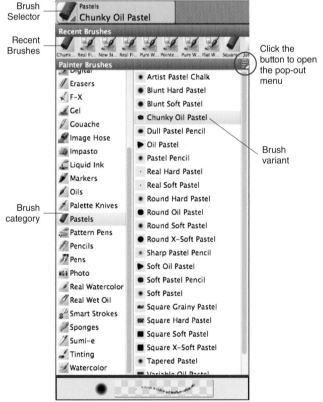

The open Brush Library with the Brush Category menu shown in List view

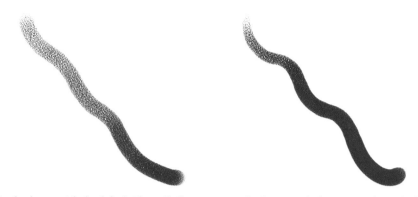

Stroke drawn with the default Blunt Chalk

Stroke drawn with the custom Blunt Chalk

CUSTOMIZING BRUSHES

You can use the controls described here to create many of the custom brushes that are described in the projects later in this book.

The majority of Painter's brushes are already programmed to take advantage of a tablet. These exercises will help you understand what's going on "under the hood" so that you can customize brushes for your own personal feel. You can modify a default brush variant to change its stroke width and opacity based on the pressure you apply to the stylus. To try out the brush settings, begin by choosing the Brush tool in the Toolbox and opening the Brush Controls by choosing Window > Brush Control Panels. (In the Brush Controls, open the Dab Preview, Stroke Preview, and Size panels.) The Dab Preview shows the size and shape of the dab, while the Stroke Preview panel gives a helpful live brushstroke preview.

Choosing a brush and painting a stroke. In the Brush Selector, choose the Chalk & Crayons category and the Blunt Chalk variant. Apply varied pressure to your stylus while painting a waxy stroke. You'll notice that the default brush reveals more grain when you apply less pressure.

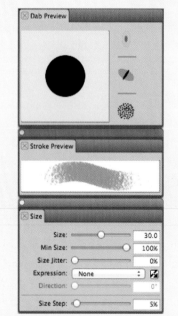

Dab Preview, Stroke Preview, and Size panel settings for the default Blunt Chalk

Setting the brush to change its stroke width. In the Size panel of the Brush Controls, set the Min Size to 32%; then set the Expression pop-up menu to Pressure. Make another stroke, and you'll see the thickness of the stroke change based on the pressure that you apply to your stylus.

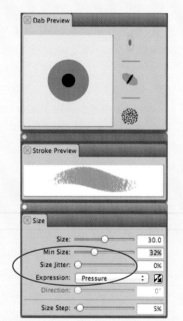

The Min Size is adjusted and the Expression menu is set to Pressure

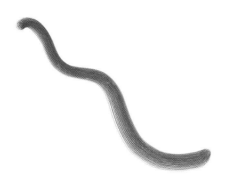

The default Thick Bristle brushstroke

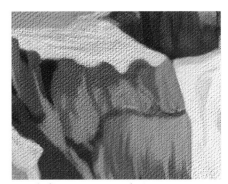

Detail of Downstream Path, Summer

More colorful brushstrokes. For this exercise, choose the Thick Bristle variant of Impasto. This brush (and others that use the same brush model) is actually a bundle of brush hairs, rather than a dab-based brush. You can load each hair with a different color. By default, the brush changes its opacity and stroke width based on the pressure that you apply to the stylus. Paint a stroke using the default Thick Bristle. By varying the pressure, you can achieve a sensitive range of opacity and stroke width. The bristles on this brush also spread out based on the direction that you tilt the stylus.

 More expression. You can set all of the Expression pop-up menus in the Brush Controls to Velocity, Direction, Pressure, Wheel, Tilt, Bearing, Rotation, Source, and Random. (The Wheel operates with the airbrush pen fingerwheel.)

Open the Color Variability of Brush Controls. Notice that the brush already has a small amount of Value variability built into it. Now set the Hue variability to about 15%, and then make a new brushstroke. You'll see subtle variation of color in the brush hairs.

Adjusting the color variability

You'll find examples of oil and pastel brushes used in the projects in Chapters 9 and 12. In *The Porte d'Aval Cliffs and Beach at Etretat* on page 136, I painted textured strokes using a Chunky Oil Pastel. In *Downstream Path, Summer* on page 186, I used a Thick Bristle brush to add details of thick Impasto paint to the cliffs and then added texture accents with a pastel.

Saving a new brush category. To avoid losing custom brushes when you reset Painter to defaults or do a reinstall, it's a good idea to save your brushes into your own brush category (think of the brush category as a container that holds your brushes). To save a new brush category, you must first choose an image that you want to use as its icon. Open an image and make a 30-pixel square selection. From the Brushes menu, choose New Brush Category, and give it a name. You'll find the brush you had chosen when you captured the icon in your new category. You can now copy brushes from other categories into your new container. So you can make a back-up copy of your new brush category for safekeeping, export the category. First select it in the Brush Library, from the Brushes menu choose Export > Brush Category and save it to your desired location.

This is a palette layout that I often use while painting. Notice the custom oil pastel palette.

CUSTOMIZING YOUR PAINTER WORKSPACE

Painter has tools that allow you to set up your workspace for various kinds of projects. For instance, you can build a custom palette to store your brushes, tools, and commands. You can also create and save a palette layout or workspace for painting and a different one for compositing that might include the Layers and Channels panels. Additionally, you can create new brush categories,* and import alternative brush and art material libraries* into the program.

LEARN MORE ABOUT. . .

＊ new brush categories. . . page 71
＊ your own brush library. . . page 64

Making your own custom palettes. For the *Etretat* study above, I created a custom palette to hold my oil pastels and papers. To create your own custom palette, choose a brush variant (I chose the Chunky Oil Pastel), press the Shift key and drag the brush icon from the Brush Selector. A small palette with the brush will automatically appear. Drag the lower-right corner to expand the size of the palette. Choose another variant and drag and drop it onto the palette. To add a paper texture, open the Paper library (Window > Paper Panels > Paper Libraries. Click on a texture, press the Shift key, and drag the paper texture from the Paper library onto your palette. To save and name your palette using the Organizer, choose Window > Custom Palette > Organizer, and enter a name for your palette.

Saving a custom palette layout. For more intuitive painting, it's helpful to simplify your workspace by closing panels and palettes that you don't need while painting. If you're not using layers, you might need only the Navigator, Color panel and the Mixer. To save a custom layout, choose Window > Arrange Palettes > Save Layout. Name your palette layout in the Palette Layout Name dialog box and click OK.

In this detail of Path to Water, West 2, *you can see the pastel, oil paint, and palette knife strokes.*

Useful brush cursors. To specify a Brush Cursor type and to set the orientation of the cursor, choose Corel Painter > Preferences > Interface (Mac OS X) or Edit > Preferences > Interface (Windows). (I prefer using a Triangle when the Enhanced Brush Ghost or Brush Ghost is not enabled.)

In this chapter, you learned about setting up your tablet and artists' basics for Painter and Photoshop. In the next chapter, you'll work with more brushes and paint.

The Drawing Cursor settings in the Preferences > Interface dialog box

Using libraries. Libraries are containers that hold the brushes, paper textures, and other items that you can create using Painter.

Every panel that has a resource list of materials has an Open Library (or Import Library) command. Let's use the Brush Selector and Brush Library as an example. Choose Window > Brush Selector. On the Brush Selector, click the small triangle to open the Brush Library panel, and then click the button in the upper right to open the pop-up menu. Next, choose Import > Brush Library to display a dialog box that lets you search through folders on your hard disk until you find the library you want. Then double-click to open it. The Import Library choice is also available under the Brushes menu: Choose Brushes > Import > Import Library. (Although you can load libraries directly from a CD-ROM like the Painter X3 CD-ROM or the *Painter Wow! Book* CD-ROM, it's more reliable to copy the libraries from the CD-ROM into your Painter application folder.)

The open Brush Library panel and its pop-up menus, with Import Brush Library chosen

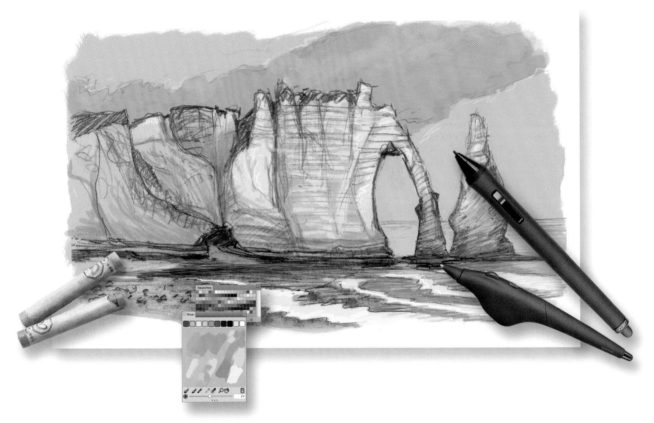

Brushes and paint with a study of Etretat

4

ASSEMBLING BRUSHES AND PAINT IN PHOTOSHOP AND PAINTER

The first part of this chapter focuses on the process of assembling your brushes and paint, and mixing colors. Then you'll explore some exciting brushes in both Photoshop and Painter. You'll gain experience with using the default brushes, combined with a pressure-sensitive tablet, and discover the unique capabilities of each brush. This experience will be helpful when you work through the drawing and painting projects in the following chapters, and also when you create the custom brushes in later chapters.

 Now you'll pick up your stylus, mix paint, and have fun exploring the brushes. My favorite Wacom Intuos pressure-sensitive tablet used in combination with the brushes in Photoshop and Painter allows for creativity and control when painting a wide variety of brushstrokes. For this chapter I chose to use default brushes that are easy to use in each program. Each program offers unique brush features. For instance, Photoshop offers a variety of brushes that respond to pressure or to the tilt of the stylus (such as the Airbrush Soft High Density Grainy), which paints a thick-to-thin stroke as you tilt the stylus as you draw; Painter offers its own unique brushes that respond to pressure, tilt, and the rotation of your hand as you draw. For instance, the Thick Oil Bristle brush allows you to spread the bristles of the brush as you tilt the stylus or while you make a curved stroke. I hope you enjoy your exploration.

CP

Exploring Brushes and Paint in Photoshop

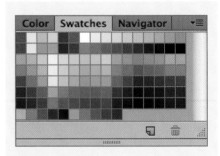

Selecting a dark red from the Swatches panel

ARTIST'S MATERIALS

Tablet: Medium pressure (set in the Tip Control Panel)

Program: Photoshop

Paint: Choose a dark red color from the Swatches or from the Color Picker; I used R 115, G 27, B 32

Brushes:

- Hard Round: line thickness varies with pressure

- Soft Round: line thickness varies with pressure

- Airbrush Soft High Density Grainy: stroke width varies with tilt and angle

Continued on page 78

1 **Setting up.** In this exercise, you'll explore using some of the default brushes in Photoshop with your tablet and stylus. First, you'll need to set up a new file and choose a color in preparation for experimenting with the brushes. Make a new file that measures 600 × 600 pixels. (I suggest using the same size file for all of these exercises.) In the Color Mode pop-up menu, choose RGB Color.

The New dialog box set up for the file

LEARN MORE ABOUT. . .

⋆ choosing colors. . . page 60

⋆ the Brush Presets panel. . . page 61

2 **Choosing paint color.** Now choose a dark red from the Swatches (Window > Swatches).⋆

 The Color Picker. You can also use the Color Picker to select your paint color. To display the Color Picker, click the Foreground Color in the Toolbox. To choose a hue, click in the vertical bar. To make the color less saturated, click on the left side of the Select Foreground Color field. To give your color more saturation, click on the right side of the field. To darken the color, click lower in the field; to lighten it, move higher.

Select Foreground Color field   Hue

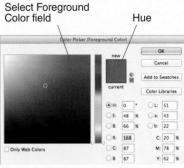

The dark red shown in the Color Picker

Hard Round, scaled to 60 pixels

Soft Round, scaled to 65 pixels

Airbrush Soft High Density Grainy preset

3 Drawing thin-to-thick strokes with hard edges. Choose the Brush tool, and then open the Brush Presets panel (Window > Brush Presets).* Click the triangle on the Brush Presets tab, and then choose Small List (which allows you to see a small picture of the brush dab and its name). Choose the Hard Round preset. Next, open the Brush panel, click its Shape Dynamics tab and set the Size Jitter Control pop-up menu to Pen Pressure. Press lightly on your stylus, and gradually increase pressure as you draw a horizontal line. Now draw a wiggly line that varies in thickness based on pressure.

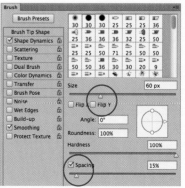

The Brush panel's Shape Dynamics window

4 Drawing thin-to-thick strokes with soft edges. Choose the Soft Round preset. Set the brush to recognize Stylus pressure, as you did with the Hard Round. Click the Shape Dynamics tab and set the Size Jitter Control pop-up menu to Pen Pressure. Apply light pressure for a thin stroke and heavier pressure for a heavier stroke.

Adjusting spacing. When I increased the size of the Hard Round preset, my brushstroke had rough edges because the dabs did not overlap sufficiently to make a smooth-edged stroke. To give the brush smooth edges, I decreased the spacing between the dabs of paint. Click on Brush Tip Shape and increase the diameter of the brush to 60 pixels; then decrease the spacing to make the dabs overlap. Experiment with the spacing of your brush. (I chose 15%.) Overly tight spacing can cause slower performance.

5 Making strokes that vary with tilt. Now choose the Airbrush Soft High Density Grainy preset. Hold the stylus upright and draw a horizontal line. Next, tilt the stylus as you draw a wavy line. Notice that the stroke thickness increases with more tilt, and the Airbrush sprays directionally.

Top stroke rough; bottom stroke smooth

Adjusting the Spacing slider for the brush

Round Watercolor

Rough Round Bristle

ARTIST'S MATERIALS

Continued from page 76

Brushes:

- Rough Round Bristle: line thickness and edges vary with pressure

- Watercolor Loaded Wet Flat Tip: flat tip; line thickness varies with stylus orientation

- Charcoal Large Smear: flat tip; opacity and thickness of stroke vary with stylus orientation

6 Making strokes with varied opacity. Choose the Brush tool in the Tools panel and the Round Watercolor preset. Press lightly on your stylus, and gradually increase pressure as you draw a horizontal line. Now draw curved lines that vary in opacity based on pressure.*

Loading brushes. Photoshop ships with several additional groups of brushes, and it's easy to load them into your Brush Presets panel. Click the arrow on the top right of the Brush Presets panel to access the pop-out menu, and look near the bottom of its list. Choose one of the libraries. After making your choice, you'll see a dialog box that asks whether you want to "replace the current brushes" with the new library you've chosen (click OK) or add the new brush set to your list (click Append).

7 Painting thin-to-thick strokes with varied edges. Choose the Rough Round Bristle preset and apply light pressure for a thin stroke with smooth edges. For a thicker stroke with rougher edges, apply heavier pressure.

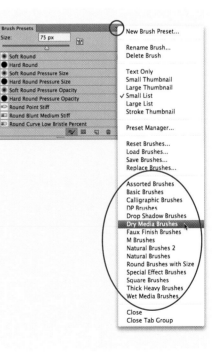

Watercolor Loaded Wet Flat Tip

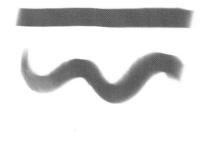

Charcoal Flat

Flat Point Medium Stiff

8 **Painting with flat brushes.** The Watercolor Loaded Wet Flat Tip preset has a flat tip. Press lightly on your stylus, and gradually increase pressure as you draw a translucent horizontal line. Now draw a wiggly line that varies in thickness based on pressure applied. You'll notice that the thickness of the stroke also changes based on the orientation of the stylus. Then draw a stroke that overlaps an existing stroke, and notice the transparency of the paint.*

Next, choose the Charcoal Flat preset. This brush features an erodable tip,* that wears as you draw. Press lightly on your stylus, and gradually increase pressure as you draw an opaque horizontal line. Now draw a wiggly line that varies in thickness based on the pressure applied. You will notice that the thickness of the stroke also changes based on the orientation of the stylus.

The Flat Point Medium Tip preset also has a rectangular tip. This preset offers more expression when used with the Mixer Brush tool.* Choose

the Flat Point Medium Stiff in the Brush Presets panel, and choose the Mixer Brush tool in the Tools panel. Press lightly on your stylus, and gradually increase pressure as you draw a horizontal line. Notice how the opacity and thickness of the stroke increases as you apply more pressure. Now draw a wiggly line that varies in thickness based on the pressure applied. You'll notice that the thickness of the stroke also subtly changes based on how the stylus is rotated in your hand as you draw. Now make a few smaller strokes that overlap. New paint builds up nicely on top of existing paint.

Exploring Brushes and Paint in Painter

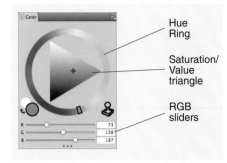

Hue Ring

Saturation/ Value triangle

RGB sliders

Choosing a nice medium-blue in the Color panel

ARTIST'S MATERIALS

Tablet: Light to medium pressure (set in the Tip Control Panel)

Program: Painter

Paint: Choose a blue color in the Color panel (R 73, G 138, B 187 is shown here), mix a blue using the Mixer or type these RGB values into Color Info: R 73, G 138, B 187

Paper Texture: Basic Paper

Brushes:

• Grainy Variable Pencil: stroke changes depending on the tilt and angle of the stylus

• Square X-Soft Pastel: stroke changes depending on the tilt and angle of the stylus; texture changes with pressure applied

• Round Camelhair: stroke changes in thickness and opacity with pressure

Continued on page 82

1 **Setting up.** Now you'll explore some of Painter's brushes using a tablet and stylus. Begin by making a new file that measures 600 × 600 pixels. (I suggest using the same size file for all of these exercises.) Then set Brush Tracking* so that you can customize Painter to the nuances of your hand on the stylus and tablet.

The Mixer. You can mix color on-the-fly using the Mixer. (If the Mixer is not open, choose Window > Show Mixer.) You can choose a color from the Swatches or from the Color panel and apply it to the Mixer Pad using your stylus and the Apply Color tool in the Mixer. Blend the colors with one another using the Mix Color tool, just as you would on a traditional artist's palette. The Dirty Brush Mode allows the Apply Color tool to smear new color with color already on the pad. To adjust the size of the Mixer's Apply Color or Mix Color tools, use the slider at the bottom of the panel. Increase the size of the Apply Color tool to 30 pixels and add a new color to a painted area. You'll notice that the smeariness of the Brush tool and character of the stroke are affected by how you brush over existing color with your stylus.

2 **Choosing paint color.** Next, choose a medium-blue color in the Color panel (Window > Show Colors). Click in the round Hue Ring to select a hue; then click in the Saturation/Value triangle to lighten, darken, or adjust the saturation of the color. You can also create paint color using the Mixer.

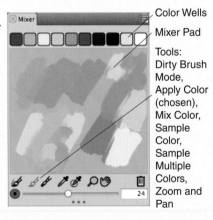

Color Wells

Mixer Pad

Tools: Dirty Brush Mode, Apply Color (chosen), Mix Color, Sample Color, Sample Multiple Colors, Zoom and Pan

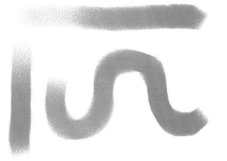

Grainy Variable Pencil strokes, painted while varying the angle and direction of the stylus

Square X-Soft Pastel strokes, painted with lesser pressure applied at the beginning of strokes

Round Camelhair strokes, painted with lesser pressure applied at the beginning of strokes

3 Drawing with pencils. The Grainy Variable Pencil is sensitive to the angle, direction, and pressure of the stylus as you draw. Choose the Pencils category and the Grainy Variable Pencil variant. Hold the stylus comfortably in your hand. Now draw a wavy line, and vary the tilt and the pressure on the stylus as you draw. The character of the line will change as you make variations in pressure, as well as subtle hand and wrist movements, such as the angle of the pen changing as you draw. Experiment with other variants in the Pencils category.

4 Brushstrokes with texture. Brushes with the word "grainy" in their names will paint a grain-sensitive stroke. Others will reveal texture based on their traditional counterparts, such as the Chalk and Pastels categories. Choose the Square X-Soft Pastel variant of Pastels. Hold the stylus comfortably in your hand, draw a wavy line, and vary the angle and the pressure of the stylus. The stroke will change as you vary the pressure and the angle of the pen as you draw. Applying less pressure will reveal more texture.

5 Painting brushstrokes of varied width and opacity. For a brushstroke with varied thickness, try the Round Camelhair variant of Oils. Begin your stroke by pressing lightly on the stylus and then gradually building up pressure. If you've carefully controlled the pressure, you'll notice that your stroke gradually expanded in width from thin to thick, depending on the pressure you've applied.

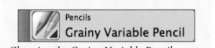

Choosing the Grainy Variable Pencil

 Revealing texture. When you draw with a texture-sensitive brush (such as the Grainy Variable Pencil and Square X-Soft Pastel), the texture will be revealed in the stroke as you draw. (When you boot Painter, a texture is loaded automatically.) You can choose a new texture by clicking the Paper Selector in the Toolbox and then choosing from the pop-out menu. You can open the Papers panel* by choosing Window > Paper Panels > Papers.

LEARN MORE ABOUT. . .

* Brush Tracking. . . page 86
* the Papers panel. . . page 212

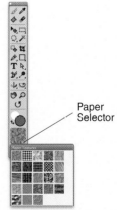

Paper Selector

Choosing a paper texture in the Paper Selector

Real Dry Flat strokes drawn with stylus held at more of an angle

Real Dry Flat stroke drawn with stylus rotated in hand while drawing

6 Painting thick and thin strokes with flat brushes. With the flat brushes, you can paint wide or narrow strokes, depending on the way you hold the stylus and the pressure that you apply. When practicing the strokes that follow, position your stylus with the button between your index finger and thumb (toward the left if you are right-handed, or toward the right if you are left-handed). With the Brush tool chosen in the Toolbox, choose the Real Dry Flat variant of Acrylics from the Brush Selector. The Real Dry Flat has RealBristle qualities for very realistic natural-media marks. To paint a thick horizontal stroke, pull the brush straight across your image using even pressure. To make thin lines, pull down. To make a wavy line of varied thickness, use light pressure on your stylus for the beginning of the stroke, and more pressure as you sweep up and rotate the brush to come back down.

 A softer Airbrush. The Digital Airbrush paints a soft spray. This brush is useful for subtle touch-up work, but the spray pattern does not change when you hold the stylus with an angle, as it does with the continuous stroke Airbrushes such as the Fine Spray described in step 8. The Tapered Detail Air and Soft Airbrush are also "soft" airbrushes.

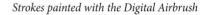

Strokes painted with the Digital Airbrush

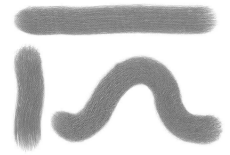

Thick Oil Bristle strokes, painted with stylus held nearly upright

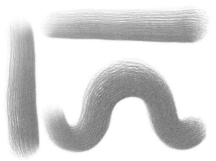

Thick Oil Bristle strokes, drawn with stylus held at more of an angle

Fine Spray Airbrush strokes, painted with stylus held at various angles

7 Making bristles spread. For a brush that spreads its bristles as it applies thick paint (depending on how you hold the stylus), choose the Oils category from the Brush

Brush Search. Available in Painter X3 and later, the useful Brush Search function in the Property Bar allows you to type in a topic such as "Real Bristle" to generate a list of brushes with these features.

The useful Brush Search feature displays a list, and a brushstroke preview when the cursor is hovered over a brush name.

Selector, and then choose the Thick Oil Bristle variant. Hold your stylus as upright as you can, and draw a stroke. Notice the bristle edges at the beginning and end of the stroke and the thick paint texture. Next, hold the stylus in a more natural, slightly angled position (with the top of the pen tilted toward you), and draw a second stroke. See how the bristles on the top of the second stroke appear to splay, or spread out, just the way a conventional brush does when you press it down and pull a stroke across your canvas?

RealBristle brushes. Brushes with RealBristle capabilities offer expressive, natural brushmarks. Examples are the Real Dry Flat and Real Wet Brush variant of Acrylics and the Real Fan Short and Real Round variants of the Oils.

8 Painting with Airbrushes. The Fine Spray variant of Airbrushes allows you to spray paint just like a traditional airbrush. Hold the stylus vertically in your hand, and paint a horizontal stroke. Now hold the stylus comfortably in your hand in a more angled position, and paint a stroke. See how the paint sprays farther out across the canvas; the more you angle the stylus, the farther the brush will spray. Other Airbrushes (such as the Coarse Spray) also allow this kind of control.

In this chapter, you've learned how to set up your brushes and paint, and you've experimented with brushes. Now you're ready for the tablet and drawing exercises in the next chapter.

California Pottery Fish: *Gesture, clean line, modified contour, and "sketchy line" styles of drawing*

5
Drawing and Tablet Exercises

In this chapter, you'll begin by choosing a subject and setting up a still life. Then you'll do exercises that will help loosen up your hand and help you to build control using the tablet and stylus. Next, you will use four different drawing methods (or ways of seeing) to sketch the subject: gesture, contour, clean line, and "sketchy line." The objective is not to draw photo-realistic illustrations, but to draw with sensitivity and expression. After completing these exercises, you will intimately know your subject.

 To simulate the look of various graphite pencils, I drew these drawings using a dark gray. I drew the California Pottery Fish *illustrations using Painter and my favorite Wacom Intuos tablet and pen. The pressure-sensitive tablet used in combination with the great variety of brushes in Painter allowed me to have control and expression while drawing different kinds of lines. For the subject, I chose a favorite ceramic pottery fish, and placed it on a light-colored surface. I lit the fish using a small spotlight, which I positioned behind and to the left of the subject. Prior to beginning the drawings, I carefully studied the forms and space around the fish, which were enhanced by the lighting. Then I relaxed and used a sensitive hand while drawing. I use one or more of these drawing methods as I'm warming up before a painting session.*

Warming Up and Sketching

A digital photo of the subject

The artist with still life set up and computer

PHOTOGRAPH: MELINDA HOLDEN

1 **Setting up a still life.** Choose a simple ceramic figure, or a cup or vase and set up your still life on a light-colored surface. I chose this fish as a subject because of its graceful flowing curves, and the interesting simple forms. The shape of the fish and the negative space around it are intriguing.

Choose a small spotlight that will cast interesting shadows on the table surface. After my still life was set up, I photographed it with a digital camera so I could save it as a reference for readers of this chapter.

When practicing the exercises that follow, remember to relax and enjoy the drawing process. The computer is forgiving—you can "undo" a line if you don't like it—or start over in a new file without wasting a precious sheet of expensive drawing paper.

2 **Practicing warm-up exercises.** Before beginning to sketch your subject, perform the following exercises to loosen up your drawing hand and to get comfortable with your tablet and stylus.

You'll begin each of the warm-up exercises with a new 600 × 600 pixel file (File > New). In the Color panel,* choose a dark gray color for sketching. I suggest using the same dark gray for all of the exercises.

More sensitivity. Brush Tracking helps interpret your input through the tablet more accurately, including parameters like pressure and speed. Choose Preferences, Brush Tracking, and make a single stroke in the window that varies from soft to hard pressure, including slow to fast movement. The speed is essential for accurate input while doing quick gesture drawings.

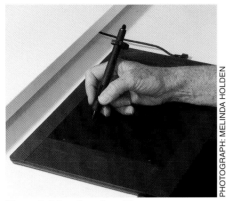

The artist's hand on the tablet

Circles: Grainy Variable Pencil

Square: Real 2B Pencil

3 **Drawing loose circles.** For the circle exercise, choose the Brush tool in the Toolbox. Click the Brush Selector to open the Painter Brushes library, then choose the Pencils category and the Real 2B Pencils variant. Place your tablet in a comfortable position on the table near you, or on

Pencils
Real 2B Pencil

The Brush Selector with the Real 2B variant of Pencils chosen

your lap. Hold your stylus comfortably in your hand, as you would a pen or pencil when writing. Move your hand in a circular motion a few inches above your tablet, in a way that feels natural and smooth. Now that you have the motion, touch your stylus to your tablet, and rotate your hand and stylus in a circular motion. Bear down harder on one side of the circle than the other, and notice how the stroke darkens with the heavier pressure.

4 **Sketching a square.** Now choose the Real 2B Pencil variant of Pencils, and sketch a square. Begin the square by applying a medium pressure and drawing a horizontal line. Using a similar pressure, draw a second horizontal line, lower in the image, parallel to the first. Position your stylus on the left edge of the top line, and pull down using medium pressure on the stylus, drawing a vertical line. Draw a second vertical line to finish the right side of the square.

Drawing cursor. You'll be using Pencils variants with small tips for this project, so it's a good idea to set the Preferences for the Drawing Cursor to show the Brush cursor at all times. This cursor is easier to see as you're drawing with a fine pencil than when using the Brush Ghost or Enhanced Brush Ghost.* Under the Corel Painter 12 menu, choose Preferences > Interface (Mac) / Edit > Preferences > Interface (PC) > and set the Drawing Cursor to Brush. Make sure to uncheck the Enable Brush Ghost check box. Click OK to close the Preferences dialog box.

Cursor Type:
○ Enhanced brush ghost
○ Brush ghost
◉ Iconic   Brush
○ Single pixel

The Preferences > Interface dialog box showing the Cursor Type setup

⬭ ✎   *The Brush Ghost for the Flattened Pencil (left) and the Brush cursor (right)*

LEARN MORE ABOUT. . .

★ the Color panel. . . pages 67, 68, 138
★ the Brush Ghost. . . page 73

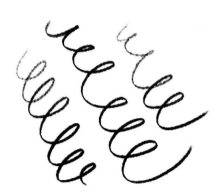

Horizontal Lines: Mechanical Pencil

Ringlet Squiggles: Flattened Pencil

A quick gesture drawing of the fish

5 **Drawing parallel lines.** Now you'll practice developing more control when using consistent pressure while drawing a set of horizontal lines. Choose the Mechanical Pencil variant of Pencils. Position your wrist on your tablet to support your hand and allow more control while drawing the lines. Try experimenting with holding your stylus more erect for this exercise. Press the stylus firmly on the tablet and use careful, consistent pressure while drawing the first horizontal line. Then draw several more lines under the first using the same consistent pressure.

6 **Drawing squiggles.** Next, you'll use the Flattened Pencil to sketch a series of loose ringlets. Choose the Flattened Pencil variant of Pencils and draw a series of curved ringlet lines. Press lightly on your tablet, and then use heavier pressure. Allow your hand to rotate naturally while drawing the lines. The Flattened Pencil is sensitive to pressure, as well as the angle you hold the stylus while drawing. This added expression contributes to a satisfying artist experience.

Open a new file—I recommend using the same size file for the remainder of the exercises. My file measured 1500 × 2000 pixels.

7 **Drawing a gesture.** A gesture is drawn quickly and loosely— it captures the movement and energy of a subject. Gestures are often drawn of people and other living things. Although the ceramic fish is an inanimate object, it has beautiful flowing curves, which make it an ideal subject for gesture. Choose the Grainy Variable Pencil variant of Pencils. Carefully observe your subject, and let your eyes sweep around its forms.

Press your stylus firmly on your tablet and sketch a movement gesture of your subject with fast, loose strokes. Experiment with varying the pressure while sketching. Focus on quickly sketching the essence of your subject in just a few seconds. You might want to repeat this exercise several times to become better acquainted with your subject.

 **For Photoshop users.** If you don't have Painter, you can follow along with these exercises in Photoshop using two default brush presets, the Pencil and Charcoal Pencil. Use the Pencil for steps 1–8. Try the Charcoal Pencil for steps 9 and 10. (Although they're useful, the performance of the brushes will not be identical.)

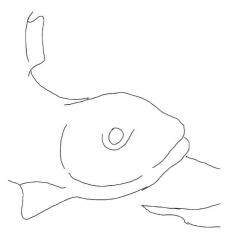

A detail from the "contour" drawing

A detail from the modified contour drawing

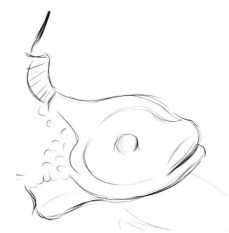

The "sketchy line" style is shown in this detail.

8 Drawing a contour. A contour drawing is a sensitive, careful drawing style that usually shows the edges of forms in space. During this exercise, you'll imagine that your stylus is actually moving along the edges of the subject, and draw using a controlled, consistent line. This exercise will help you to develop more control over the pressure that you exert on the tablet. Choose the Mechanical Pencil variant of Pencils. This pencil will allow you to draw a line of even thickness and value, provided that you apply a consistent pressure to the tablet. Carefully observe your subject. To achieve a consistent line, apply pressure to the pen on the tablet as evenly as possible. Let your hand move in a controlled manner as you draw. See if you can draw around the outside of the subject without lifting your stylus from the tablet (as you would your pencil from the paper).

9 Making a modified contour. This adaptation of the contour method will allow you to be more expressive with the line quality. Making a modified contour drawing will help you to become more sensitive and observant while becoming more intimate with your subject. You'll also develop more control over varied pressure using your stylus and tablet. Choose the Thick and Thin Pencil. Touch the stylus to your tablet, and let your eye follow the edges of the forms as you draw. Vary the pressure as you draw an indented area of a form. In an area where you see a highlight or a raised form, decrease your pressure slightly, so that the strength and opacity of the line vary in an expressive way. Pretend that you are tracing around the edges of the forms with your stylus. If you like, add a few important internal contours.

10 Using a "sketchy line" style. This kind of line is composed of multiple overlapping strokes (hence its name). Take the time to study your subject carefully and analyze its basic forms and shapes. Think about how you can simplify the subject so that in the beginning, you draw just the basic shapes using loose strokes. Using the Real 2B Pencil, apply light pressure to your stylus as you rough in the basic shapes. Don't draw a continuous line around your subject. Instead, sketch in a way similar to how you would use a pencil, with sketchy lines that overlap one another to suggest the curves and straighter lines. As you begin to refine the edges of your drawing, embellish the most important areas by applying heavier pressure to create bolder marks. (Apply heavier pressure, and then let up gradually as you come out of a curve, for instance.) Congratulations! You've completed the drawing exercises. An instructional sidebar follows.

Sketching in Photoshop

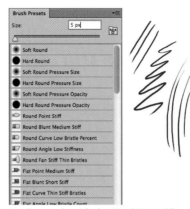

Strokes made with the Hard Round brush preset, and a toy duck drawn using a favorite "sketchy line" style

Artists who love responsiveness while doing quick sketches will enjoy many of Photoshop's simpler brush presets. (Simple means "no performance-hungry settings in the Brush panel like the Dual Brush setting.") In the first example, you'll use a brush that is ideal for drawing lines similar to a round-tipped ink pen or pencil. For the second example, you will load a brush that will allow you to draw lines of variable thickness based on the angle you hold the stylus.

Setting up for drawing. Create a new file that measures 1500 × 2000 pixels. (All of the examples presented in this sidebar use the same size file.) Choose a dark gray in the Color Picker (to simulate graphite). Now choose the Brush tool in the Toolbox. In preparation for the second drawing example, load the Calligraphic Brushes as follows: Choose the Brush tool; then click on the tiny arrow on the top right of the Brush Presets panel and, when the menu pops open, choose the Calligraphic Brushes from near the bottom of the list. A dialog box will appear asking "Replace current brushes with the brushes from the Calligraphic set?" Click the Append button to add them to your existing Brush panel.

Drawing with a "sketchy line." For the toy duck drawing, I used the "sketchy line" method,* in which the strokes gently overlap one another, to create curves and to render straighter lines. This type of drawing has an energetic approach, and it is forgiving because you build up areas of emphasis gradually.

Photoshop's Hard Round brush preset is ideal for drawing smooth lines with crisp edges, and for the technique that follows. Choose the Brush tool in the Toolbox; then open the Brush panel (Window > Brush). Click the triangle on the Brushes tab and choose Small List (which allows you to see a small picture of the brush dab and its name). Now click on Brush Presets and scroll to choose the Hard Round 5 pixels preset. To vary the opacity and size with pressure, set the Opacity and Size buttons on the Options Bar.

After choosing the brush, set its Opacity and Size to be controlled by pressure. Turn on the buttons on the Options Bar.

I suggest making a few practice marks to get to know your brush. This brush is already set up to vary opacity and stroke width with pressure, so to achieve a darker line, press harder with your stylus, and to draw a lighter line, apply lighter pressure. While drawing, avoid doing any erasing, because building up layers of line work adds character to your drawing. When you sketch a

Strokes made with the Flat 7 pixels Calligraphy brush preset, and loose drawings using the "calligraphic" style.

line, begin with a lighter pressure and, if you like the line, sketch over it again to emphasize it. Above all, relax and enjoy the drawing process.

Drawing with a calligraphic line. For the second sketch, you'll use a brush that draws lines of varying thickness depending on the angle and pressure applied to your stylus, using a modified contour method.

Begin by creating a new file and choose the Flat 7 pixels brush that was imported when you loaded the Calligraphic Brushes set earlier. Click on the little arrow to the right of the brush tip preview in the Options Bar to pop out the Brush Preset picker; then

LEARN MORE ABOUT. . .

∗ the "sketchy line" method. . . page 89

∗ the contour method. . . page 89

choose the Flat 7 pixels preset from the list. (As you did with the Hard Round, enable the Opacity and Size buttons in the Options Bar.) Make some practice marks and notice how the line varies if you start a stroke from the right or the left and pull up or down.

Observe your subject, and imagine tracing your stylus around the edge of the forms.∗ To steady your hand while using this controlled drawing method,

place your forearm or the base of your hand on the edge of the table and hold your stylus as you would a writing pen. Touch your stylus to the tablet and begin drawing. Don't worry if your lines wiggle a little; it will add to the hand-drawn look.

I hope you've enjoyed this exercise. Now you're ready to move on to learning about volume in Chapter 6, "The Illusion of Volume."

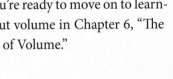

Loading more Photoshop brushes. In Photoshop's Dry Media Brushes, you'll find the #2 Pencil, which is a great brush for doing methodical drawings (such as the contour method described on page 89), but if you sketch quickly as I do, the performance can lag. To load the Dry Media Brushes, choose the Brush tool; then click on the tiny arrow on the top right of the Brush Presets panel. When the menu opens, choose the Dry Media Brushes from near the bottom of the list. A dialog box appears, asking if you'd like to Append or Replace the brushes with the new set. Choose Append to add them to your existing Brush panel.

California pottery

6

THE ILLUSION OF VOLUME

To begin, you'll draw a cube and an orange, which will help you to understand how to model solid objects using Painter. After the cube and orange, there is a project that features modeling rounded forms using Photoshop. After completing these exercises, you'll set up a still life using a more complex object and paint it so that it has volume, weight, and mass.

 It's helpful to practice the process of modeling form in a monochromatic painting before moving on to using both color and value together, because the composition of a color painting will not hold up without well thought-out values. I drew the cube, the orange, the salt shaker, and the vase using my Wacom tablet and stylus. The pressure-sensitive tablet used in combination with the brushes in Painter and Photoshop allowed me to have control while drawing the lines and shaded areas. For a more complex subject, I chose a California pottery vase and placed it on a light-colored tabletop near my computer. I lit the vase using a small lamp, which I positioned to the upper left of the subject. Prior to beginning the drawing, I carefully studied the forms and space around the subject, which were enhanced by the lighting.

My objective was to create an interpretive drawing, but not a photo-realistic rendering. I purposely simplified forms and sometimes slightly distorted them to enhance the composition. Also, to give depth and interest to the image, I kept remnants of the original sketch, the lines along the rim of the vase, and the horizon line behind the vase.

Sketching a Cube

Sharp Pastel Pencil, *varied pressure*

Square Hard Pastel, *light pressure*

Square Hard Pastel, *heavier pressure*

The sketched diamond shape

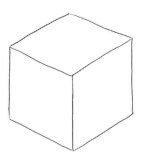

The line drawing of the cube

ARTIST'S MATERIALS

Tablet: Medium pressure

Program: Painter

Paper: Basic Paper: versatile, medium-grain texture

Paint: Dark gray, chosen in the Color panel

Brushes:
- Sharp Pastel Pencil: ideal for sketching; reveals texture and produces an expressive line that varies with pressure

- Square Hard Pastel: allows subtle building of values while revealing paper texture; heavier pressure also creates a varied texture effect

1 **Warm-up: A solid cube.** This exercise will help you understand the concept of volume and solidity of a form in space. If you are familiar with the concept, you can skip step 1 and move on to step 2.

You'll draw a cube that is lit from the upper left. Imagine a "solid" cube—one that is cut from granite. Thinking of it as a heavy, solid cube will help you to draw it as one.

You'll begin the exercise with a new 600 × 600 pixel file. In the Color panel, choose a dark gray.* In the Paper Selector (Toolbox), select the Basic Paper texture.*

Choose the Sharp Pastel Pencil variant of Pastels from the Brush Selector. Next, I recommend setting Brush Tracking* so that Painter can customize itself to the pressure and speed of your hand on the stylus and tablet. You'll start the cube by drawing a diamond shape. Now sketch an angled line. Add a second line,

parallel to the first. Draw two more angled lines that connect the first two. Try to maintain an even pressure on the stylus so that all of the lines are a similar shade of gray.

To sketch the sides of the cube, draw three vertical lines. For the bottom of the cube, draw two diagonal lines that connect the bottom of the vertical lines. I used Painter's Page Rotation tool* to rotate the image, which made it easier to draw the straight, angled lines.

LEARN MORE ABOUT. . .

* the Color panel. . . pages 67, 68, 138
* the Paper Selector. . . pages 81, 190
* Brush Tracking. . . page 86
* Page Rotation tool. . . page 95
* shading and value. . . pages 120, 126

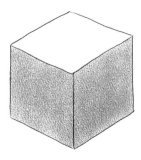
The cube sketch partially shaded

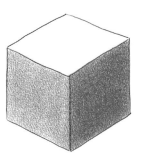
Suggesting a light source by adding shading

The final cube with cast shadow added

2 Shading the cube. Adding tone to the sides of the cube will help to suggest volume. Envision a light source shining from the top left.

Now you'll use the same gray that you chose for the lines to add shading to two sides of your cube. Choose the Square Hard Pastel variant of Pastels from the Brush Selector. Use a light pressure on your stylus, and build up the shading for an even coverage on the two side planes. Aim for a medium-gray value.*

Tone and value. Tone (or value) is the lightness or darkness given to a surface by the amount of light reflected from it. Black in the shadow areas is the darkest value, and white in the highlights is the lightest value.

3 Building up darker shading. To emphasize the light source shining from the upper left, use soft, controlled strokes to build up darker shading in the right side of the cube.

Page Rotation. With the Page Rotation tool, you can rotate the image to a comfortable drawing position, which makes it easier to sketch angled lines. Choose the Page Rotation tool in the Toolbox. Click and drag with the tool on your image to rotate it. To return the image to its original position, double-click on the Page Rotation tool in the Toolbox.

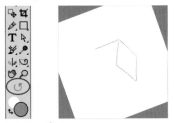
Rotating the page

4 Adding a cast shadow. A cast shadow will help to place your cube on a surface and add to the illusion of space, and its volume or weight. Draw your cast shadow darker as you get closer to the edge of the cube, and let it gradually fade out at its outer edge.

For Photoshop users. If you don't have Painter, you can follow along with these exercises in Photoshop using the Dry Media Brushes. See the instructional sidebar on page 91 on how to load the brushes. Use the Charcoal Pencil for the cube. For the orange on page 96, try the Pastel on Charcoal Paper or the Square Charcoal. (Although they're useful, the performance of the brushes will not be identical.)

Drawing a Textured Round Object

Soft Pastel Pencil, *varied pressure*

Square X-Soft Pastel, *light pressure*

Square X-Soft Pastel, *heavier pressure*

The sketched outline of the orange

The apple partially shaded with medium gray

1 **Warm-up: A round object.** This exercise will help you understand the concept of drawing a round form that has volume and solidity. Using a similar set-up to the fish (Chapter 5), I looked at an orange and drew it.

You'll make a loose drawing of an orange that is lit from the upper right. Think of your orange as being solid and heavy. This will help you draw it with weight and mass.

Begin by starting a new 600 × 600 pixel file; then choose a medium gray (40–50% value) in the Color panel.* Select Basic Paper* in the Toolbox and choose the Soft Pastel Pencil variant of Pastels from the Brush Selector. So that Painter can customize itself to the pressure and speed of your hand on the stylus and tablet, set up Brush Tracking.* Now sketch a rough outline of your orange. Keep your wrist loose.

2 **Adding the first tones.** Because it helps me to establish a balance or tension in my composition, I often prefer to rough in the darker shadow areas first, before modeling the overall subject.

Observe the light source shining from the upper right onto the orange. You'll use the same gray you chose for the sketch to suggest the deepest shadow areas on the side of the orange. Choose the Square X-Soft Pastel variant of Pastels from the Brush Selector, and using a light pressure on your stylus, lay in the shading for an even coverage on the side of the orange that is hidden from the light. Aim for a medium-gray value.*

LEARN MORE ABOUT. . .

* the Color panel. . . pages 67, 68, 138
* Brush Tracking. . . page 86
* underpainting. . . pages 131, 192

The base tone, and layered darker values

The final highlights and shadows

Close-up detail of the final image

3 Layering values. Now rough in the foundation (underpainting) values by choosing a light gray and brushing it onto the lighter areas.* Then choose a darker gray and use gentle pressure on your stylus to paint curved strokes onto the shaded side of the orange.

4 Adding highlights and shadows. Continue to observe your subject, and model its surface using strokes that follow the rounded form. If needed, add darker values to the cast shadow in the area nearest to the orange. Brighten the "hottest" highlight with pure white. If you apply the white with a light touch on the stylus, you will preserve the subtle

tone and texture underneath. A cast shadow will help to place your orange on the surface. Paint your cast shadow darker nearer to the edge of the subject, and let it gradually fade out at its outer edge. Finally, remember that this exercise is a loose drawing, not a photo-realistic one. Relax and enjoy your drawing process.

Lighting and form. Setting up a single light source will make it easier for you to perceive the forms. You'll notice that the areas closest to the light are lighter, and that the object becomes darker in areas that are farther from the light. Directional lighting can make a huge difference in the appearance of a form. Here are four oranges in different positions, with a light source shining overhead. These sketches show that different dimensional effects can be achieved depending where the object is in relation to the light source. The brightest highlight will be the area closest to the light source. Notice the reflected light—light that reflects from the table surface onto the side of the object—and notice the darkest shadow on the object, which will be the area farthest from the light source and directly under the subject.

Drawing Rounded Forms

Pastel Medium Tip, small

Pastel Medium Tip, default (top),
Pastel Medium Tip, modified (bottom)

Pastel on Charcoal Paper, default (top),
Pastel on Charcoal Paper, modified (bottom)

ARTIST'S MATERIALS

Tablet: Medium pressure

Program: Photoshop

Paint: Grays chosen in the Color panel

Brushes:

• Pastel Medium Tip: low opacity brush that applies subtly textured strokes

• Pastel Medium Tip: modified to cover underlying paint and to make stroke thickness vary with pressure

• Pastel on Charcoal Paper: low opacity brush with texture saved in the preset

• Pastel on Charcoal Paper: modified to cover underlying paint and to make stroke thickness vary with pressure

The first values

Building up darker values

1 Setting up and laying in values. Create a new file that measures 1500 × 2000 pixels. Choose a medium gray in the Color panel, click on the Brush tool in the Toolbox, and choose the Pastel Medium Tip preset from the Dry Media Brushes.* Set the Opacity to 100% in the Options Bar. Click to open the Brush Preset picker on the Options Bar, and reduce the size of the Pastel Medium Tip to about 5 pixels using the Brush Size slider. Make a new layer, and draw a loose sketch.

Now click on the image background. Using the default Pastel Medium Tip preset, block in large areas of value, starting with the midtones. The midtones will help to unify your image, and will connect the lighter and darker values. I simplified the number of values at this stage, using a medium gray, a light gray, and a darker gray.

2 Painting more values. Before beginning to paint the darker values, I set the Pastel Medium Tip brush to vary its opacity with stylus pressure and saved the new preset.* While applying light pressure, gradually build up darker values, changing the size of the brush as you work. Let your strokes follow the curves of the forms.

Next, I feathered in the highlights on the side of the shaker and on its base. By applying very light pressure to the modified Pastel Medium Tip, I was able to subtly brush lighter value over the darker tones to give the impression of a blend.

LEARN MORE ABOUT. . .

* Dry Media Brushes. . . pages 91, 95
* saving a brush preset. . . pages 61, 99

Painting highlights and adding details

The final image

Close-up detail showing texture added

3 **Painting the cast shadow and details.** Next, to give the salt shaker more of a sense of space, I painted a gradation onto the cast shadow, and refined the reflected light on the edge of the base near this shadow and the underside of the shaker. Then I added more contrast to the edges of the shaker.

4 **Adding texture and smudging.** As a final step, I added a subtle texture to areas using the Pastel on Charcoal Paper preset. To brush more texture onto your image, choose the Pastel on Charcoal Paper preset. Open the Brush panel, and modify the brush so the Opacity varies with pressure. Save your new preset. Now sample color from the area

where you want to paint and darken or lighten it slightly. You will achieve more texture if you apply a lighter pressure. Brush very lightly over the area to slightly blend tones and add texture. Photoshop does not allow you to blend in the same way Painter does, but with carefully chosen colors and values, you can achieve a similar effect.

Painting with pressure. When using the Pastel Medium Tip, see what it's like to control the buildup of paint using pressure on the stylus. Choose the brush and click on Transfer in the Brush panel. Then set the Opacity Jitter Control pop-up menu to Pen Pressure. Experiment with the Opacity Jitter slider if you like. (To slightly vary the opacity, I set it at 4%.) Save your new brush by choosing New Brush Preset from the pop-out menu and giving it a unique name.

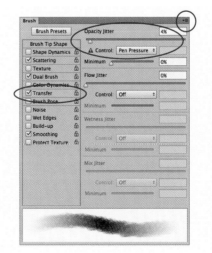

Drawing a Hollow Rounded Form

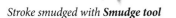

#2 Pencil varied pressure

Square Charcoal varied pressure

Stroke smudged with Smudge tool

A color digital photo of the pitcher with light source on the tabletop

A black-and-white version of the photo might help you to think in values instead of colors.

1 **Setting up a still life.** In this exercise you'll use Pastel brushes to paint a three-dimensional pitcher that has volume and weight. Choose an object that has an obvious rounded form (such as a cup or a vase), and set it on a light-colored surface. I chose this vintage pottery vase for my subject because of its rounded, retro shape and its interesting design. I arranged the pitcher using a slight angle to add interest to the composition and to create intriguing negative space around it.

Position a small lamp that will cast an interesting shadow on the subject and table surface. I positioned the light source so it would shine from the upper right of the pitcher.

2 **Visualize in black and white.** Observe the lighting on your subject, and notice how the lighting enhances the presence of the forms in three-dimensional space. Study the tonal values of the blacks, grays, and whites and how they help to reveal the round body, rings, and hollow interior.*

LEARN MORE ABOUT. . .

* shading, tone, and value. . . page 95
* the Color panel. . . pages 67, 68, 138
* cross-hatching. . . page 115
* Dry Media Brushes. . . pages 91, 95
* Brush Presets panel. . . pages 77, 78

The rough sketch showing basic shapes

Refining the shapes using the #2 Pencil

3 **Sketching basic shapes.** Now create a new file with a white background. For a rectangular format like this one, set the Width and Height at 1400 × 1200 pixels.

To begin, I sketched the basic shapes of the vase using loose, simple strokes.* As you'll notice, I added an imaginary horizon line, which will help to create more of a sense of space.

The #2 Pencil is located in the Dry Media Brushes.* Choose the Brush tool; then click on the tiny arrow on the top right of the Brush Presets panel* and, when the menu pops open, choose the Dry Media Brushes from the list. A dialog box will appear asking "Replace current brushes with the brushes from the Dry Media set?" Click the Append button to add them to the existing Brushes. Choose the #2 Pencil in the Brush Presets panel.

Now choose a dark gray in the Color panel.* Study your subject, allowing your eye to trace around its forms. Rough in the shapes and proportions. Keep your wrist loose, and apply more pressure to your stylus when you want to emphasize a line (by making it darker). Apply less pressure when you want lighter lines. As you draw, continue to take time to observe your subject.

4 **Building a more detailed drawing.** When you have the proportions established, begin to refine your drawing. You can leave the lines you sketched earlier, because they will add character to your drawing. Drawing over the existing lines will also help you to refine your drawing.

As the drawing began to develop, I continued to use the #2 Pencil, using expressive strokes and varying pressure in the stylus to "sculpt" the forms. You can accomplish this by making your strokes follow the rounded forms—let them sweep curved lines around the vase. You could also accomplish this with cross-hatching.* (Remember to carefully observe the perspective of the vase and to adjust the angle of the lines, as in the illustration above.) Continue to keep your wrist loose as you draw with your stylus so that you have a relaxed, natural feeling while sketching.

Laying in the first tones with the Square Charcoal

Sketching darker values onto the shadow areas

5 **Building up tone with charcoal.** The Square Charcoal is a versatile tool for drawing that features an erodible tip that wears flatter with use. The tip can be sharpened by clicking the Sharpen button in the Brush panel. Choose the Brush tool in the Tools panel and the Square Charcoal from the Brush Presets panel.

To paint a stroke with a square edge, hold the stylus with its button up. To paint a stroke with a pointed end, hold the stylus with the button facing to the side (right or left). (To reduce the size of the Square Charcoal, click the small arrow on the Options Bar to open the Brush Presets picker and move the Size slider to the left.) Continue to "sculpt" the forms by adding darker values.

To develop the forms of the vase using light to medium tones, I used light to medium pressure on the stylus. I worked over broader areas first, and then gradually added more detailed strokes (the rim and handles).

Next, keeping my light source in mind, I began to add darker and lighter tones for more contrast. To suggest a

cast shadow, I used similar grays. Study your subject. If your light source is positioned in the upper left like mine, consider adding lighter tones to the upper-left planes and darker tones to the lower-right planes.

The Brush Tip Shape window shows controls for the Erodible Square tip and the Sharpen button.

Using a small brush to sketch the darker values on the vase

Smudging and brushing to soften transitions between the tones

6 **Refining the forms.** Using a dark gray and the Square Charcoal in a smaller size (7–12 pixels), I drew over the rim and handles to refine them. When I was satisfied with the look, I chose a light gray and added new highlights.

To blend areas of the pitcher and cast shadow, I used the Smudge tool. For subtle blending, apply a light pressure and work back and forth on the edge of the shadow to "feather" it, or make it more graduated. Pull out from the dark area into the light area using a heavier pressure when you want to pull some dark tone into a light area.

When observing the vase, I noticed that the rim had some extremely bright highlights. To brighten these

highlights in my study, I used a smaller Square Charcoal (5–7 pixels). I zoomed into the rim area using the Zoom tool, and carefully added very light gray and white strokes to areas of the lip and handles. (I chose not to go around the entire rim because it would not look natural.) Next, to enhance the feeling of space, I used the Square Charcoal and varied grays to rough in a gradation to the background. I also varied the light grays to add a gradation to the cast shadow. Brushing very lightly (using a technique known as *scumbling*) allowed me to apply a little tone while revealing underlying values. You can see the entire final image on page 92.

Softly painting graduated tones using the Square Charcoal

 Erodible tip. The Square Charcoal features an Erodible Square tip that wears broader with use. Softness can be adjusted using the Softness slider in the Brush panel. To sharpen the tip, click the Sharpen button in the Brush panel.

White Orchid

7
SENSITIVE TONE AND MODELING

Making studies in black and white will help you to understand your subject and will lead to more successful work later when you use color. In this project, you'll set up a still life and practice the process of observing your subject and painting it with sensitive tone and modeling, giving it presence in realistic three-dimensional space.

 I drew White Orchid *using my favorite Wacom tablet and pen. The pressure-sensitive tablet used in combination with the Charcoal brushes in Painter allowed me to have control while drawing lines and building up interesting shading and texture on the flower petals. For the subject, I chose a beautiful white Phalaenopsis orchid and placed it near my computer. I lit the plant using a small lamp that I positioned on the upper right of the subject. Before beginning to draw, I studied the negative space around the orchid and its delicate forms that were enhanced by the lighting.*

My objective was to create a sensitive, expressive drawing, instead of a photo-realistic one. I chose to draw a single orchid, rather than the entire group that was on the stem, so that I could focus on one subject, and create a stronger statement. For a more dynamic composition, I exaggerated the angle of the orchid. Also, I exaggerated the value contrast to add drama and to enhance the focal point. I painted a cast shadow behind the flower using dark, multi-directional, hatched strokes, which added subtle interest, while increasing the depth.

Using Sensitive Tone and Blending

Hard Charcoal Pencil, varied pressure

Hard Charcoal Stick, varied pressure

Hard Charcoal Stick stroke blended using **Soft Blender Stump**, **Pointed Stump**, and **Grainy Water**

ARTIST'S MATERIALS

Tablet: Soft-to-medium pressure

Program: Painter

Paper: Basic Paper: a versatile, medium-grain texture

Paint: Grays, chosen in the Color panel

Brushes:
- Hard Charcoal Pencil: ideal for sketching; opacity and texture vary with pressure

- Hard Charcoal Stick: allows subtle building of values, while revealing paper texture

- Soft Blender Stump: for blending larger areas

- Pointed Stump: for blending details

- Grainy Water: for blending while revealing paper grain

A color digital photo of the subject

A grayscale version of the photo might help you to think in black and white.

1 **Setting up a still life.** Choose a houseplant or a flower picked from your garden and set up your subject in front of a simple, non-distracting background. I chose this orchid as a subject because of its graceful shapes, unique texture, and interesting details. I found the shapes of the petals and the negative space around them to be fascinating.* I set up a small spotlight to cast interesting shadows on the flower.

2 **Visualizing in black and white.** Study your subject, allowing your eye to trace around the edges of the forms, and to take in the feel of the delicate texture. Absorb the affect of the lighting on your subject that enhances the feeling of its form in space. Study the tonal values of the blacks, grays, and whites and how they give the forms solidity.*

LEARN MORE ABOUT. . .

* setting Paper Color. . . page 189
* the Color panel. . . pages 67, 68, 138
* the Paper Selector. . . pages 81, 190
* Brush Tracking. . . page 86
* tone and value. . . page 95
* erodible tips. . . pages 102–103

 Positive and negative spaces. Think of the forms of your subject as "positive space," and the area or "air" outside and around the subject as "negative" space. Positive and negative space are equally important to drawing and to good composition.

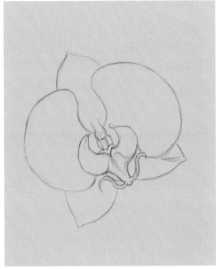
Sketching with the Hard Charcoal Pencil

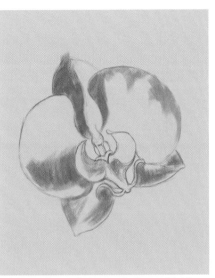
Adding value with the Hard Charcoal Stick

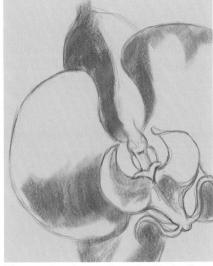
The curved strokes are shown in this detail.

3 **Sketching the shapes.** Open a new file that is 700 × 900 pixels. Set up a light-to-medium gray background color so that you can work with dark shadows and whiter highlights on a mid-toned ground.* Next, choose a dark gray in the Color panel*, and choose Basic Paper in the Paper Selector.*

Set Brush Tracking to customize Painter to the feel of your hand on the stylus.* Then choose the Hard Charcoal Pencil variant of Charcoal & Conté from the Brush Selector. Using your stylus, sketch in a way that is similar to how you would use a pencil, with lines that gently overlap one another to suggest the shapes. Focus on the simple shapes at this stage. If you like, embellish the most important areas by applying heavier pressure to create bolder strokes.

4 **Adding the first tones.** Now that the shapes are roughed in, you'll begin to build dimension by blocking in the first tones. For this task, I recommend using the Hard Charcoal Stick because of its rectangular, chisel-like shape, which allows you to expressively paint broad areas while revealing texture. You can build up value quickly or slowly, based on the pressure you apply to the stylus.

Sculpt the darkest areas of your subject first by using a dark gray. Observe and analyze your subject. Where are the darker values? (They are usually in the deepest shadow areas.)*

When painting the curved flower petals, I used curved strokes that followed the contours of the forms, as you can see in the close-up view above.

For Photoshop users. If you don't have Painter, you can follow along with this exercise using Photoshop's brushes. Photoshop CS6 features Charcoal brushes with erodible tips,* with which you can achieve similar results. Choose the Brush tool in the Tools panel, then use the Charcoal Pencil for sketching. For blocking in large areas of value, try the Square Charcoal. If you'd like to paint with more texture, try the Pastel on Charcoal Paper preset. Note: The Pastel on Charcoal Paper preset does not feature an erodible tip. See the "Painting with pressure" tip on page 99 to learn how to set up the Pastel on Charcoal Paper preset to vary opacity with pressure.

Developing more value

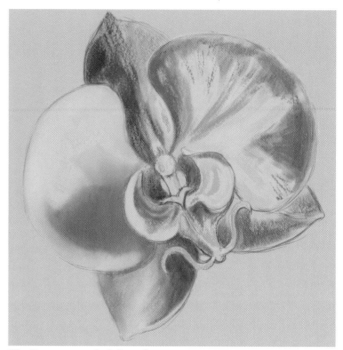

Blending tones on the left petal

5 **Building form.** Continue to observe your subject; study the values, from light to mid-tone to dark; and then carefully work the shaded areas to establish a value range. I added the mid-tone areas using the same gray color in the Color panel, but used a lighter pressure on the stylus. If you prefer to build up the tone more slowly, lower the Opacity of the brush using the slider in the Property Bar. If your drawing still needs more contrast, darken the strongest shadowed areas.*

6 **Blending.** Use a Blender brush to subtly smudge or smear some of the areas, and blend the light and dark values. I suggest leaving traces of texture as you blend, by applying gentle pressure on the stylus. You will notice blended areas on the petals on the left of the flower in this example.

To blend* with control in small areas, I suggest using the Pointed Stump; for blending larger areas, try the Soft Blender Stump or the Grainy Water variant of Blenders.

LEARN MORE ABOUT. . .

* textures to build value. . . pages 111, 173
* blending. . . pages 165, 166
* the Color panel. . . pages 67, 68, 138

Close-up view of the blended area

Adding brighter highlights and deeper shadows

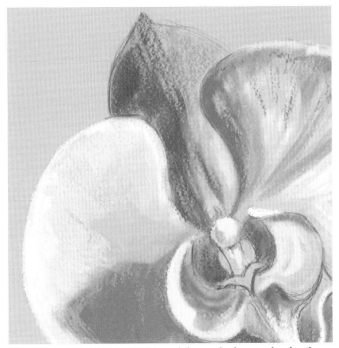
You can see the brighter highlights and deeper shadows in this detail.

7 **Adding highlight and shadow.** For a more dramatic, high-contrast look, I added stronger highlights using white and lighter gray tones.

Choose a bright white in the Color panel* and the Hard Charcoal Stick variant of Charcoal & Conté from the Brush Selector. (If needed, reduce the size of the Hard Charcoal Stick by moving the Size slider to the left in the Property Bar.) As you paint the brighter highlights, continue to use curved strokes that complement the forms. If you'd like to reveal more texture in some areas, as I did, apply less pressure to your stylus. To end a stroke showing more texture, gradually lift your stylus from the tablet at the end of the stroke.

After adding the highlights, you might want to add some deeper tones to the darker shadow areas if they need "punching up." In areas where you want a darker shadow without as much texture, reduce the size of the Hard Charcoal stick and apply more pressure. To achieve a crisper edge in some areas, I sampled color using the Dropper tool, and then zoomed in and used a small version of the Hard Charcoal Stick to carefully draw along the edges.

 Value, volume, and depth. You can use value to suggest volume and depth. Darker values tend to recede, whereas lighter values will come forward. Strong value contrast will help to emphasize the focal point in a composition.

Painting the cast shadow and stem

Brightening details in the interior of the flower

8 **Adding the stem and cast shadow.** You may want to paint a cast shadow (as I did) to create more of a sense of space and atmosphere around the flower. For dappled light and interest, I used the Hard Charcoal Stick to paint varied angled strokes (wide, overlapping hatching marks) behind the left side of the subject.

9 **Emphasizing details.** Again, it's a good idea to step back and look at your painting. Does your drawing need more contrast? Are there edges that you'd like to emphasize? At this point, I decided to emphasize a few important internal contours. I used the Hard Charcoal Pencil to strengthen edges of the highlighted interior curves, and I also redefined edges of the lower petals. The emphasized edge is most evident in the lower-left petal. Congratulations! You've completed the last step in this technique.

You've learned about using sensitive tone and value in your images. In the next chapter, you'll learn about creating the look of atmosphere in your images.

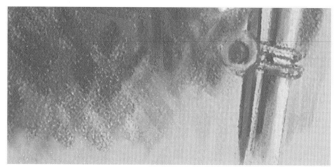

Close-up view showing the angled hatched marks on the shadow

Using Interesting Strokes to Build Tonal Variations

There are many ways to build tonal variations, from blended gradations, to linear hatching, cross-hatching and stippling, to name a few. Here are some examples that can serve as inspiration for your own experimentation.

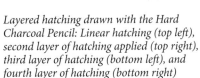

Layered hatching drawn with the Hard Charcoal Pencil: Linear hatching (top left), second layer of hatching applied (top right), third layer of hatching (bottom left), and fourth layer of hatching (bottom right)

Hatching drawn with the Hard Charcoal Stick: Overlapping linear hatching (top left), layer of light marks over dark (top right), soft angled hatching (bottom left), and angled lines, using harder pressure (bottom right)

Patched hatching drawn with the Hard Charcoal Pencil builds tone and an abstract pattern

Overlapping tight circular squiggles drawn with the Hard Charcoal Pencil build tone and suggest activity

Dots drawn with the Hard Charcoal Pencil using varied pressure suggest a gradient with sparkle

Lines and dabs of different tones drawn with the Hard Charcoal Stick and Hard Charcoal Pencil using varied pressure add depth and interest

Expressive strokes drawn with the Hard Charcoal Stick for tone and energy

Gradient drawn with the Hard Charcoal Stick shows sketchy vertical strokes

Gradient (from left) blended with the Soft Blender Stump (Blenders) for a softer look

Broad lines of darker tone drawn with the Hard Charcoal Stick using varied pressure to create a subtle gradient

Conch Shell Study

8

A Sense of Atmosphere

You can achieve atmosphere in a variety of ways, two of which are cross-hatching (overlapping strokes that work together to build value) and pointillism (small dabs of tone that blend in the eye of the viewer). In this technique, you will simulate the effect of air, which is heavy with moisture or particles of pollen, and how it can add depth to an image. You'll use varied color to draw with cross-hatched strokes, which overlap but do not cover the sparkling light and texture. This will give the drawing an amorphous, dreamy quality. For this project, you'll set up a still life and practice the process of observing your subject and drawing it so that it has shimmering light quality, as well as volume and mass. Following the feature project is a Painter sidebar, where you'll have the opportunity to put these concepts of light and texture to work in a black-and-white drawing.

 I drew Conch Shell *from life using my favorite Wacom tablet and pen. The pressure-sensitive tablet used in combination with Square Pastel brush presets in Photoshop gave me expression and control while drawing the shaded areas. For the subject, I chose a large, graceful conch shell, and placed it on a tabletop near my computer. Then I set up a small spotlight to shine on the shell.*

I use this approach when creating an atmospheric mood in a loose painting. As the drawing develops, the subject gradually emerges through layers of cross-hatched or dabbed strokes. Near the end of the process, I add a few linear details to bring areas into focus.

CP

Building Form and Atmosphere Using Hatching

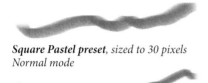

Square Pastel preset, *sized to 30 pixels Normal mode*

Square Pastel preset, *sized to 15 pixels, Normal mode*

A digital photo of the shell

Square Pastel preset strokes, 100% opacity, Normal mode

ARTIST'S MATERIALS

Tablet: Medium pressure

Program: Photoshop

Paint: Colors chosen from Swatches panel and Color Picker

Brushes:

• Square Pastel: erodible tip; ideal for pressure response; reveals Canvas texture saved with the brush

• Eraser: used to remove tone for highlight areas

1 **Arranging a still life.** Choose an object that has simple, intriguing forms (such as a sea shell or a pear with a unique shape), and set it on a light-colored surface. I chose this shell for my subject because of its graceful shape and its texture. Then I placed it at an angle to give the composition more depth, and to create interesting shapes in the negative space around it.

Position a small lamp that will cast a shadow on the subject and table surface. I positioned the light source to shine from the upper right.

 Which Pastel preset? Photoshop has several Pastel presets with similar names that perform very differently. For this exercise, use the Square Pastel preset.

2 **Visualizing and setting up.** Observe your subject. Notice how the lighting helps you to observe the forms in three-dimensional space.

Now start a new file with a white background. For a square format like mine, set the Width and Height at 1500 × 1500 pixels, and set the Color Mode menu to RGB Color.

Next, choose the Brush tool in the Toolbox, and then open the Brush Presets panel (Window > Brush Presets). Scroll to find the Square Pastel preset. This preset features an erodible dab.* The brush has a texture saved with it, which allows you

LEARN MORE ABOUT. . .

* erodible tip. . . pages 102–103, 107

* choosing a color. . . page 60

* stroke variations. . . page 111

Square Pastel preset strokes, varied opacity, Dissolve mode

The rough sketch in process, showing with cross-hatching on the background, without darker shading or details

to draw textured strokes, similar to hard pastel on canvas board. Choose a medium blue in the Swatches panel (Window > Swatches). (I chose R 100, G 167, B 205 for the blue.) I planned to use a complementary color palette for the painting, blues for the background and accents, and oranges and golds for the sea shell.*

Using your stylus, practice making hatching strokes. Experiment with lowering the opacity if you like. (I varied the opacity from 40–80% depending on the density of tone I wanted to paint.)*

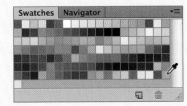

Choosing a medium blue

3 Building a sense of atmosphere.

This atmospheric approach uses both line and mass to build a composition. Overlapping hatched lines blend in the viewer's eye to create areas of tone that sparkle with light. For additional texture and sparkle, change the Blend Mode for the brush to Dissolve in the Options Bar. If you'd like a smoother look, leave the Blend Mode at the default, Normal.

For flexibility, I sketched onto a layer. Add a new layer to your image by clicking on the Create A New Layer button near the bottom of the Layers panel. Using a light touch on your stylus, use cross-hatch strokes to lay in the background first. The shape of the object should begin to emerge. Starting with the background, or the negative space

around the shell, will help you to see the shape of the shell apart from the background as you sketch. Continue to observe your subject and analyze its basic forms. This method will keep your drawing loose. Don't focus on detail in this stage; continue to work over all your drawing, until your basic composition begins to emerge. I added a few very loose strokes to suggest the contours of the shell. I planned to draw over the light strokes later with darker tones.

 Texture with Dissolve. The default painting mode is Normal. For a different texture look, try changing the mode to Dissolve using the pop-up menu in the Options Bar. Crisp texture can be achieved while building up layers of hatching.

Drawing light-medium tones using hatching strokes, and laying in a broad area of gold for the body of the shell

Close-up of the in-progress modeling with light-medium-toned strokes in oranges and rose

4 Modeling form and space with hatching. For more dimension, add darker hatched strokes to the background, and begin to add more value to your subject.

I overlapped strokes, using several directions, to add activity and dappled light to the background. Because darker values tend to recede, this helped to bring a lighter subject forward in the composition.*

I planned for the body of the shell to be mostly golds

 Resizing a brush. To resize your brush as you work, click to open the Brush Preset picker in the Options Bar and then use the Brush Size slider to adjust the size. (I used a 40-pixel size for broader areas, and then reduced the size to 20 pixels for modeling areas of the shell, and then to 10 pixels for more detailed areas.) You can also use the bracket keys on your keyboard to resize a brush. To reduce the brush size, press the left bracket ([), and to increase the size, press the right bracket (]).

and oranges. So I wouldn't paint over the drawing in blue, I sketched in the first gold color onto a new layer. I positioned the layer with gold color under the layer with the blue drawing. Add a new layer to your image, and using the Square Pastel, make broad hatching strokes to lay in color for the body of your subject.

When the base of gold was laid in, I merged the gold layer with the blue sketch layer by selecting both layers in the Layers panel, and choosing Merge Layers from the pop-up menu. Merging the two layers will allow you to draw over the sketch with more color and tone.

Now that the composition was established, I began to sculpt the forms of the shell, using varied shades of gold, orange, brown, and blue. I recommend using broad cross-hatching strokes to sketch the larger areas of the

LEARN MORE ABOUT. . .

* value and depth . . . pages 126, 135
* modeling form. . . pages 103, 111, 118

Using hatching strokes to build up medium tones and basic forms

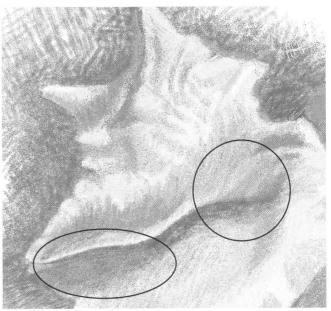

The darker strokes on the inside of the shell

subject first (for instance, in my image, the curves above the opening of the shell). Then gradually add thinner hatched strokes (I added curved hatched strokes on the opening of the shell, and the thinner lines on the top protrusions).

When drawing your subject, "sculpt" the forms by building up curved hatching that follows the direction of the forms.* If you've chosen to use lighter values on your subject, as I did, consider leaving pure white areas for the highlights.

Next, to build more dimension, I added varied darker blue strokes to the background, cast shadow, and the shell in a few places. As you work, layer the strokes, but be careful not to fill in areas with solid color. You will add darker blues, and browns to a few areas in the last step.

Keeping my light source in mind, I used overlapping linear strokes and cross-hatch strokes in varied orange, rose, brown and blue to darken the opening edge of the shell. I paid careful attention to the curved forms and to the raised and indented areas as I worked.

Rescuing an overworked area. If you've overworked an area of your drawing, it's easy to step back a few stages using the History panel. (If the panel is not open, choose Window > History.) Click backward in the history states until you have undone the overworked strokes. (The default number of history states is 20. You can increase this number in Preferences, but Photoshop requires more memory with a larger number of states.) You can also switch to a small Eraser and use the same cross-hatching stroke pattern to "hatch" the light areas back in.

Stepping back in the History panel

Painting darker blues on the background

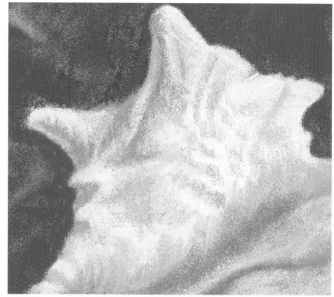

Modeling more detailed forms on the shell, and painting highlights

5 **Refining the shell and background.** Consider making a print of your image when the forms and background are established. After making a print of my image and studying the shape of the shell, its proportions, and values, I noticed that the upper "lip" of the shell needed to be redrawn, and more highlights and shadows needed to be brought out in some areas. I set up the Eraser tool in Brush mode with a hard-edged tip; then I saved a preset for the Eraser tool.* Using this Eraser (in sizes of 9–15 pixels, with 10–30% opacity), I sketched the highlights.*

 The Eraser tool and the Wacom stylus eraser. If you turn your pen upside down and use the eraser on your stylus, Photoshop will choose the default Eraser tip or the most recent Eraser tip that you've used. To set up my Eraser for this project, I chose the Eraser tool in the Toolbox, and then chose the Hard Round brush tip in the Brush Preset window. I could easily switch between my Brush tool and the Eraser by turning my stylus as I worked.

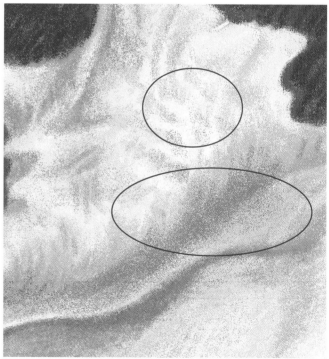

Using a larger brush and light pressure on the stylus to brush darker rose colors onto the opening of the shell. The highlights are subtly brightened using the Eraser tool with a 10-pixel Hard Round tip, set to 20% opacity.

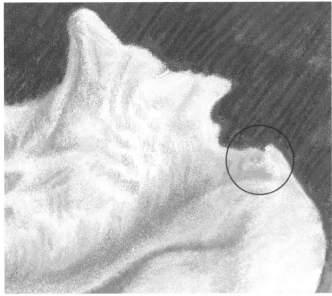

The top lip of the shell needed to be corrected

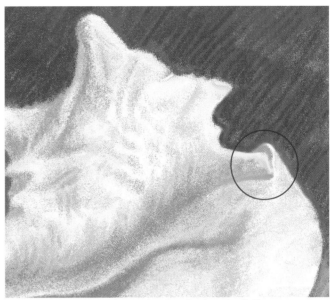

The redrawn top lip, and more details refined on the shell

6 **Redrawing areas and adding more contrast.** If you notice areas of your image that need to be redrawn, continue to observe your subject as you make the refinements. After any corrections are complete, add the final details. For editing flexibility, you might want to draw these final details on a new layer, as I did.

After zooming in to 100%, I used a 10-pixel version of the Square Pastel preset and used a light cream color to redraw the lip, and then painted shadows using light brown and rose colors. Next, I used a smaller brush and darker versions of these colors to refine a few details on the interior of the shell, and I also embellished the curved shapes at the bottom, leading into the opening of the shell. To carry the color theme throughout, I loosely painted a few varied brown and blue strokes on the background. As a final touch, I strengthened a few edges, including the cast shadow along the lower edge of the shell.

LEARN MORE ABOUT. . .

* Eraser tool presets. . . page 65, 118
* Eraser tool. . . page 128

A close-up view of the cross-hatched background, and the in-progress raised and indented areas on the outside of the shell

Achieving Sparkling Light

Square Soft Pastel, soft to firm pressure

A digital photo of the apples

Using hatching to start the basic composition

Square Soft Pastel, hatching

ARTIST'S MATERIALS

Tablet: Medium pressure

Program: Painter

Paint: Grays: mixed on the Mixer Pad or in the Color panel

Paper: Charcoal Paper: a rough even-textured paper

Brushes:
• Square Soft Pastel: opacity and grain vary with pressure; the pastel strokes also change subtly, depending on the bearing (direction) of the stylus

1 Setting up and visualizing. Choose an object that has a rounded form (such as an apple or a orange), and set the object on a light-colored surface. Position a lamp that will cast a shadow on the subject and table surface.

Now, create a new file with a white background. For a rectangular format like this one, set the Width and Height at 1800 × 1400 pixels. From the Brush Selector, choose the Square Soft Pastel variant of Pastels, and choose Charcoal Paper from the Paper Selector.

 More atmosphere and light. This Painter technique is a variation on the atmospheric concept described on page 138. Painter allows more complex layering of pastel or chalk-like media (without covering texture) than Photoshop does, so it's an ideal tool to use for this atmospheric approach.

Then, using the Color panel and Mixer panel, I created a palette of grays.

 Mixing grays. You can create grays for your value studies using the Mixer. (To open the Mixer, choose Window > Show Mixer.) Choose grays from the Color Wells at the top of the panel or from the Color panel. Apply them to the Mixer Pad using your stylus and the Apply Color tool in the Mixer panel. Use the Mix Color tool to blend your gray paints.

A palette of grays

LEARN MORE ABOUT...

★ Brush Tracking... page 86

Working more values in the background, and onto the apples

Roughing in the cast shadow and adding more tone to the apples

2 **Laying in general forms and space.** After setting up Brush Tracking, use cross-hatch strokes to lay in the basic composition, roughing in a graduated background and the general light on your subject.* Try to keep your strokes loose, using the cross-hatch method and avoiding adding details at this early stage. Adjust the brush size as needed using the Size slider in the Property Bar.

3 **Building space and form.** Next you'll use darker grays (about 80%) and more cross-hatched strokes, because they will weave a pattern of sparkling light and create a wonderful sense of space. If you use a light touch on the stylus, you won't completely cover the texture or values underneath. Use curved strokes that follow the forms when painting the apples.

Building layers of modeling on the apples and values on the background

Adding subtle detail to the apples

4 **Modeling with smaller hatched strokes.** To deepen the values on the apples, I used a darker gray, and applied it using shorter strokes, focusing on the deepest shadow areas on the apples, and also the darkest areas of the cast shadows. Next, I used a lighter gray to emphasize the gradient on the right side of the background.

5 **Finessing and adding details.** Your finished image should not look photo-realistic, but it should have an amorphous quality with a feeling of shimmering light. As a final touch, I used a variety of grays and a smaller brush size to add details (such as the stem), and to strengthen a few edges.

The Porte d'Aval from Across the Bay

9
STARTING WITH A SCANNED DRAWING

In the first part of this chapter, you'll learn how to scan a drawing that you can use as a basis for artwork in the computer. In the first technique, you'll rework a scanned drawing in Photoshop to resolve its composition, and then use the reworked sketch as the starting point for an expressively painted study completed in Photoshop, reminiscent of a traditional gouache painting technique. For the second project, you'll start with another drawing and paint right over it using the Oil Pastel brushes in Painter and develop a painting with energetic brushwork and atmosphere. Following these two projects are helpful sidebars that demonstrate how to paint watercolor washes over a drawing.

 For many years, I had dreamed of visiting the small town of Etretat on France's Normandy coast. Etretat, with its spectacular limestone cliffs, was a favorite painting location of many of my favorite master artists—Eugene Delacroix, Gustave Courbet, and Claude Monet, among others.

In 2000, my husband and I visited this scene at Etretat several times when we stayed in a small hotel in the village. I loved the towering limestone cliffs, the negative spaces around the arch and needle, and the way the light-colored cliffs picked up the light at different times of the day. I sat on the beach and drew on Vellum finish Bristol board and in my sketchbook using HB and 2B graphite pencils. The Bristol and sketchbook have subtle texture and are ideal surfaces for drawing with pencils. To record details and different moods, I drew several sketches. The drawings have now become the basis for a series of color paintings of the area. After scanning the drawings, I used a Wacom tablet and pen, and Painter and Photoshop to color the drawings and to create the paintings.

CP

Scanning a Pencil Drawing

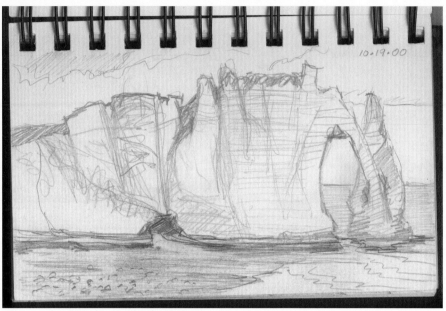

The raw scan of the close-up sketch of Etretat

The scanning process digitizes an analog image by sampling data into pixels, making it available for use in Photoshop and Painter.

How will your scan be used? Before beginning to scan, you should know how you will use the scan, and if you plan to incorporate it into another image, how large that final image will be. (Please refer to the sidebar on pixels and resolution on pages 6 and 7.)

The Epson 4870 Pro Scanner I used has a handy software plug-in that allows scanning directly into Photoshop. (The Epson Perfection V750-M Pro Scanner is also recommended for professionals.). (Many other manufacturers have plug-ins, as well. There are many different scanner interfaces, so you might need to do some experimenting.) I chose

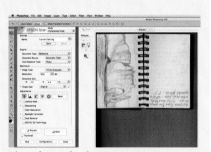

The software for the Epson 4870 scanner set up to scan the 4 × 6-inch pencil drawing at full size and at 500 ppi

File > Import > Images From Device. My drawing measured 6 × 4 inches. Because of its small size, I set the resolution at 500 pixels per inch—which would capture the detail that I wanted into a 3000 × 2000-pixel file. From the Scan Type pop-up menu, I chose the 16-bit grayscale mode, which would capture the subtle range of grays in the drawing. The spiral-bound sketchbook with

loose pages was challenging to get the sketch perfectly straight on the scanner. No worries! We can easily straighten a scan in Photoshop.

Straightening and cropping. To automatically adjust the straightness of your scan, choose the Ruler tool (it's nested with the Eyedropper tool) and drag out a measure line along the top of the scan, and then choose Image > Rotate Canvas > Arbitrary. Photoshop will enter the correct angle of rotation into the Rotate Canvas dialog box. To crop your scan, choose the Crop tool. Set the tool to its defaults by clicking the Reset button. Now drag a marquee around the area that you want to keep, and then double-click inside the marquee (or press the Return or Enter key) to accept the crop.

The scan of the sketch with editing complete

The crooked, raw scan (above) and the straightened, cropped scan (below)

Adjusting the tonal range. For more contrast, I reduced the gray tones in the sketch (while preserving the texture of the pencil marks) using Photoshop's Levels command. Choose Image > Adjustments > Levels. If the white paper

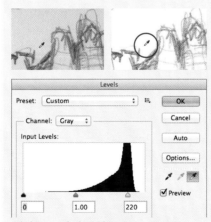

Clicking with the White Point Dropper in a light area of the drawing brought it back to white, and changed the Input Level (originally 255) to 220.

in your drawing looks muddy, choose the White Point Dropper and click a blank paper area. (It's also possible to set the white point in the scanner software if you choose.)

Adding Canvas Size. I wanted to add more image to the sky and water, so I chose Image > Canvas Size, and increased the Height and Width of the scan.

Increasing the Canvas Size on the top and bottom of the image

Using Photoshop to Work Over a Pencil Drawing

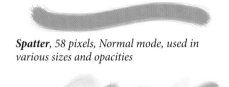

Charcoal Pencil, 9 pixels, Normal mode, used in various sizes and opacities

Spatter, 58 pixels, Normal mode, used in various sizes and opacities

Round Blunt Medium Stiff and *Flat Blunt Short Stiff*, 38 pixels, used with the Mixer Brush tool in various sizes and wetness

ARTIST'S MATERIALS

Tablet: Medium pressure

Program: Photoshop

Paint: Choose a color in the Color Picker or from Swatches

Brushes:

• Charcoal Pencil: ideal for pressure response; stroke width based on pressure

• Spatter: ideal for pressure response; leaves bristle marks at end of stroke

• Round Blunt Medium Stiff: used with Mixer Brush tool and varying wetness

• Flat Blunt Short Stiff: used with Mixer Brush tool and varying wetness

The scan of the close-up sketch of Etretat

My scanned drawing had a lot of texture, which would work well with the painting that I planned to do in Photoshop.

I planned to integrate the sketch into the image by making it semi-transparent and coloring it with a sepia tone that would complement the color theme. Leaving the pencil texture in the sketch would add interesting texture and tonal values to the image, which would help the color have more personality.

After I painted areas of flat color for an underpainting, I planned to overlay semitransparent glazes that would model form and create depth.

1 **Drawing and scanning.** In the previous spread, I told the story of how I drew the sketches while traveling in France. Likewise, you can choose a sketch from your sketchbook, or use pencils and paper to create a new drawing to scan.

I drew the pencil sketch shown above in my 4 × 6-inch travel sketchbook. After scanning the drawing into Photoshop at 500 pixels per inch at actual size, in grayscale mode, I cropped the scan and adjusted its tonal range.*

LEARN MORE ABOUT. . .

* scanning. . . pages 124–125
* cropping an image. . . page 124
* adjusting tonal range. . . page 125

Using the stylus to draw the freehand Lasso selection

Using Free Transform to give the towers more height

2 **Transforming for a more dramatic perspective.**
Take time to examine your image. Would you like to refine the composition of your drawing? Will your composition have more impact if you change the size of one of the elements?

For more drama in my drawing, and to enhance its focal point, I increased the height of the towering cliffs at the end of the point.

To transform an element, choose the Lasso tool and use your stylus to draw a freehand selection around the area that you want to edit. The stylus is extremely useful for drawing selections because it gives you much finer control and is faster to use than a mouse.

Next, choose Edit > Free Transform, and while pressing the Shift key (to constrain the proportions), use the Move tool to change the size. (I increased the size of the "towers" by pulling on the handles.) When you have

adjusted the Free Transform handles as you like them, double-click inside the marquee (or press the Return or Enter key) to accept the transform. Now deselect the selection by choosing Ctrl/Cmd-D.

Putting your drawing on a layer. You'll have more flexibility during the painting process if you put your drawing on a layer. To cut the final drawing to a layer, leaving the Background layer white, choose Select > All, and from the Layer menu, choose New, and then Layer Via Cut (Shift-Ctrl/Cmd-J). To copy the drawing to a layer and leave a copy on the background, choose Select > All, and from the Layer menu choose New, and then Layer Via Copy (Ctrl/Cmd-J). To rename your new layer, double-click on the layer name, and when the text field appears, type a useful name into the field. (I named my layer "sketch.")

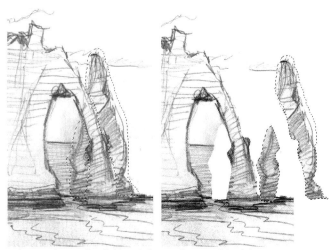

Selecting the needle, (left) and the needle moved (right)

The needle is moved outside the arch and redrawn.

3 **Selecting and moving the needle.** You can improve your composition by moving elements in your image. (To create interesting negative shapes around the arch and the needle, I moved the needle outside the arch.) Using the Lasso tool and your stylus, draw a freehand selection around the area you want to move, use the Move tool to drag it (I moved the needle to the right), and then deselect.

Cleaning up. To clean up areas of the drawing (for instance, the sea waves, the needle, and the beach), I used the Eraser tool with a hard-edged tip, in various sizes.

Notice the areas between the wiggly water lines in the illustration above, and the fine scratch marks near the base of the needle.

4 **Redrawing the needle and other elements.** Now that your elements are where you want them, you can use the Brush and Eraser tools to redraw areas of your image. With the Brush tool chosen in the Toolbox, click the brush "footprint" in the Options Bar to open the Brush Preset picker, and choose the Charcoal Pencil preset. Press Alt/Option to switch from the Brush to the Eyedropper, and sample a dark gray color from the image.

Using a dark gray color and a small Charcoal Pencil (9–15 pixels), I sketched in the missing areas on the needle, and strengthened the lines on the edges of the arch.

After a careful look at the composition I added more canvas around the drawing to allow for more foreground, water, and sky. My file now measures 4000 × 3700 pixels. To add more space around your sketch, select white for the background color, and choose Image, Canvas Size. In the dialog box, make sure the Canvas Extension Color pop-up menu is set to Background Color. Click the Relative check box and enter the desired values into the fields. Click OK. Next, I used the Charcoal Pencil preset to sketch the waves, foreground beach, and clouds.

The reworked drawing, ready for color

The drawing colored with sepia

5 **Coloring the sketch with sepia.** Coloring your drawing helps integrate it into your painting. I planned to use a color theme that included warm browns, so I gave my sketch a sepia brown color, which worked well with the color palette I planned to use.

Before coloring the sketch with sepia, change the Color Mode to RGB, and preserve the layer. (Because it was easier to complete the edits on the gray file, I didn't add the sepia before cleaning up and editing the scan.)

Tint your drawing by filling the sketch with sepia. In preparation for the painting to come—I cut the final tinted drawing to a layer, leaving the Background white. (The instructional sidebar on page 127 describes how to cut the sketch to a layer, and how to copy it to a layer. For this technique, it's best to cut it to a layer.)

Then set the blend mode of the "sketch" layer to Multiply in the Layers panel so the white areas of the sketch appear to be clear, allowing you to use your sketch as a guide when you paint color on underlying layers later.

Tinting the sketch lines. You can quickly tint your drawing with color. If your sketch is grayscale, begin by choosing Image > Mode > RGB. (Don't flatten the image when changing the mode.) In the Layers panel, target the sketch layer; then in the Color Picker, choose a warm, dark brown for the Foreground Color (I used R 70, G 58, B 51), and choose Edit > Fill, with Foreground Color; Mode, Color; and Opacity, 100%. The Color Mode fills your sketch with transparent color while preserving the tones in your drawing.

The settings in the Fill dialog box

The paint dabs in the upper-left corner of this image detail

The warm orange-ochre base color is laid in on the new layer.

6 **Designing a color palette.** Think about the kind of color palette that you'd like to use. Will it feature warm browns, oranges, and blues like mine, or will it have primarily cooler blues and purples? I remembered how the afternoon light lit up the white cliffs with a golden glow. I would need a rich, earthy color palette to carry out this color theme.

I recommend adding a new layer to store your paint dabs, as you plan your color theme. Use the Color Picker to mix colors;* then make small dabs of paint in an upper corner of the image. (If you choose to leave the paint dabs on this layer, you can hide or show the layer as needed when you want to sample color from it using the Eyedropper. You can also save your colors into a custom Swatches palette and then delete the layer.

7 **Laying in an opaque base color.** In this step, you'll paint a base color (underpainting) that will establish the color theme for the entire image. (I used a light orange-ochre color.) Choose the Brush tool, and then choose the Spatter 59 pixels preset and scale it up to about 150 pixels. Make a new layer* and name it "base color." Using loose, broad strokes, block in color behind the sketch. (When you complete a stroke and lift up on the stylus, you'll notice the bristle marks at the end of each stroke.)

LEARN MORE ABOUT. . .

* using the Color Picker. . . page 76
* adding a new layer. . . page 68
* Brush panel. . . pages 61–64
* Mixer Brush tool. . . pages 132–134, 169
* saturation. . . pages 76, 176

Strokes painted with the Spatter Brush, Flat Blunt Short Stiff, and Round Point Stiff presets

The in-progress underpainting, with brushwork painted with the Spatter Brush, Flat Blunt Short Stiff, and Round Point Stiff presets

8 **Building an underpainting.** Next, make a new layer for the underpainting, and name it to keep your painting organized. Choose a medium sky blue from your color palette. (I chose a blue that would be dark enough to contrast with the cliffs.) To rough in large areas of color, I used the Spatter Brush preset; with it, you can use a large brush size and paint quickly. When the large areas of the sky and water were blocked in, I switched from the Brush tool to the Mixer Brush tool and used two versatile brush presets. These brushes require more computer power to paint in real time on a large file, but they offer beautiful strokes and the look of oil paint.

Next, practice with the Mixer Brush tool and the two brushes that I used. Choose the Mixer Brush tool* in the Tools panel and the Flat Blunt Short Stiff brush preset, and make a few practice strokes to get the feel of the brush. Now choose the Round Point Stiff preset and practice painting strokes. When you are comfortable with

the brushes, choose the Flat Blunt Short Stiff preset, size it to about 60–80 pixels, and paint more color on to the sky. Use expressive strokes, and dots and dabs of color, varying the pressure on the stylus as you work. Scale the brush smaller to work in the tighter areas at the top of the cliffs and inside the arch. (I scaled my brush down to about 25 pixels.)

Follow up by choosing a more turquoise blue and adding more paint to the water. For the water, I used a varied palette of cool, blue-green hues from my palette about the same value and saturation as the sky.* I envisioned the water moving as I painted it. I left the broken areas of the waves alone for this stage, so that when I painted them with lighter color later, some of the underpainting would show through. Then using a light creamy brown, block in the lighter areas of the distant cliffs.

Painting dabs of color onto the sky, using the Flat Blunt Short Stiff preset and a Dry setting

Adding more paint to the landforms, sky, and water, and laying in the foreground using two Mixer Brush tool settings, Dry and Wet

9 **Painting with dry and wet paint.** The Mixer Brush tool and accompanying brushes allow you to paint with varying viscosities of paint. When the Mixer Brush tool is chosen, choices in the Options Bar allow you to choose Useful Mixer Brush Combinations from the pop-up menu, for instance, Dry, Moist, Wet, and Very Wet. The Dry setting allows the application of more opaque color, and the Moist and Wet settings offer variations of wetness and blending when new paint is applied.

Varying paint qualities using the Mixer Brush tool settings. The Useful Mixer Brush Combinations pop-up menu in the Options Bar allows you to choose from a variety of Dry, Moist, Wet and Very Wet settings, and also create custom combinations of your own. The illustration below illustrates some of the paint effects possible using two colors and four of the choices.

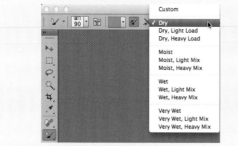

The Useful Mixer Brush Combinations pop-up menu

Strokes painted with the Round Blunt Medium Stiff preset, from left to right: Dry, Moist, Wet, and Very Wet.

Adding warmer browns to the sunlit areas on the cliffs and darker purples to the shadows with the Flat Blunt Short Stiff preset

Varying the color in the reflections on the water with the Round Blunt Medium Stiff preset, using a Moist setting

If you want your brush to load with paint with each stroke, enable the Load the Brush After Each Stroke button in the Options Bar. To load your Mixer Brush preset with fresh paint, click the paint swatch on the Options Bar to access the pop-up menu and choose Clean Brush; then choose Load Brush to fill your brush with paint.

Continue to block in your color areas, refining your composition as you work, using the Flat Blunt Short Stiff and the Round Blunt Medium Stiff presets. I added more

color and brushwork to the ocean to suggest reflections, and painted cream and varied colors—purple, brown, rose, and gray—into the shadows on the cliffs. For the sky, I used the Round Blunt Medium Stiff and a Dry setting to lay in patches of opaque color; then, using a Moist setting, and a lighter touch on the stylus, I softened the edges of some of the clouds. I used a similar brushing process for the water, landforms, and foreground.

Load your brush. Choose the Mixer Brush tool, click the paint swatch on the Options Bar to access its pop-up menu, then choose Load Brush to load the preset with fresh paint.

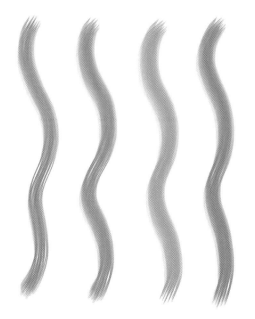

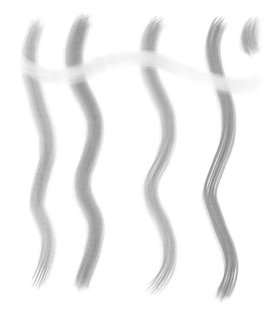

The vertical strokes are painted with the Round Blunt Medium Stiff preset with the Useful Mixer Brush Combinations menu set to Dry, and Flow set to 20%.

Strokes painted with the Round Blunt Medium Stiff, set to Dry, and Flow set to 20%. The horizontal stroke is painted with the Useful Mixer Brush Combinations menu set to Moist, and a Flow of 20%.

10 Adding glazes and details. Now you'll use tints and glazes (and a technique similar to conventional oils) to build dimension in your painting. Add a new layer and name it "glazes."* Choose the Mixer Brush tool and the Round Blunt Medium Stiff brush, and reduce its Flow to about 10–20% in the Options Bar. A low Flow setting will allow you to build up color slowly, with some transparency. To lay down drier color without mixing

The settings in the Options Bar for glazing with the Mixer Brush tool and Round Blunt Medium Stiff preset. I used both Dry and Moist settings and adjusted the Flow between 10–20%.

 Paint blending and layers. For the look of blended paint, I used several layers in Photoshop. With Painter, you need fewer layers because you can blend and make the media interact more easily.

as you paint, set the Useful Mixer Brush Combinations pop-up menu to Dry. For more mixing of existing color as you lay down new paint, set the Useful Mixer Brush Combinations menu to Moist. Sample color from your image, and then use the Color Picker to make it lighter or darker.* Using varied pressure on your stylus, paint expressive brushstrokes. Let your brushstrokes be fun and loosely descriptive. This is an expressive study, not a tight rendering.

I remembered the mass of the towering limestone cliffs. For more interest on the cliff face, I added lighter tones and highlights using the glazing technique. After mixing a lighter version of the ochre, using the Color

LEARN MORE ABOUT. . .

* adding a new layer. . . page 68
* using the Color Picker. . . page 76
* value and depth. . . pages 126, 135

Painting the striations and shadows on the cliffs using a small Round Blunt Medium Stiff preset, with a low Flow of about 10–20%. I used both Dry or Moist settings.

Using the Round Blunt Medium Stiff preset, with a Dry setting and low Flow, to paint short, dabbed strokes, for more varied color and activity in the clouds and sky.

Picker, I used the Round Blunt Medium Stiff preset with a Dry setting to brush and dab color onto the cliff face. Making areas of the cliffs lighter would help bring them forward in the composition, and would also enhance the focal point. Then, I used shorter, dabbed strokes of varied purple, brown, and rose to suggest the indentations in the cliff. To emphasize the horizontal striations on the cliff, I varied the pressure on my stylus while painting a graceful strokes of varied thickness.

What does your image need? Do you want to add darker shadows, or more foreground detail? To create more depth, consider adding darker tones behind your subject (as I did behind the "cliff towers").* Using the Round Blunt Medium Stiff preset in various sizes, I brushed thin glazes of darker color onto areas of the sky. Making the clouds darker behind the lighter cliffs helps to enhance the focal point. To finesse the reflections on

the water, I laid in color using the Round Blunt Medium Stiff preset and a Dry setting; then I set the brush preset to a Moist setting; then, using light pressure on my stylus, I painted lightly to soften edges along some of the strokes.

To finish the painting, I brightened a few highlights on the cliff. The brown lines in my drawing add interest to the painted study. For a subtle look, I reduced the opacity of the sketch layer to 30% in the Layers panel. The completed final image is shown on page 122.

Step back and take a good look at your painting. Congratulations! You've completed the technique.

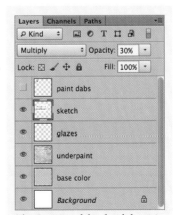

The Opacity of the sketch layer is set to 30%.

Using Painter to Work Over a Pencil Drawing

Chunky Oil Pastel, *using various sizes and opacities*

Variable Oil Pastel, *using various sizes and opacities*

The completed oil pastel study: The Porte d'Aval Cliffs and Beach at Etretat

ARTIST'S MATERIALS

Tablet: Medium-soft pressure

Program: Painter

Paper: Basic Paper: a versatile, medium-grain texture

Paint: Mix color using the Mixer

Brushes:

- Chunky Oil Pastel: opacity and grain vary with pressure; also blends with underlying color based on pressure

- Variable Oil Pastel: opacity and grain vary with pressure; strokes also change subtly, depending on the bearing (direction) of the stylus

This technique was inspired by my traditional experience with conventional pastel and oil pastel. Here I've combined a scanned pencil drawing with digital oil pastels in Painter. I colored the scan with a dark sepia brown that blended with the color theme. After painting with the oil pastels, I composited the sketch with the image because it would contribute value and detail.

 Automatic color mode conversion. Painter's native color mode is RGB. If you open a grayscale scan in Painter, the image will be converted automatically to RGB color.

1 **Drawing and scanning.** Draw a detailed sketch. (I drew the pencil sketch shown above on 9 × 12-inch vellum-finish Bristol board.) Now scan your drawing into Photoshop. My settings were 300 pixels per inch, at actual size.* Then crop your scan and adjust its tonal range.*

 Copying your sketch to a new layer. To put a copy of your sketch onto a layer for safekeeping, choose Select > All, hold down the Alt/Option key, and choose Select > Float. To rename your new layer, double-click the layer's name in the Layers panel, and enter a new name in the Layer Attributes dialog box.

The sketch colored with the Sepia Browns gradation

 Adjusting the tones. You can use the Equalize feature in Painter to adjust the tonal range of your scan. To add more contrast to your sketch and reduce gray tones, choose Effects > Tonal Control > Equalize. When the Equalize dialog box appears, move the black point marker and the white point marker under the histogram closer together to reduce the gray tones. Move them right or left to affect the line thickness and quality. You can preview the adjustment in your image before you click OK to accept.

2 Coloring and making a layer. For this study, tint the sketch with a color that will complement the color palette you plan to use in your painting (I chose a brown).

Next, put a copy of the sketch onto a layer, leaving the original on the Canvas.* Reduce the Opacity of the layer to 20% using the Opacity slider on the Layers panel; and then temporarily turn its visibility off in the Layers panel, so you can see the pastel strokes more clearly as you begin to paint over the drawing.

LEARN MORE ABOUT. . .

★ scanning. . . pages 124–125

★ cropping an image. . . page 124

 Coloring with sepia. Open your sketch in Painter. Open the Gradient Libraries panel by choosing Window > Media Library Panels > Gradients. To view the Gradients in List View, click the small triangle on the top right of the panel and from the pop-up menu choose Gradient Library View > List. Now choose the Sepia Browns gradient from the list. Next, open the same pop-up menu and choose Gradient Control Panel. Click the small triangle in the upper right of the Gradient Control panel to open its pop-up menu and choose Express in Image. Click OK. The Sepia gradient will automatically be mapped to your image.

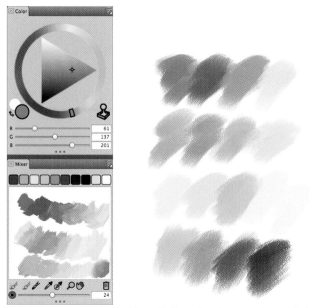

Using the Color panel and Mixer (left), and trying out colors with the Chunky Oil Pastel over Basic Paper texture (right)

Blocking in the first light tones

3 **Mixing paint and trying out colors.** You can use the Mixer panel* to try out colors on-the-fly as you paint. The Mixer features an oily brush to apply color and a palette knife to blend paint.

In this technique, you'll use the texture-sensitive Oil Pastels that can blend and smear color, so it's a good idea to experiment with how these Oil Pastels will react with the texture on an image as you try out the colors. Open a new file (mine was 700 × 1000 pixels) and try out the Chunky Oil Pastel and Variable Oil Pastel variants of Oil Pastels using your stylus. Experiment with color until you settle on a color theme that you like, and your "palette" is complete. For this painting with soft, warm light, I chose a color theme of primarily pastel colors; a few brighter, more saturated colors; and a few grays and browns.*

LEARN MORE ABOUT. . .

* using the Mixer. . . page 80

4 **Laying in paint over the sketch.** To begin painting, choose the Chunky Oil Pastel variant of Oil Pastels and block in color right over the top of the original sketch on the Canvas. (If I painted over an area completely and then needed to see it, I could always make the sketch layer visible, and turn up its opacity.) I recommend using light- and medium-toned colors with lower saturation for the underpainting. This will create a rich layering of color as you build up more Oil Pastel strokes over the underpainting.

A sense of atmosphere. In this project, you will use an atmospheric technique that employs hatched strokes to build the volume of the land mass and to suggest the planes of rock. The layered brushwork will also create shimmering light on the beach and water. For variations on this technique, see Chapter 8, "A Sense of Atmosphere."

Chunky Oil Pastel strokes (left) and Variable Oil Pastel strokes (right)

Beginning to model the forms of the cliffs

5 Understanding the brushes. The Oil Pastels offer great expressiveness when combined with a tablet. Vary the pressure on the stylus, and these brushes vary the opacity and also reveal more or less grain. The Chunky Oil Pastel slightly smears new color into existing paint, and it has an uneven broken edge, just like a traditional, crumbled soft oil pastel. The Variable Oil Pastel allows a natural-feeling stroke that changes as you rotate your hand while painting, and it allows you to smear new color into existing paint more easily. Experiment with the brushes by making squiggly lines, while varying pressure. Notice how wonderfully the colors blend as you overlay the colored strokes.

6 Sculpting the forms. Look at your sketch, and plan how you'll sculpt the forms. The Variable Oil Pastel 30 has a rectangular tip that makes it ideal for blocking in the crevices and cracks near the top of the towering cliffs. Using the Variable Oil Pastel, paint the larger crevices. Begin at the top and pull a stroke down, while slightly rotating your wrist as you paint. You'll notice a wonderful variation in the density of the stroke. When you've painted the deeper, darker top crevices, switch to a smaller brush—the Variable Oil Pastel. To suggest the horizontal stratification on the cliff face, use lighter pressure.

Looking at my sketch and remembering the crevices and indentations in the cliff face, I began modeling the cliff by pulling medium-toned purple strokes vertically down the top crevices. The cliff also had intricate horizontal stratification, which I chose to simplify, by painting subtle horizontal strokes in just a few areas.

Painting vertical brushstrokes while rotating the stylus and varying the pressure

Defining the arch and needle

Adding brighter color to the horizon, and darker shadows to the arch and needle

7 Adding brighter color and deeper tones. Next, use both brushes as you add more color. Switch back and forth between the Chunky Oil Pastel and the Variable Oil Pastel, as you continue to block in the planes on the cliffs. I added warmer colors to create an afternoon glow on the cliffs, and on the backlit arch in my painting.

 Smearing and scumbling with Oil Pastels. When you apply a new color, the Variable Oil Pastel can smear the new color into the existing paint, which is helpful when building up layers of varied color. The pressure you apply affects smearing. If you apply heavy pressure, more new color is applied. If you use medium pressure and pull at the edge's existing color, you smear more color. The Chunky Oil Pastel smears more subtly. Both of these Oil Pastels paint a grainier stroke when you apply a light pressure, which is useful for scumbling new color over the top of existing pastel.

Blocking in a large shaded area on the cliff using a purple-gray

Using feathered strokes to suggest the planes on the cliffs and the motion of the water

Painting overlapping feathered strokes of blues, greens, and purples in light and mid-tone values on the water

8 **Feathering and sculpting with hatched strokes.** Now that your painting is laid out, step back from the image to look at its overall composition. Do you need to add more detail or contrast in certain areas? Is there movement in the brushwork to help guide the viewer's eye around the composition?

To add movement and varied color while sculpting the forms of the cliffs, I overlaid cross-hatched strokes, using a conventional pastel technique known as feathering. I wanted to create motion in the water, rather than have it appear smooth. The water was moving up and down on the beach, so I lightly sketched in light aqua and blue horizontal strokes, varying the brush work using slight angles. I used the Variable Oil Pastel, and sized the brush smaller to lay feathered strokes over the top. By varying the pressure on my stylus, I was able to control the opacity of the brushstrokes. (This brushwork is shown in the illustration on the right.)

Painting the beach and water using feathered hatched strokes of varied colors, creating shimmering light and color on the beach and in the water

You can see the reflected light and the final linear details on the cliffs in this close-up view.

Using similar colors on the sunlit areas of the cliff and the beach helps to carry the effect of the soft afternoon light, as shown in this detail.

9 **Adding final details.** It's good to make a proof print before completing your painting, so you can see where you want to paint final accents and details. My proof print showed me where to add darker tones; for instance, in the small cave, the lower crevices, and at the base of the arch.

Before beginning to paint your final details, add a new layer, and position it above the Canvas and below the sketch layer. Then, using a small Variable Oil Pastel, paint the details that your image needs.

I darkened the cave, the crevice, and also added definition to the outer edge of the arch. Using more saturated purples and oranges and golds, I used the Variable Oil Pastel 20 to add lively accents of varied color to the beach and water. The water was moving up and back, rising and falling on the gently curved beach. To emphasize the motion of the surges, I added short overlapping angled strokes. These layered strokes added more complexity, giving the water a more natural, shimmering look with broken color. This brushwork is shown in the upper-right illustration.

The angled, hatched strokes overlap, and are drawn using many directions. This helps to suggest the layers of limestone rock on the cliff. Layers of overlapping strokes also help to build the reflection. It is sketched right over the top of the moving water.

The grainy, scumbled texture on the sky lends to the atmospheric effect. Hatched strokes help to sculpt the rounded hills, and angled strokes add energy and character to the planes on the shady cliff face.

The overlapping strokes of purples, grays, and golds add interest and color activity to the beach. Thick and thin horizontal and angled strokes add motion to the waves, and squiggly lines suggest the rolling surf line.

Next, I used varied pressure to paint thin strokes of light orange and gold (using the Variable Oil Pastel 10) on the cliff face in areas where it was hit by the sun, and in areas where light reflected on the cliffs from the water. I also added loose overlapping angled strokes to the gently curved beach. Then I used a small Variable Oil Pastel to add gentle, curved strokes to suggest the rolling surf line, where the waves spilled onto the sand.

To carry the reflected light to the foreground, I recommend using similar colors to those you used to paint the brighter accents on the cliffs. Finally, add more texture to the sky by "scumbling" with very light blue pastel. Here's how: Choose the Chunky Oil Pastel, and a color that is different from the underlying color. Apply light pressure to your stylus as you paint new color just on the peaks of the paper texture, over the top of the existing color.

You can see the entire final image on page 143. In the next four pages, you'll learn about painting washes over a drawing. Then you can take a break, or move on to the next chapter.

The final image. To achieve a look of oil pastels with a complex texture, I needed only a few layers. The sketch layer contributes subtle line work to the composition, and sits at the top of the layer stack in the Layers panel, with its opacity set to 20%.

Adding Washes to a Drawing Using Painter

I recommend that you use color tints with a value of 50 or lighter when working with Digital Watercolor. This sky blue has a value of 90.

The Porte d'Aval viewed from the west

Painter's Digital Watercolor is ideal for painting light tints over scanned drawings, such as this pen-and-ink sketch. I laid in light-colored washes over the ink drawing quickly and was able to blend paint easily and smoothly.

1 Setting up. Open a scanned drawing, and cut the drawing to a layer by choosing Select > All and then Select > Float. Set the layer Composite Method to Multiply in the Layers panel. Then click on the Canvas in the Layers panel.

For most of the coloring, it's a good idea to use light tints that will set off the ink drawing. Choose a light blue for the sky; then select the Digital Watercolor category in the Brush Selector. For the washes, choose the Soft Broad Brush variant.

 Watercolor media. Painter offers two basic kinds of watercolor media: Digital Watercolor and Watercolor. Digital Watercolor is faster and simpler to use. It can be painted on the image Canvas or on a default layer set to Gel mode. Real Watercolor and Watercolor require a special Watercolor media layer. The Watercolor media layer allows for more realistic watercolor effects like media pooling and runny pigment, which are amazing to watch and to paint with!

Digital Watercolor brushstrokes   *Watercolor brushstrokes*

Laying the first washes and brushstrokes on the Canvas

2 **Painting washes.** Using light-to-medium pressure on your stylus, paint soft strokes on the sky and water using the Soft Broad Brush. You can vary the opacity of the paint with the pressure you apply to the stylus.

Using the Soft Round Blender to smoothly blend the water

3 **Blending and smoothing.** Choose the Soft Round Blender and use a light pressure on the stylus to pull and smooth paint. I pulled my strokes using various directions to emphasize the lighting on the water.

The washes on the Canvas are complete.

4 **Adding more washes.** Using the Soft Broad Brush, continue to lay in washes over all your painting. If you want crisper-edged strokes, try the Simple Water variant. For a diffused effect, try the Soft Diffused Brush.

The darker washes painted on a new layer

5 **Painting glazes.** Add a new layer (in Gel mode) and use the Simple Water and Soft Broad Brush to apply a few darker glazes. (I applied glazes around the edges of the image, leaving the center lighter to enhance the focal point.)

Applying Washes to a Drawing Using Photoshop

The Porte d'Aval viewed from the west

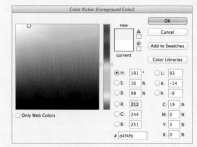

Choosing a light blue in the Color Picker

I n this exercise you'll use transparent washes on layers to create a water-color look over a drawing.

 Glazing on layers. To achieve this watercolor look, I painted glazes on several layers, each set to Multiply to allow the colors to blend. Photoshop does not allow the same interaction with media (smearing, blending, or diffusing) that Painter has, so glazing on layers is a great solution to achieve the look of blended paint. An additional plus, using lay-ers also helps with editing flexibility.

The Layers panel for the final image

1 Getting set up. Open a scanned drawing, convert it to RGB color mode, and cut the drawing to a layer by choosing Select > All and then pressing Shift-Ctrl/Cmd-J. Set the layer Blending Mode to Multiply in the Layers panel. Then make an empty new layer to hold the first washes, and set it to Multiply.

Just as you might with conventional watercolor, I recommend starting out with light color tints and then gradually building up to darker-toned washes as the painting develops. Choose a light blue for the sky, and then select the Watercolor Small Round Tip from the Brush presets. To paint the broader wash areas, I sized this brush up to 72 pixels, and saved the larger-size preset so it would be easy to choose later. I also saved a 40-pixel version of this preset. For the first washes, choose the 72-pixel preset.

 Flatter brushes. These default brushes allow you to paint thick and thin strokes depending on how you rotate the stylus, which makes them nice for calligraphic brushwork, such as the motion lines on the waves.

Watercolor Loaded Wet Flat Tip strokes

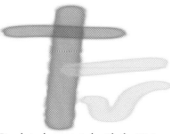

Brushstrokes painted with the Watercolor Small Round Tip, sized to 72 pixels. This default brush is named "round" but it is actually elliptical.

Using a large round preset to paint the first washes on a new layer

2 **Painting broad washes.** Using medium pressure on your stylus, paint light tints on the sky and water using the Watercolor Round 72 preset. I used light colors and reduced paint opacities, from 10–40%.

The underpainting layers are complete in this step.

3 **Completing the underpainting.** After adding a new layer (in Multiply mode), use the Watercolor Round in sizes from 20 to 72 pixels, and medium pressure on your stylus to lay in the underpainting for the cliffs and the hills.

Painting details on the cliffs and beach using a smaller brush

4 **Painting darker glazes.** After adding new layers (in Multiply mode) for the cliff glazes, the hills, and the beach, use a smaller Watercolor Round to paint darker glazes on the landforms.

Adding slightly darker washes to the water on a new layer

5 **Adding final glazes.** Now add a new layer for the final shadows. Use the Watercolor Round and Watercolor Loaded Wet Flat Tip brushes to apply a few darker glazes. (I added shadows to the beach and activity to the water.)

The Three Engines

10

Using a Photo Reference for Painting

In this project, you'll use a photo reference as a guide for sketching and painting. You'll set up a still life and photograph it, and then create a palette of colors and build custom brushes to use with a tablet and stylus. After that you'll use the photo as a guide for sketching and painting. To organize the illustration, you'll separate the elements of the image—the photo, sketch, loose color, and details—on individual layers, so that you can make changes to one without affecting the others. Following this project, there is a Painter sidebar that demonstrates using the Tracing Paper feature as a guide while sketching and painting.

 I painted The Three Engines *in Photoshop using custom brushes and my favorite Wacom tablet and pen. The pressure-sensitive tablet used in combination with the custom-built brushes and Photoshop's paint engine allowed a great deal of control and expression in creating a wide variety of brushstrokes.*

I developed this colorful, expressive approach especially for product illustrations of children's toys and clothing. The technique involves analyzing the objects and reducing them to simple shapes in a sketch, and then painting the shapes using areas of flat, loose color. For this illustration, I used my nephew Brady's train engines on a light-colored surface. I lit the trains using a full-spectrum light shining from above, and to the right of the trains. Carefully observing the light and how it subtly changed the colors on the shapes helped me develop the dimension of the forms.

My approach to the illustration was interpretive rather than photo-realistic, with lots of experimentation with color and brushwork. I used a palette of primary colors (red, yellow, and blue), with some pastels and secondary colors as accents. The primary and pastel color palette added to the playful feeling of the illustration.

CP

Using a Photo Reference While Painting

Sketcher, varied pressure

Gouache, varied pressure

The original digital photo

1 **Setting up and photographing a still life.** Start out by setting up a still life on a light-colored surface. A full-spectrum light casts interesting shadows on the surface, which is a technique often used for product shots. (If you don't already have one, you can buy a full-spectrum light from a home improvement store.) After you've set up the still life, photograph it with a digital camera.

Open your photo in Photoshop. If you like, you can crop it or change its dimensions.*

To set up a digital "lightbox" for sketching, first make sure the background color is set to white. (Press the "D" key.) Then move the photo to a new layer by pressing Ctrl/Cmd-A to select all, and then Shift-Ctrl/Cmd-J to cut the image to a new layer, leaving behind a white background. (If you do not see a white background, set the background color to white in Transparency and Gamut Preferences.) Reduce the new layer's Opacity to 40% in the Layers panel.

To help keep track of your layers as you build the file, it's a good idea to give each layer a meaningful name. Double-click on your new layer's name in the Layers panel and type "original photo."

Photoshop's Layers panel showing the "lightbox" setup

LEARN MORE ABOUT. . .

* the file size you need. . . pages 6–7
* cropping in Photoshop. . . page 124

Experimental dabs of paint color

Marks made with the pressure-sensitive brushes

2 **Choosing colors and making a "palette" file.** To begin experimenting with color, create a new document with a white background.* Choose the Brush tool from the Tools panel, and then click on the Foreground color swatch at the bottom of the Tools panel to open the Color Picker.* Choose colors from the Picker, or sample them from the "original photo" layer (with its Opacity restored to 100% in the Layers panel)* and make pigment dabs in your new file.

Try out colors until you settle on a color theme that you like, and your "palette" is complete. Then save the file. When you paint (in Steps 5 and 6), you can sample color from your palette file, or you can make a custom Swatches panel.*

Reducing the colors by posterizing. It can be difficult to accurately sample color in a photo. For instance, you might click with the stylus in what looks like a uniformly red area, but the sampled color may turn out to be darker or lighter than expected. To make it easier to sample, add a Posterize Adjustment layer to reduce the number of colors: Click the Create New Fill or Adjustment Layer button at the bottom of the Layers panel. Try out different settings (between 4 and 8 Levels) until you get a set of colors that you like. At any time, you can click in the "eye" column of the Posterize layer to turn its visibility off or on. Or double-click on the layer's thumbnail* and change the number of colors. Use the Dropper tool to sample colors from the photo layer.

3 **Making brushes.** Before you start painting, you'll need to build two brushes specially designed to take advantage of a pressure-sensitive tablet and stylus. You'll need one brush for loose sketching and one for applying flat, opaque color like that of gouache or oils.* Both brushes will increase in size as you apply more pressure, so you can easily make your brushstrokes thick, thin or tapered. "Making Brushes for Sketching and Painting" on pages 152–153 explains how to build these brushes.

LEARN MORE ABOUT. . .

* starting a Photoshop file. . . page 76
* using the Color Picker. . . page 76
* making a Swatches panel. . . page 60
* using the Layers panel. . . page 60
* traditional artists' materials. . . page 42

Making Brushes for Sketching and Painting

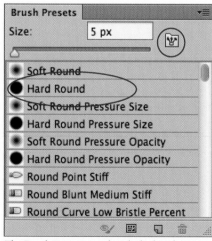

Strokes made with the sketcher brush

To start building brushes, first choose the Brush tool from the Tools panel. Then open the Brush Presets panel (Window > Brush Presets).

A brush for sketching. To make a brush that's good for loose sketches, you'll make it responsive to stylus pressure and you'll build in texture to make it look like your pencil is interacting with the surface of the paper.

The sketching brush is based on Photoshop's Hard Round brush, so click on the Hard Round preset in the Brush Presets panel.

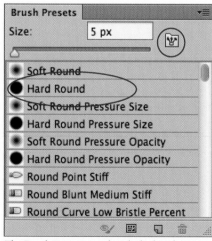

The Brush Presets panel with the brush presets displayed using Small List view. The Toggle Brush Panel button is near the top of the panel.

To open the Brush panel, click the Toggle Brush Panel button on the Brush Presets panel. To set the controls so that the brushstroke gets wider as you apply pressure to the stylus, click on the name "Shape Dynamics" (not the check box, but the name) in the Brush panel, and in the Size Jitter Control pop-up menu near the top of the panel, choose Pen Pressure.

The Brush panel's Shape Dynamics panel showing the control for size set to Pen Pressure

To build in some "paper texture," click on the name "Texture" in the Brush panel. Choose the Fine Grain texture, which performs much like a traditional drawing paper when it is scaled down.

Choosing the Fine Grain texture. The texture list is shown using Small List view.

Wrinkles is a fairly coarse texture, but you can get a finer-textured look by reducing it to 25% using the Scale slider. Leave other settings at their defaults.

Scaling the texture

There's one more thing you have to do to make sure your new brush is available in the Brush panel and the Brush Preset picker so that you can choose it whenever you want to draw with it: Click the little arrow to the right of the Brush panel name and choose New Brush Preset from the panel's menu.

Choosing New Brush Preset from the pop-up menu on the Brush panel

In the Brush Name dialog box, name your brush (you could call it "sketcher"), and click OK.

Strokes made with the gouache brush

Sketcher and gouache used together

A gouache brush with a custom, "captured" brush tip. This pressure-sensitive brush applies flat color with subtle bristle marks. Instead of starting with one of Photoshop's existing brushes, you'll start this brush by creating a round custom "bristly" tip in a new file. Open a new document (Ctrl/Cmd-N) with Height and Width set at 72 pixels and Resolution set at 72 pixels/inch.

Make a round selection with the Elliptical Marquee tool. (To constrain your selection to a circle, press the Shift key.) Make sure to leave several pixels of space between the edge of the selection and the edges of the file. Choose the Brush tool (press "B"), and then choose the Soft Round 100 pixels brush from the Options Bar's pop-out Brush Preset picker. In the Options Bar, change the Mode to Dissolve and the Opacity to about 75%.

Modifying the Soft Round 100 pixels brush to make a "bristly" dab. The Options Bar shows the Preset Picker and the Mode and Opacity settings.

Now click inside the round selection in the file you created.

Painting a custom tip inside the circular selection boundary

Next, using the Rectangular Marquee tool, make a selection around your brush tip image. Choose Edit > Define Brush Preset, and give your new brush a name (such as "gouache"). The size of the sampled dab determines the size of the new brush.

Selecting the custom tip

Brushes with sampled tips usually must have their Spacing adjusted to paint smooth strokes. You can do this in the Brush panel by clicking on the name "Brush Tip Shape" and reducing the Spacing to between 6–10%.

Additionally, open Shape Dynamics, and in the Size Jitter Control pop-up menu near the top of the panel, choose Pen Pressure.

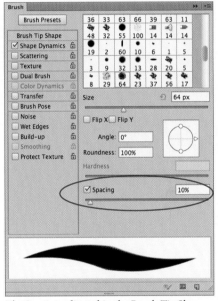

The Spacing adjusted in the Brush Tip Shape window

Add your new gouache brush to the Brush panel and Brush Preset picker, just as you did for the sketcher. You'll notice two gouache brushes in the Brush Preset list. Click on the first one with the looser spacing in the presets list, and choose Delete from the Brush Preset picker menu.

Sketching using the "lightbox"

The completed sketch, with visibility for the "original photo" layer turned off

4 Sketching. Next, you'll sketch the basic forms of your subject. You can then use your sketch as a guide for painting, instead of constantly looking at your photo.

With the Brush tool chosen in the Tools panel, click the brush "footprint" in the Options Bar to open the Brush Preset picker, and choose the sketcher brush that you made in Step 3. Use the Color Picker* to choose a dark gray color for sketching.

 Better observation. If you can, leave your still life set up as you paint. Observing your subject from life and toggling the visibility of the reference layer on and off while painting gives you a different perspective on your subject, helping you to become better acquainted with its forms and color nuances.

Make an empty, new layer for your sketch (Ctrl/Cmd-Shift-N), and rename it "sketch" by double-clicking its name in the Layers panel. If your new sketch layer isn't at the top of the Layers panel, drag its name up to that position.

The Layers panel with the "sketch" layer added

Now draw a loose sketch. Let your hand move in a relaxed and expressive manner as you draw with the stylus. Press lightly to draw a lighter, thinner line, and heavier to sketch a thicker, stronger line. The reduced

opacity of the "original photo" layer (set up in Step 1) makes it easy to see your contrasting dark gray sketch lines. You can toggle the "original photo" layer on and off by clicking in its "eye" in the Layers panel.

Visibility turned off for the "original photo" layer and "Posterize 1" layer

LEARN MORE ABOUT. . .

* the Color Picker. . . page 76
* programming your stylus. . . pages 48–52
* changing brush size. . . page 116

Beginning to lay in flat color areas

The first flat color areas roughed-in

The roughed-in color, including shadows

5 Roughing-in the color. Now add another empty layer, this time for painting, and drag this new layer under the "sketch" layer in the Layers panel. Name it "loose color" to help keep your Layers panel organized, as you did with the other layers in Steps 2 and 3. If you like, you can merge your Posterize Adjustment layer with your photo layer (as I did), by selecting it in the Layers panel menu and choosing Merge Down. Now you can

The Layers panel showing the "loose color" layer added and visibility of the "original photo" layer turned off

click the "eye" icon to hide your "original photo" layer.

To lay in areas of flat color, choose the Brush tool (press "B"). Then click on the brush footprint in the Options Bar, and select your gouache brush preset from the Brush Preset picker. To make the pigment look opaque like gouache, make sure the Opacity of the brush is still set to 100% in the Options Bar and Mode is set to Normal.

Load your brush with paint by holding down the Option/Alt key and clicking in your "palette" file (from Step 2) to sample color; then release the key and paint. Or use the rocker button on your stylus, programmed to act like the Option/Alt key.* As you paint, you can also sample existing color from your painting, instead of just your "palette" file.

Your brushstroke will change as you vary the stylus pressure. But to work with a larger or smaller brush, you can change the overall size range of the brush by opening the Brush Preset picker on the Options Bar and adjusting the Brush Size slider, or by using the bracket keys to increase or decrease its size.*

As you observe your subject or your reference photo, look carefully at the shadows. You will see subtle reflected light, rather than solid gray. In areas of the multicolored shadows where you want more complexity, you can make the pigment partially transparent by moving the Opacity slider in the Options Bar.

Adjusting size and opacity of the gouache brush

The in-progress loose color for Engine #1 with the sketch turned off

The color for Engine #1, showing the reworked shadows and background

6 **Completing the loose color.** At this point, you can turn off visibility for the "sketch" layer (unless you decide to keep the sketch lines as part of the illustration).

I continued to refine the painting. For instance, I added brighter color overall in the image. Then, using a steadier hand on my stylus, I cleaned up a few edges on the trains. I was careful not to overwork the clean-up process, because I did not want the painting to look mechanical, but to have a hand-painted look. I subtly reworked the shapes in the shadows to be more simple, pleasing curves that would complement the composition. Also, I toned down the shapes and colors in the background by using a low opacity version of the gouache brush to paint a wash of warm gray behind the trains,

which helped to enhance the focal point. Then I added a few linear details using a smaller version of the gouache brush.

 A consistent texture. For a realistic, consistent look overall, plan to use the same texture at the same scale for any textured brushes that you use to paint a particular piece. That way, all brushes will seem to "reveal" the same paper texture.

The "Fine Grain" texture, scaled to 50%

The completed painting for Engine #1 with textured details

A detail of the Engine #2 showing the textured brushwork

7 **Adding more details and texture.** Next, add another new layer to your file, and name it "details." Drag this layer above the "loose color" layer. By painting details on a separate layer, you can experiment with finer brush-work without changing the "loose color" layer below. Choose the Brush tool and the gouache brush preset. Reduce the brush size using the Brush Size slider in the Brush Preset picker, as described in Step 5. To add a subtle texture to the strokes of this smaller gouache brush, open the Brush panel (Window > Brush) and click on the word "Texture." Then click on the texture thumbnail and choose Wrinkles; finally, scale it to about 25%. Save this new brush preset as "gouache with texture."

Where does your painting need details? Where would adding texture complement your image? Using your

stylus, press harder where you want a thicker line and gradually decrease the pressure when you want to taper a line. I used this approach when painting the brighter highlights on the wheels. For most of the linear details, I used a small, smooth gouache brush (without the texture), saving the textured brushwork just for accents. In the final image, I used a medium-sized, smooth gouache brush to add richer darks in the shadows under the trains. I also painted brighter highlights along

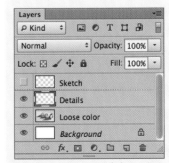

The final Layers panel showing the "details" layer selected

Close-ups of the completed painting for Engine #2 and Engine #3, including the linear details and textured brushwork. The texture can be seen on the blue trains, on the edges of the highlights, and more subtly on the front of the yellow train.

some of the edges where the light was the strongest. To paint shiny highlights on the metal screws on the wheels, I used almost pure white. Finally, I sampled color from the image and added textured edges to some of the flat color areas, such as the light green areas of color on the two engines. I also added a few textured details to the highlight areas on the red and yellow engine, as I finished the painting.

You've done it! Step 7 is the last step in this technique. I hope you've enjoyed the painting process. In the sidebar on the facing page, you'll see how easy it is to simulate the look of gouache in Painter. You'll be able to apply the painting processes you've learned in this chapter in the later projects in the book.

 The long journey of the "digital lightbox." Many artists who use the computer and a tablet and stylus also use digital or scanned photos, incorporated into their painting files as a reference while sketching. Although the digital technology is quite recent, this "tracing" technique goes back a long way. Master painters have used various forms of cameras and photography as references for their paintings, ever since those technologies became available. Vermeer, for instance, used the camera obscura. More recently, master painters developed the technique of projecting a photo onto a canvas, to help them map out a composition. And illustrators have long used light tables and luci-graphs to trace proportions from photo references. Using a photo on a layer in a digital file is just the latest step in a long journey.

Using Painter's "Digital Lightbox."

The Tracing Paper feature in Painter was designed to help you trace a reference image quickly. It's also useful when painting with Painter's cloning brushes.*

The reference photo

The cloned image with Tracing Paper enabled, and the in-progress drawing

The final illustration painted with the Gouache brushes. The sketch layer is hidden.

1 Setting up for tracing. For this exercise, begin by opening a reference photo. Make a clone by choosing File > Clone, and leave your original image open. (Painter's powerful cloning function includes an important feature, called Tracing Paper.) To sketch as I did, delete the contents of the clone Canvas by choosing Select, All and then pressing Backspace/Delete. Enable Tracing Paper by choosing Canvas, Tracing Paper or pressing Ctrl/Cmd-T. Next, make a new transparent layer for your sketch by clicking the New Layer button at the bottom of the Layers panel.*

2 Sketching and painting. Now choose a dark gray in the Color panel, and the 2B Pencil variant of Pencils in the Brush Selector. Using your stylus, draw a loose sketch.

I added a new layer and painted colored brushwork using the Gouache brushes. If you like, use the Dropper to sample colors from your photo. First, I laid in the large, flat areas of color on the body of the engine using the Flat Opaque Gouache brush. To paint the smaller areas, I used the Fine Round

LEARN MORE ABOUT. . .

★ cloning. . . pages 211, 215
★ making a new layer. . . page 68

Gouache brush, varying its size as I worked. Toggle Tracing Paper off and on as you work so that you can see the color in your painting more accurately. (The Tracing Paper toggle button is in the top right of the image window.) The Gouache brushes offer a variety of expressive strokes when used with a tablet and stylus.

A close-up detail of the blue train illustration

Quiet Moment

11
Defining the Focal Point

These projects demonstrate the thought process behind the composition design of two paintings that have strong focal points. You'll begin the projects using your own reference sketches. In the first project, you'll use Painter to create a piece that has a cool, luminous color palette and a composition with dynamic diagonals and contrast that enhance the focal point. A sidebar with suggestions for creating oil painting looks in Photoshop follows. The second project features a warmer color palette and mixed media. The center of interest is enhanced by the composition's color, contrast, and dramatic brushwork.

 My approach to these paintings is interpretive rather than photo-realistic. Using traditional composition techniques, I designed the compositions to lead the viewer's eye into the paintings.

While teaching in Germany, Steve and I visited the palace of King Ludwig and its gardens in Schwetzingen, and we especially enjoyed the peaceful feeling prior to sunset at the end of the day. I enjoyed sketching on location in my sketchbook, and the drawings have become the basis for a series of paintings of the gardens. Quiet Moment was painted in Painter, using Oils brushes, Palette Knives, and Blenders. Laying down paint and moving and blending it is important to the digital oil painting experience.

Path to Water, West 2 was inspired by a favorite location near home, and is featured on the cover of this book. Its composition features rich textures, dramatic brushwork, and lighting in the center of interest. With this piece, I began by sketching on location. Later, back at my studio, I enjoyed painting with my Wacom tablet and pen in Painter using Pastel, Oils, and a Palette Knife.

Strengthening the Focal Point

Oily Bristle, using various sizes and opacities

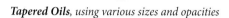

Tapered Oils, using various sizes and opacities

Wet Oily Palette Knife strokes used to blend, using various sizes and opacities

The quick color study created on location

For *Quiet Moment*, I designed a composition with the focal point off center, with reflections on the water lit by distant sunlight, leading the eye to the swan in the foreground. To invite the viewer's eye into the composition, I painted the brilliant blue area on the lower left, with the light area moving up through and past the swan, and deeper into the composition. To create tension and a more dramatic composition, I built the inverted "v" shape of the light from above shining on the water. Also, I used atmospheric perspective (less contrast, detail, and color saturation in the background trees) to give more attention to the swan and grass in the foreground that have more detail and contrast.

1 **Gathering references and designing the composition.** To begin, draw conventional sketches and scan them; or if you prefer, draw directly in Painter using a Pencils variant.

If you've scanned a drawing, cut the image to a layer so you can lower the opacity of the reference and use it as a guide while tracing and reworking the composition.

If you choose to sketch directly in Painter, open a new file and add a new transparent layer for your sketch. Drawing on the layer gives you more flexibility with how you incorporate your sketch into the image.

I made the pencil and watercolor studies shown above on location in my 8 × 10-inch travel sketchbook.

This sketch shows the reworked composition.

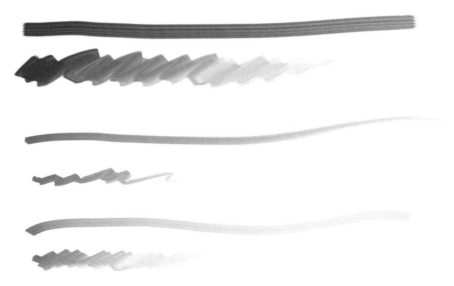

Exploring brushes. Brushstrokes painted with the Oily Bristle (top), Tapered Bristle (center), and Wet Oily Brush (bottom).

The color sketch notes the inspiration for the color theme and the composition, including the lighting, which help to define the focal point. The pencil sketch notes linear detail on the reflections and grass in the foreground. After scanning the color drawing and pencil sketch into Photoshop at 300 pixels per inch at actual size, I cropped the scan.

I combined some of the elements from both sketches. To rework the composition, I added a new layer and drew using the Real 2B Pencil variant of Pencils. As you see in the drawing above, I have added more tall grass in the right foreground area and have sketched a small swan in to the background.

2 **Building a color palette and trying out brushes.** You can sample color from your study if you like using the Dropper tool, choose colors from the Color panel, or you can do as I did and design a color palette with different colors for your

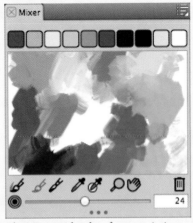

The Mixer with colors for my painting

painting. I used the Mixer panel to mix a palette of colors for my color theme.*

Next, open a new image in Painter. (My image measured 2000 × 2000 pixels.) Click the Brush Selector to open the Brush Library and choose the Oils category. Try out the brushes on the Canvas, rather than on a layer. The brushes I used incorporate Artists' Oils capabilities.* These brushes will feel more oily and will blend more easily when working on the Canvas. Begin by applying color to the Canvas using the Oily Bristle

LEARN MORE ABOUT. . .

* Mixer. . . page 80
* Artists' Oils. . . pages 164, 222

Blending and moving color with the Wet Oily Palette Knife and the Blender Palette Knife

Roughing in base colors on the sky and background trees

variant. Begin by pressing firmly on the stylus and then gradually use less pressure. Now paint strokes using the Tapered Oils and Wet Oily Brush. Notice the taper in the strokes and the amount of paint applied. Next, practice blending between colored areas using the Wet Oily Palette Knife and the Blender Palette Knife variant of Palette Knives as shown above. When you are familiar with the brushes, choose Ctrl/Cmd-Backspace/Delete to remove your paint experiments from the Canvas.

 The Artists' Oils brushes. With the default Painter Brushes libraries in Painter 12 and X3, the Artists' Oils have been distributed into the Acrylics, Blenders, Impasto, Oils, and Palette Knives categories. However, you can easily access the entire Artists' Oils category by loading the Painter 11 Brush library: click the Brush Selector to open the Brush Library Panel and then click the button on the top right to open the menu and choose Brush Library > Painter 11 Brushes. In the Painter 11 Brush Library, choose Artists' Oils.

3 Laying in the base colors for an underpainting. If you have scanned a sketch, or drawn a sketch in Painter, put the sketch on a layer. To put a copy of your sketch onto a layer, choose Select > All, hold down the Alt/Option key, and choose Select > Float. To rename your new layer, double-click the layer's name in the Layers panel, and enter a new name in the Layer Attributes dialog box. So the white areas of your sketch view as transparent, in the Layers panel, set the Composite Method to Gel.

When your composition is as you like it, choose the Oily Bristle variant of Oils in the Brush Selector. In the Layers panel, select the Canvas layer. Using your stylus, begin to brush large areas of color onto your painting. Turn the visibility of your sketch on and off as needed, using the eye icon in the Layers panel. Keep your subject, lighting, and the atmosphere in mind as you work.

Working from background to foreground, I began with the sky, trees, and water, and then painted the reflections and foreground plants. After laying in overall color with the Oily Bristle, I switched to the Tapered Oils to rough

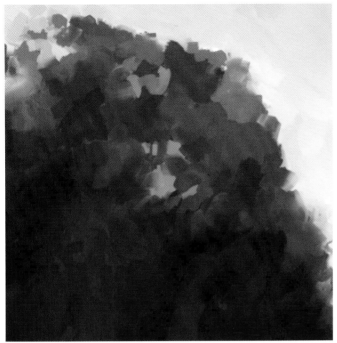

Painting highlights and varied color using the Tapered Oils

The overall base colors are blocked in. The sketch layer is hidden.

in highlights and small patches of varied color on the trees. When less pressure is applied to this brush, the stroke will taper. When the stylus is held straight up, the tip of the brush appears more flat; when it is held at an angle, the tip of the stroke will have a subtle point.

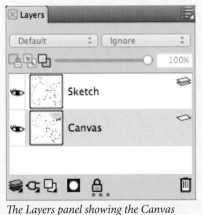

The Layers panel showing the Canvas selected

4 **Modulating color.** Now that your underpainting is complete, it's time to add character and interest to the paint and blend areas that you want to soften.

To add subtle interest, I sampled color from the image and changed it slightly, and then used an oils brush with reduced opacity to apply the strokes. Choose the Blenders category and the Blender Bristle variant in the Brush Selector. Reduce the size of the brush to about 10–15 pixels using the Size slider in the Property Bar, and reduce its opacity to about 10–30% using the Opacity slider. For more activity in the brushwork and color, practice varying the size of your brush as you work, using the Size slider in Property Bar. At this stage, I used a smaller brush and short dabs of paint to layer varied color over color on

Blending areas of the water, with the sketch layer hidden

Adding small brushstrokes of warmer color to the trees

Adding touches of color and blending the distant trees and water

the foliage. To modulate color in your painting, sample color from your image with the Dropper tool, and change the value slightly using the Color panel.* You might want to soften the transitions between colors in your image. One of Painter's strengths is being able to blend and pull paint easily and expressively. Experiment with blending areas of the sky. Pull from a darker area into a lighter area using your stylus.

In my underpainting, I had painted light-and medium-value blue-purples and warmer colors onto the sky. To soften the colors and to suggest afternoon sunlight shining through soft clouds, I used the Just Add Water variant of the Blenders. The opacity of the Just Add Water brush changes as you apply pressure to your stylus—if you apply more pressure, the opacity increases, and with less pressure the opacity is reduced.

To blend areas of the water, I used the Blender Bristle, at a low opacity from 10–30%. The Blender Bristle incorporates Artists' Oils capabilities, and applies blends while applying new color. The low opacity allows you to blend

existing color while building up a little more color slowly. Apply light pressure on the stylus, as you pull strokes to blend. I applied loose, long, subtly curved strokes.

With this brush, you can also apply subtle color in glazes, much like wet traditional oils. Using light to medium pressure on the stylus, I varied the colors as I painted loose horizontal strokes on the water and reflections, using both warm (red-purple), cool (blue-purple) colors, and shades of gold and green.

The foreground swan is painted.

Adding details, contrast, and brighter color to the foreground.

5 **Refining the foreground and painting the swan.**
While visiting the pond, I had also made drawings of the swans. The composition called out for a figure in the foreground. Painting the foreground swan on a layer would allow me to adjust its placement in the composition. I added a new layer and used a small Oily Bristle brush to rough in the swan. Then I switched to a small Tapered Bristle brush, to model the forms.

6 **Adding more brushwork to the foreground and trees.** Examine your image. Do you need to add details in the foreground or in the focal point areas? Will your image benefit from brighter color and more contrast in the focal point areas?

As I looked over my composition, the foreground called for more brighter color and loose shapes that would play against the dynamic foreground swan. Using

The swan sketches used for inspiration

You can see the highlights and shadows on the foliage, as well as the blended areas.

Using a small Wet Oily Palette Knife to blend and vary the edges of the trees

Painting the small swan with muted colors and values

warmer, lighter greens, I used the Oily Bristle and the Tapered Bristle brushes to paint longer leaves of grass in the lower right. To blend and pull color, I used the Wet Oily Palette Knife variant of Palette Knives. The Wet Oily Palette Knife is a wonderful tool for moving and pulling the Artists' Oils paint.

Next, I zoomed into the background trees and used a small Wet Oily Palette Knife (7–10 pixels) to blend and vary the edges of the trees. I wanted a loose look, not a photo-realistic look, so I used short, curved strokes, varying the pressure on my stylus (to vary the opacity) as I worked.

Choose the Palette Knives category, and the Wet Oily Palette Knife variant. Practice pulling color using short, curved strokes, and then longer strokes. Vary the pressure on the stylus; when heavier pressure is used, you will pull and move more paint.

Next, I painted darker tones on the shadow areas of the trees using the Oily Bristle, all the while keeping in mind the activity in the color.

7 **Painting finishing touches.** To accent the foreground swan, I envisioned a small swan in the background. I used a sketch drawn on location for inspiration. After adding a new layer to my image, I used a small Oily Bristle brush to paint the small swan. This swan is a supporting element in the composition, and in the shadow of the trees, so I painted it with muted color and values.

To finish, I added a few touches of brighter highlights to the foreground swan and to the tall grass. The finished painting can be viewed on page 168.

In this technique, you learned ideas for enhancing the focal point in your images. A Photoshop sidebar follows on the next page.

Oil Paint Looks with Photoshop

Using Photoshop CS6 and later (combined with the Mixer Brush tool and special presets), you can achieve oil paint looks similar to the process and brushwork in *Quiet Moment*. Choose the Mixer Brush tool in the Tools panel. (It is nested with the Brush tool.) In the upper left of the Options bar, click on the tiny arrow to open the Brush Presets picker and, when the menu pops open, choose the Round Point Stiff preset. Choose a color in the Color panel

and make a few strokes with the brush. Add more strokes of another color, and experiment with how the paint interacts. Try out more presets. Some of my favorites are the Round Blunt Medium Stiff, Round Fan Stiff Thin Bristles, Flat Point Medium Stiff, Flat Blunt Short Stiff, and Flat Angle Low Bristle Count. Here are some examples that can serve as inspiration for your own experimentation.

Strokes painted with the Mixer Brush tool and presets from left to right, (top) Round Point Stiff, Round Blunt Medium Stiff, Round Fan Stiff Thin Bristles, and (bottom) Flat Point Medium Stiff, Flat Blunt Short Stiff, Flat Angle Low Bristle Count.

Blocking in base colors using the Mixer Brush tool and the Round Point Stiff and Flat Blunt Short Stiff brush presets. The brush presets respond to stylus pressure. Use light pressure for lower opacity or thinner paint, and heavier pressure for more opacity or more opaque paint.

Layering colors using the Mixer Brush tool with the Round Blunt Medium Stiff and the Flat Blunt Short Stiff brush presets. To apply new color and blend subtly as with moist paint, from the Useful Mixer Brush Combinations pop-up menu in the Options Bar, choose Moist, and then apply new strokes.

Layering small, thin strokes of color, using light pressure on the stylus, to blend colors and values. For the feeling of wetter paint, while applying more color, set the Useful Mixer Brush Combinations pop-up menu to Wet. The Wet setting in the Options Bar is set to 50% to allow for more blending while applying new color.

Path to Water, West 2

Enhancing the Focal Point

Square Grainy Pastel strokes

Real Flat and Real Tapered Round strokes

Real Tapered Round and Palette Knife strokes, using various sizes

ARTIST'S MATERIALS

Tablet: Medium-soft pressure

Program: Painter

Paper: Artists Rough Paper

Paint: Mix color using the Mixer

Brushes:

• Square Grainy Pastel: opacity and grain change based on pressure and stroke changes with the rotation of the stylus

• Real Flat and Real Tapered Round: strokes change based on pressure and the bearing (direction) of the stylus

• Palette Knife: thickness of the paint and stroke width change based on pressure and the bearing (direction) of the stylus

The colorful plein air sketch drawn using Brushes on the iPad was inspiring.

For *Path to Water, West 2* (shown on the facing page), I designed a square composition with depth, atmosphere, and perspective. To focus attention on the pathway, water, and sky, I set the horizon about one-fifth of the way from the top of the painting. The meandering path leads the viewer's eye into the heart of the composition and into the light.

Path to Water, West 2 is a mixed media piece. I began by sketching freely with Pastel, and then painted over areas with the Oils and a Palette Knife.

Rather than follow every detail of the painting process, this project focuses on the composition process, simulating natural-media textures and creatively resolving the work.

This plein air pencil sketch also gave inspiration for the painting.

1 **Planning the composition.** To begin, make conventional sketches and scan them, or sketch on your iPad* using an application such as Brushes, as I did. (The color sketch shown above is profiled in Chapter 2 on page 14.) You can also draw directly in Painter using a Pastel. For *Path to Water, West 2*, I wanted a square composition, so I opened a file that measured 2250 × 2250 pixels.

If you've scanned or imported a drawing, cut the image to a layer* so that you can lower the opacity of your reference and use it as a guide while creating your underpainting and reworking the composition.

LEARN MORE ABOUT. . .

* sketching on the iPad. . . pages 11–41
* putting a sketch on a layer. . . page 164

Laying in colored paint with the Square Grainy Pastel

The general values and colors are roughed in with the Pastel.

2 Laying in the base colors. In Painter, I created a color palette for my painting using the Mixer.* For the color theme, I sampled color from my plein air sketches, mixed additional colors using the Color panel, and applied them to the Mixer Pad.

For the best response with texture-sensitive brushes, set up Brush Tracking.* Using the Square Grainy Pastel, you can make rich, textured strokes. To paint the first base colors, I sketched freely using the Square Grainy Pastel with Artists Rough Paper. Some of the rich, grainy texture is preserved in the final stages of my painting.

Choose the Square Grainy Pastel variant of Pastels in the Brush Selector. In the Paper Selector, choose Artists Rough Paper. Press lightly on your stylus to apply less pastel paint and reveal more texture.* Press heavily to apply more paint. When using the Square Grainy Pastel, the texture will still be visible when heavier pressure is applied.

3 Building values and richer color. Keeping the balance of your composition in mind, gradually layer more pastel strokes to build values and richer color, and to model the forms. Paint loosely and freely, without focusing on details at this stage. As you work, use the Size slider in the Property Bar to adjust the brush size. (I varied the size about 15–40 pixels.)

Additionally, in a few areas where I wanted more subtle grain, I varied the graininess of the Square Grainy Pastel from its default of 9% to about 11%, using the Grain slider in the Property Bar.

The Mixer with colors for the painting

Painting richer color and more contrast with the Pastels and Oils to strengthen the center of interest

In this detail, the Palette Knife strokes can be seen on the water. I used the Real Tapered Round to paint details on the shrubs and trees.

4 **Adding details and accents.** For *Path to Water, West 2*, I wanted energetic, expressive brushwork to come through in the final painting. More saturated color and dramatic contrast leads the viewer's eye to the focal point in the distance. After the general forms were established, I switched from the Pastels to painting with the Oils. Using the Real Flat and Real Tapered Round variants of Oils, I added more detailed brushwork to the plant life, path, and hills. Then, to blend and dramatically move paint in areas of the sky and water, I used the Palette Knife in small and large sizes (from about 10–65 pixels).

 Painting light over dark with a grainy pastel. The Square Grainy Pastel uses the Cover method in the General panel of the Brush Controls. The Cover method allows you to paint light accents of color over darker values. Additionally, the Grainy Hard Cover submethod helps give the Square Grainy Pastel its grainy character.

The Real Flat is an expressive brush that paints thick to thin stokes depending on how you hold the stylus. I used it to add varied blue brushstrokes on the ocean. The Real Tapered Round is useful for painting leaves on the foreground plants and for adding expressive details to the trees in the background.

Now choose the Palette Knife variant of Palette Knives. In an area where you want to blend and move paint, practice with the Palette Knife. Using the Palette Knife in a small size, you can achieve an interesting, expressive brushstroke for the horizon.

Good work! You have completed this project. In the next chapter, we will work with mixed media paint, paper, and canvas.

LEARN MORE ABOUT. . .

★ Brush Tracking. . . page 86
★ the Mixer. . . page 80
★ revealing texture. . . page 81

Punta San Antonio, Spring

12
SIMULATING PAPER AND CANVAS

In this chapter, you'll learn ideas and methods for using texture and mixed media in your images. First, you'll create a dramatic painting in Photoshop using custom brushes—including one that reveals paper texture—and learn more ideas for adding texture to your work. Next, you'll use Painter's realistic Impasto to "gesso" a canvas. Then you'll use Oil brushes to rough out an underpainting using a bright color palette, and layer pastel and thick paint over the top using your stylus, without losing the texture underneath. A sidebar also covers how to add more texture to your image using surface texture.

 Punta San Antonio, Spring was inspired by a seascape in Mexico. Using watercolor sketches painted on location for reference, I created a painting inspired by the raw wildness of this coastline. I chose a palette of primarily blues and purples, accented with earth tones and bright golds. The complementary colors would work together to create an inviting painting. Using custom brushes to apply both smooth and textured paint, I painted the dynamic ocean and coastal terrain.

Downstream Path, Summer was inspired by a favorite location in San Diego, California. I made several sketches on location in my conventional sketchbook. Later, back at my studio, I created a painting that had the feeling of the hot, sunny day, with wispy clouds that allude to a coming weather change. I chose a palette of colors that included warm, earthy colors on the cliffs and varied turquoise blues for the clear ocean. In this painting, I left no area of the canvas with a flat-color look. To add varied texture to the oil painting, I added touches of grainy pastel on the beach and sea foam. To finish, I added a few details with thick Impasto paint.

CP

Achieving Texture in a Photoshop Image

Sketcher, Normal mode, used in various sizes and opacities

Gouache, Mixer Brush tool, Dry with 100% Flow (left), and Moist, with 25% Flow (right)

Gouache, showing textured dry brush effect

ARTIST'S MATERIALS

Tablet: Medium-soft pressure

Program: Photoshop

Brushes:
- Sketcher: customized with pressure response and texture for loose, expressive line work

- Gouache: customized with a sampled dab and pressure response; used with Mixer Brush

- Gouache: modified for applying "wet", translucent color

- Gouache: modified for a textured, dry brush effect

The inspirational watercolor sketch

For *Punta San Antonio, Spring,* I designed a composition with dynamic moving waves in the foreground. To invite the viewer's eye into the composition, I painted the golden light in the upper left sky, and on the lower right, with the light moving up through to the center and deeper into the composition. Also, I used atmospheric perspective (less contrast, detail, and color saturation in the distant hills) to give more attention to the foreground that had more detail and contrast.

1 **Assembling references and designing the composition.** To begin, draw conventional sketches and scan them, or if you prefer, draw directly in Photoshop using the "Sketcher" brush you made in Chapter 9.*

If you've scanned a drawing, cut the image to a layer* so you can lower the opacity of the reference and use it as a guide while tracing and reworking the composition.

If you choose to sketch directly in Photoshop, open a new file and add a new transparent layer for your sketch. Drawing on the layer gives you more flexibility with how you incorporate your sketch into the image.

The second watercolor I used as a loose reference for the distant point

The digital sketch shows the reworked cliffs, hills, and foreground.

I painted the watercolor studies shown above on location in my 8 × 10-inch watercolor sketchbook. The sketch on the left notes the inspiration for the color theme and the composition, including the lighting, which helps with the atmosphere. After scanning the watercolor studies into Photoshop at 300 pixels per inch at actual size, I cropped the scans.* I used the second drawing for reference but did not bring it into my image as a layer.

I liked my references, but I wanted to change the cliffs and foreground, and combine some of the elements from both sketches. To design the composition, I added a new layer and drew a black-and-white sketch using

the "Sketcher" brush. As you see in the digital sketch above, I have drawn a grassy cliff in the foreground area, extended the point of land in the distance, and suggested more movement in the water. I used the second sketch as a reference while loosely sketching the forms of the cliffs, hills, and waves.

 For Painter users. If you don't have Photoshop, you can follow along with this project using the Fine Point variant of Pens to draw the digital sketch. For the color painting, try using the Gouache brushes, reducing their opacity when needed to achieve the semitransparent washes. For truly transparent washes, try the Digital Watercolor brushes. You can paint the transparent washes on a new layer, with its composite method set to Gel. (The performance of the brushes will not be identical.)

LEARN MORE ABOUT. . .

∗ scanning. . . pages 124, 125
∗ Sketcher brush. . . pages 152–154

These dabs of paint applied with the custom Gouache brush and Mixer Brush tool show the starting color theme for this project.

Testing paint with the Gouache brush using the Mixer Brush tool. Dry, with 100% Flow (left), and Moist, with 10% Flow (center and right).

2 **Building a color palette and testing brushes.** You can sample from the Color Picker as you go, but I recommend planning your basic color theme before jumping into your painting. Most of the colors in my painting were purples, ocean blues, golden oranges, and warm greens that you'd see on an early spring morning. Because the seascape was relatively simple, I chose to use rich colors in the sky. The purples in the sky would complement the oranges, because they were opposite one another on the color wheel. I used the Gouache brush and my stylus to paint dabs of color for a color palette.

3 **Testing brushes and beginning the loose study.** To tune in my brushes and paint, I did some tests with the Mixer Brush tool and the custom Gouache brush. In the paint test illustration above, the strokes on the left were painted with the Gouache brush and the Mixer Brush tool, with the Useful Mixer Brush Combinations pop-up menu set to Dry and Flow set to 100% in the Options Bar. This setting is good for laying down flat, opaque areas of color. To achieve blending and translucent color, I set the Useful Mixer Brush Combinations pop-up menu to Moist and reduced Flow to 10% in the Options Bar.

Now you'll paint a base color that will establish the color theme for the image. Make a new layer and name it Paint. Using the Gouache brush (with the Mixer tool set to Dry in the Options Bar), begin laying in your basic shapes. Focus on the larger shapes first, without focusing on details at this point. Later you will paint subtle details on the hills and water, using more color and varied values.

Laying in opaque flat color on the image, beginning with painting the basic shapes. The sketch is visible in this example.

Building a custom Gouache Dry Brush preset. This brush appears to be "dry" because of the texture saved within the brush and because each "tip" is textured. To build it, begin by choosing the Gouache brush that you built in Chapter 9. Turn on the Texture check box and open the Texture window of the Brush panel. From the Pattern menu, choose Fine Grain. Now set the Scale to 50, set the Mode menu to Subtract, and enable the Texture Each Tip check box. Next, enable the Shape Dynamics check box so that the stroke thickness changes based on pressure. Save your new brush by choosing New Brush Preset from the Brush panel's main menu. (I named my brush Gouache Dry Brush.)

The Texture window of the Brush panel

Saving a custom Mixer Brush tool preset. You can save handy presets that include your custom Mixer Brush tool settings, such as the Useful Mixer Brush Combination settings and Flow settings that you used in Step 3 on page 178. Choose the Mixer Brush tool and the custom Gouache brush. For a Dry brush, set the Useful Mixer Brush Combinations pop-up menu to Dry and set Flow to 100% in the Options Bar. Try out your brush. When you're satisfied, save it for use later. Click the tiny triangle to the right of the Mixer Brush tool in the Options Bar and choose New Tool Preset from the pop-up menu. When the New Tool Preset window appears, name your preset and click OK to accept.

The basic forms and colors are laid in using the Mixer Brush tool and custom Gouache brush, in various sizes.

To carry the warm sunrise light into the foreground, golds and oranges are painted onto the water.

4 **Layering paint and modeling the forms.** First flat areas of color are painted. Then, to achieve form and depth, more color is stroked on top. To lay in the flat areas of color, choose the Mixer Brush tool and the Gouache brush preset that you used in Step 3. For flat, opaque paint, set the Useful Mixer Brush Combinations pop-up menu to Dry. As you're laying in color areas, adjust the size of the brush as you work.

To paint the dynamic ocean waves, I used a varied pressure on the stylus to pull gently curved horizontal lines to suggest the moving waves. The gently curving lines suggest motion and also light and shadow. Practice painting a flowing horizontal line that varies in thickness from thin to thick. Begin with light pressure on the stylus and gradually apply more pressure as you pull the stroke. Now paint another curved stroke next to it, and then another. Continue this brush process as you lay in the basic shapes for the water.

Next, I layered more color on the hills and modeled the forms by blending transitions between the light and dark values. Before you begin modeling the hills, set the Useful Mixer Brush Combinations pop-up menu to

Painting darker blues and purples on the distant hills and blending the transitions between the values

The shapes of the background hills are refined in this example, and more paint is applied to the waves.

You can see the expressive brush stroke textures in the paint on the water and on the background hills in this detail.

Moist, and reduce Flow to 10–30% in the Options Bar. as you did in Step 3. Apply new color, and gently brush back and forth to blend between the dark and light tones. Aim for a loose, painterly look, with expressive energy in your brushwork.

When the hills were as I liked them, I painted brighter golds and oranges onto the sky, using the same process of laying down flat color, then coming back over it with translucent glazes and blending as I did on the hills.

At this point take a careful look at your painting. My painting needed warmer colors from the sky carried down into the foreground. For the refined brushwork, I added a new layer, naming it Paint 2. I sampled color from the sky using the Eyedropper tool and painted accents of gold and orange on to the water. Finally, I loosely painted the grass on the foreground cliff, and added a few accents of gray-green to the distant hills. For the dry brush texture on the foreground water and the hills, I used my custom Gouache Dry Brush.*

In the next step you'll add a subtle texture to your painting using texture applied to a layer, as I did with this painting. The following spread features more ideas for adding texture to your Photoshop paintings.

The moving waves were painted with various sizes of the Gouache brush

The added texture can be seen in these detail images.

5 **Adding a subtle paper texture.** When you're adding a textured effect to your image, always remember that it's best to do so to fool the eye; apply the effect subtly, because too strong of an effect will look fake.

For *Punta San Antonio, Spring*, I applied texture to a new layer, and then used a transparent blend mode to composite it into the image.

Begin by adding a new layer to your image. Target the layer, and then choose Edit > Fill. In the Fill dialog box, set the Use menu to Pattern, set the Mode menu to Normal, and set the Opacity to 100%. From the Custom Pattern menu, choose Fine Grain, and click OK. You will see the new layer fill with the texture.

Now set the Blend menu in the Layers panel to Overlay to composite the texture with your image. For more creative fun, consider experimenting with the other Blend modes—especially Soft Light and Color Burn—as they also work well with textured effects. For a subtle, natural look, I reduced the opacity of the texture layer to 30%. For the final image, I hid the sketch layer. The final painting can be seen on page 174.

On the next few pages, you'll find creative sidebars that feature more solutions for adding rich textures to your artwork.

Choosing Fine Grain from the Custom Pattern menu

The Layers panel showing the settings for the "texture" layer

Adding Texture with the Texturizer Filter

In addition to the method that I used for my *Punta San Antonio, Spring* study, there are more ways to add texture to your images in Photoshop; for instance, you can use the Texturizer filter on your image.

Before applying the Texturizer filter

After applying and compositing the texture

1 Setting up a layer. In this exercise, you'll use the Texturizer filter for a coarse weave look. Open the version of a painting that has not had texture applied. You can apply the Texturizer filter directly to your image, but you will have much more control over the effect if you set it up on a layer. Now add a new layer that is filled with 50% gray by choosing Edit > Fill. (The Texturizer filter will not work on a layer that has empty pixels.) In the Fill dialog box, set the Use menu to 50% Gray, set the Mode menu to Normal, and set the Opacity to 100%.

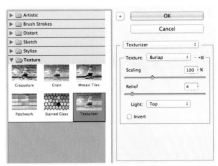

The settings in the Fill dialog box

2 Simulating a burlap texture. Now choose Filter > Texture > Texturizer. When the dialog box appears, choose Burlap from the Texture menu, and experiment with the Scaling and Relief sliders if you like. I wanted a coarse look, so I left scaling at 100%. For a realistic look, set the Relief slider to 4.

Setting up the Texturizer dialog box

3 Blending the texture with the image. When you have your texture as you like it, composite your texture layer with the image by choosing the Overlay mode from the Blend menu on the Layers panel. (You can experiment with other Blend modes; for instance, Soft Light produced a nice result with this layer.) For a more subtle texture look, I reduced the opacity of the layer to 40% in the Layers panel.

The Layers panel showing the Blend mode and opacity settings

Adding Texture with the Lighting Effects Filter

You can apply a canvas texture to your image using a lighting effect and a texture channel, as shown in this example, which uses another version of the *Punta San Antonio, Spring* painting.

A detail of the Punta San Antonio, Spring *study before applying the lighting effect*

1 **Creating a texture channel.** By putting texture into an alpha channel in the Channels panel, you make it accessible to the Lighting filter. Open an image that has no texture added to it yet, and add a new channel to the image. Select the channel in the Channels panel, and then choose Edit > Fill. In the Fill dialog box, set the Use menu to Pattern, set the Mode menu to Normal, and set the Opacity to 100%. From the Custom Pattern menu, choose Fine Grain, and click OK. You'll see the new channel fill with the texture. I used the default channel name of Alpha 1.

The new channel Alpha 1 is filled with the texture.

2 **Copying your image to a layer.** Now that your texture channel is set up, copy your image to a new layer by choosing Select > All, and from the Layer menu, choose New > Layer Via Copy. Keep the new layer selected.

The new layer is selected in the Layers panel.

A new version of the painting after the lighting effect was applied

The paint seems to melt into the texture in this close-up view.

3 Applying the lighting effect. Now choose Filter > Render > Lighting Effects. In the Lighting Effects dialog box, choose the Infinite light from the Light Type menu. Set Intensity to 25. Set the Gloss slider to –97, Material to –100, Exposure to 5, and Ambience to 8. Now set the Texture Channel menu to Alpha 1. Next, set the Height to about 5.

4 Finessing the look. A textured lighting effect can appear artificial on an image, so I recommend adjusting the layer opacity and Blend mode for a more pleasing, natural look. For a subtle effect of pigment melted into canvas, I chose the Soft Light Blend mode and settled on an Opacity of 70%.

Congratulations! In this project you learned how to apply texture with brushes and special effects.

The Layers panel with settings

The Lighting Effects dialog box with settings

The image with lighting effects applied

The lighting effects blended with the image

Downstream Path, Summer

Painting with Oil, Pastel, and Impasto Paint on Canvas

Flat Oils and Medium Bristle Oils strokes

Square Hard Pastel stroke

Thick Bristle, Palette Knife, and Distorto Impasto strokes, using various sizes

ARTIST'S MATERIALS

Tablet: Medium-soft pressure

Program: Painter

Paper: Coarse Cotton Canvas

Paint: Mix color using the Mixer

Brushes:

- Flat Oils and Medium Bristle Oils: strokes change based on pressure and the bearing (direction) of the stylus

- Square Hard Pastel: opacity and grain change based on pressure and stroke changes with the direction of the stylus

- Thick Bristle, Palette Knife, and Distorto Impasto: thickness of the paint and stroke width change based on pressure and the bearing (direction) of the stylus

This colorful conventional felt tip marker sketch inspired my colors and composition.

For *Downstream Path, Summer*, I designed a composition that emphasizes the solidity of the cliff forms and the perspective. To focus attention on the cliffs and water, I set the horizon about one-third of the way from the top of the canvas. I saw the cliffs as large topographic blocks moving back and the water's softer curves as the ideal complement to these more solid block forms of the cliffs.

Rather than follow every detail of the painting process, this technique will focus on the composition process, simulating natural-media textures and creatively mixing media to resolve the work.

1 **Designing the composition.** To begin, make conventional sketches and scan them, or if you prefer, draw directly in Painter using one of the Pencils variants.

If you've scanned a drawing, cut the image to a layer* so that you can lower the opacity of your reference and use it as a guide while creating your underpainting and reworking the composition.

LEARN MORE ABOUT. . .

* scanning a sketch. . . pages 124, 125
* putting a sketch on a layer. . . page 164

The tighter pencil sketch shows more detail in the forms.

This colored pencil sketch inspired the activity in the water and sky.

If you choose to sketch directly in Painter, open a new file and add a new transparent layer for your sketch. Drawing on the layer gives you more flexibility with how you incorporate your sketch into the image.

I began this landscape by drawing a tight sketch and a few color studies. This process helps me to get the scene and its forms ingrained in my mind. That way when I complete the painting in my studio, I can pull from my memory, because I took the time to truly observe and study my subject.

I drew the pencil, felt tip marker, and colored pencil studies shown here on location in my travel sketchbook. I scanned the tight pencil sketch, opened it in Painter, put it on a layer, and set the Composite Method to Multiply. I named my layer "sketch."

On the following page "Building a Colored Paper Textured Surface" shows you how to begin an image with a colored "ground." On the following spread "Building a Gessoed Canvas," describes how I set up a colored ground (with a canvas texture and gesso) for the painting.

Continued on page 192

Composing a landscape. Although the location I've used here is spectacular, you don't always have to look for such a perfect setting for a successful painting—it's possible to derive inspiration from any scene. Look for a good composition in a series of hills, trees, or in elements from any landscape. Frame the space by making a rectangular frame with your hands, and look for a good design. You can also get a sheet of paper and cut a rectangular or square hole in it, and use the hole to frame your viewing.

You can draw or paint any subject and make it interesting if the composition is good. A simple composition can be intriguing if it is composed dynamically with interesting angles and curves and a strong focal point. Areas of loose brushwork activity with energy in the brushstrokes and an interesting atmosphere do wonders for a simple scene.

Building a Colored Paper Texture Surface

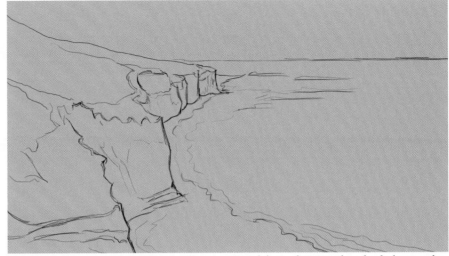

For this loose sketch of my favorite coastline view, I used the Real 2B Pencil, and a dark gray color.

Work over a colored, textured "ground" to give your drawings a more natural look. In Painter, you can apply a paper color to your image canvas, and add texture for the look of traditional paper.

1 **Giving a new image a paper color.** Begin by choosing File > New to open the New Image dialog box. Notice the Color swatch to the left of the Width and Height fields. Click the Color swatch to open the Colors dialog box and choose a color (I chose

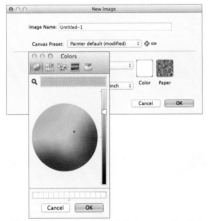

Clicking the Color swatch brings up the Colors Picker.

a light brown). Click OK to accept and close the window. The new color will appear in the New Image dialog box as shown below.

The updated New Image dialog box and the new file with light brown canvas.

2 **Adding texture.** Painter makes it easy to add texture to your image. When you launch Painter, Basic Paper is chosen in the Paper Selector. For this example I used Basic Paper. Choose Effects > Surface Control > Apply Surface Texture. In the dialog box, set the Using menu to Paper, Amount to 25–30% (for a subtle look), Shine to 0% (for a matte finish), and experiment with the Light Direction buttons. (I chose the upper-left.) Click OK to accept.

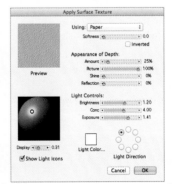

The Apply Surface Texture settings for the subtle paper texture.

Building a Gessoed Canvas

In Painter, you can set up a gessoed canvas on which you can enjoy painting with a variety of media, including pastel, oil paint, and thick Impasto paint.

Detail of the embossed canvas

Detail of the gessoed canvas

1 Making a colored ground. Open a new file with a cream colored background. (My file was 3300 × 1950 pixels, at 300 ppi. The size of the file affects the appearance of the texture.) If you find performance on your computer slow when using Impasto on a file this size, you can use a smaller file, such as 1500 × 1000 pixels.

To set the Paper Color, click the Paper Color preview in the New Image window and choose a color in the Colors dialog box. To choose a new hue or adjust its saturation, click or drag in the color wheel. To make the color darker or lighter, adjust the value slider on the right side of the window. When you have a color that you like, click OK to accept it.

2 Embossing the canvas. Now you'll brush a canvas texture onto the image surface for the look of evenly gessoed canvas. Choose a rough canvas texture from the Paper Selector. (I used Coarse Cotton Canvas.) For more flexibility, make a new layer for your embossed canvas and name it to keep your image organized. (I named mine Gessoed Canvas.) Choose the Impasto brush category in the Brush Selector, and then choose the Grain Emboss variant. If you are using a file size similar to mine, scale the brush up to about 140 pixels. Using a light, even pressure on your stylus, gradually brush the texture onto the image surface.

To give a more subtle canvas effect, I adjusted the Surface Lighting. Choose Canvas > Surface Lighting, and reduce the Amount to 80% and the Shine to 20%.*

3 Painting thicker gesso. To add more interest to your embossed canvas, add some thick paint. Choose a Thick Bristle variant of Impasto. For the look of thicker paint, increase the Depth to about 20% in the Impasto panel of Brush Controls. Choose Window > Brush Controls > Impasto.* Using varied pressure on your stylus (and the same cream color you used for your colored ground), add brushwork to your canvas. For a realistic gessoed look, I suggest not covering the entire canvas, but using well-placed brushstrokes to add interest.* Allowing the strokes to overlap occasionally provides a rich look. I suggest using a soft touch to avoid completely covering the embossed canvas texture.

Square Hard Pastel brushstrokes

Flat Oils brushstrokes

Thick Bristle and Palette Knife brushstrokes

4 **Trying out brushes.** You can achieve a variety of different media effects on your gessoed canvas. The first two brushes described here apply thin paint to the canvas, without adding thick (impasto) paint that covers the gesso texture. For more flexibility, make a new layer for your paint, and then choose the Pastel category and the Square Hard Pastel variant. (Keep the same Coarse Cotton Canvas loaded that you used to create your canvas.) Hold your pen at an angle, and make a few relaxed strokes using varied pressure. The Square Hard Pastel stroke changes based on the angle

LEARN MORE ABOUT. . .

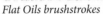

* Surface Lighting. . . page 197
* Impasto. . . page 197

and direction of your hand and the pressure that you apply. Applying less pressure also reveals more grain; applying more pressure covers the valleys in the paper grain.

Now choose the Oils category and the Flat Oils variant. This brush responds to the pressure you apply and to the angle and direction of the stylus as you paint. Make a few relaxed brushstrokes, and notice the thin wash of paint on the canvas.

The next brush that you'll try out applies thick, Impasto paint to your gessoed canvas. Choose the Thick Bristle variant of Impasto, and make a few expressive brushstrokes using varied pressure. Next, choose the Palette Knife variant of Impasto, and reduce its size to about 10 pixels. Using heavy pressure, make a few strokes into the

paint you applied with the Thick Bristle. You'll notice that the Palette Knife excavates, or digs into the thick paint. The knife is also useful for scribbling interesting marks into the gesso. I used the Palette Knife to scrape and move paint on the foreground cliff face of *Downstream Path, Summer* on page 186. When you've finished trying out the brushes, you can delete this layer by dragging it to the trash can on the Layers panel.

 A gessoed canvas. When working with conventional materials, I often apply a coating of paint to the canvas to add texture and to seal the ground so that it absorbs less paint during the painting process.

Painting on the gessoed canvas using the pencil drawing as a guide

Detail of the in-progress underpainting on top of the gessoed canvas

2 **Creating an underpainting.** For more flexibility, make a new layer to hold your underpainting, and name it. Next, you can mix your colors using the Mixer.* If your painting will depict the bright sunlit day like mine, mix light, warm, saturated colors. Then to work out the color and value relationships in your painting, begin by painting broad areas of color for an underpainting. (So that it would not be distracting while I painted, I lowered the opacity of the pencil drawing layer to about 30%.) To apply the first washes onto the Underpainting layer, use the Flat Oils or Medium Bristle Oils variants of Oils. You can experiment with the other Oils brushes, but at this point, I recommend staying away from using the brushes with "Thick" in their name because they apply Impasto paint. (You'll use Impasto brushes later in step 5.)

LEARN MORE ABOUT. . .

* using the Mixer. . . page 80
* Impasto. . . pages 180, 181

As a painting develops, I constantly rework areas and refine the composition. The pencil drawing was important to help me remember structure, but I did not let it restrict my brushstrokes when I needed to change the shape of one of the cliffs or paint looser edges.

 **For Photoshop users.** If you don't have Painter, you can paint your scene in Photoshop. See the instructional sidebar on page 91 on how to load the brushes. Use the custom Sketcher brush from page 152 for the sketch; then for the oil painting, try the technique described in the "Oil Paint Looks with Photoshop" sidebar in Chapter 11 on page 169. You can also use the Gouache brush along with the Mixer Brush tool described on page 178 of this chapter. For the grainy strokes, try the Dry Media Brushes, such as the Pastel Rough Texture and the Soft Pastel Large. (These brushes are useful and fun to paint with, but they do not produce identical results to the Painter brushes.)

The underpainting of the cliffs, sky, and beach is nearly complete in this image.

Color inspiration and interpretation. The golden afternoon light reflecting off the ocean cliffs on a clear sunny day was my inspiration for the color palette. I love the use of Impressionist color. Rather than toning down the color for my shadows using black to give the illusion of atmosphere and depth, as a colorist, I find ways to enhance the natural richness found in reflected light on my study's surfaces. During the development of the painting, I looked at my earlier color studies and visited the location again in afternoon sunlight to make more color notes for the lighting on the cliffs and beach. You can take a photo for reference, but often a photo does not record all of the impressions that you can see. While looking at the color in nature, I relax. Then, to simplify the forms and see larger areas of color, I squint and gaze at the area to see the subtle colors of the reflected light coming from the beach onto the cliffs. Try not to think about the details in the landscape when analyzing the color because this can cause you to miss important but subtle variation in the colors. The colors you use in a painting help to set the mood and evoke the emotion of the work.

The in-progress painting with the sketch layer hidden

Painting the planes and forms of the cliffs

3 **Building more complex color and form.** When you're satisfied with the underpainting, move on, to resolving your composition. When my underpainting was complete, I hid my sketch so that it would not distract me. (Click the sketch layer eye icon closed to hide the layer.)

For more flexibility, add a new layer to hold your new paint. (I named my layer "paint.") In the Layers panel, enable the Pick Up Underlying Color check box. Using the Flat Oils and the Medium Bristle variants of Oils (in various sizes), paint brushstrokes to sculpt and refine the forms progressing from the back of your composition (farther away) to the mid-ground and foreground. The Flat Oils brush is ideal for blocking in the planes of the cliffs and for laying in broad areas of color on the water and sky. The Medium Bristle is a round brush that changes size and opacity subtly depending on the pressure you apply. I customized this brush so that it would paint strokes of more varied thickness.* Then I used this

A more tapered brush. You can customize the Medium Bristle Oils to paint sensitive thin-to-thick strokes based on the pressure you apply, similar to the way a conventional round brush performs. Select the Medium Bristle Oils, and then open the Size panel of the Brush Controls (Window > Brush Controls > Size). Make sure that the Size Expression is set to Pressure, and then set the Min Size to 20%. In the Spacing panel (Window > Brush Controls > Spacing), reduce the Spacing to 9% and Min Spacing to .05%. To save your new variant, choose Save Variant from the Brushes menu, and give it a name.

I named my brush Tapered Medium Bristle. Now return the default Medium Bristle to its original settings by choosing Restore Variant from the Brushes menu.

Painting varied gold strokes on the cliffs with the Medium Bristle Oils

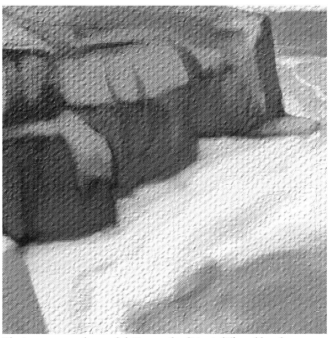

The in-progress color modulation on the distant cliffs and beach

brush to refine edges and to paint linear details (for instance, the wavy blue brushstrokes where the waves spill onto the beach).

To help the faraway landforms recede into the distance, I recommend using less contrast than you'll use in the foreground. Instead of painting the shadows using high contrast in this seascape, I chose to use moderate contrast and to modulate the shadows with varied color. For the details in the shadows, I used subtle changes in color, with warm and cool purples and blues. Where the sun was brightest on the cliffs, I painted vibrant golds and oranges and warm browns.

 The evolving painting. Continue to work over your painting; relax and respond to your design and color as the image develops. Experiencing a dialogue with the painting is a wonderful sensation for an artist. As you work, let your painting evolve. At some point, you'll begin to look at your references less and respond to the paint as you make decisions. If the balance of the painting calls for brighter hues in the water than you'd originally planned for, go ahead and experiment by painting with the brighter colors on a new layer. You'll be able to control the strength of the color by adjusting the opacity and the composite method. I continually compose and rework the composition throughout the painting process. Sometimes it's as if the painting takes on a life of its own.

LEARN MORE ABOUT. . .

★ saving custom brushes. . . pages 64, 71

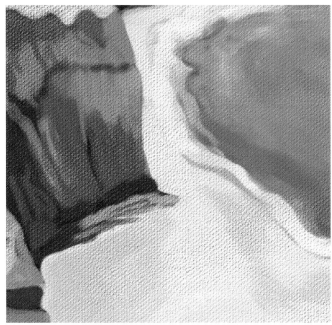

The first layer of grainy pastel brushed onto the beach

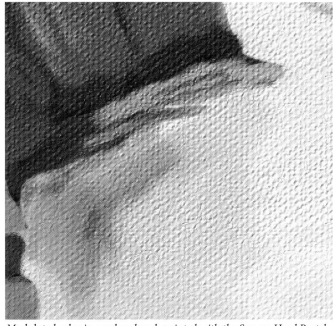

Modulated color in sand on beach painted with the Square Hard Pastel

4 **Painting grainy pastel for texture interest.** You learned several ideas for enhancing the focal point of a painting in Chapter 11. Using the right combination of mixed media can also help to strengthen the center of interest. Now that your painting is nearly complete, take the time to look at your composition. Are there areas that would benefit from more or less contrast? Where do you need to refine details? Are you satisfied with the feeling of atmosphere and mood in your painting?

To achieve a subtle layering of texture, you can paint with grain-sensitive brushes over the oil paint on canvas. The grainy brushes are ideal for simulating the look of sand or to achieve the look of sparkling light reflecting from the sea foam. This mixed media technique would be very messy if you combined oil paint and pastel traditionally. Painter and the computer give you the ultimate in flexibility. For the most realistic texture effect, choose the Coarse Cotton Canvas texture in the Paper Selector. Choose the Pastels brush category and a Square Hard

Pastel variant. As you paint with the Square Hard Pastel, you'll notice that the opacity and grain vary with pressure and that the strokes also change subtly, depending on the bearing (direction) of the stylus, as you work.

To create interesting layered texture on the beach, begin with broader strokes in a color just a little bit darker than the existing paint. Apply the pastel using a light touch to allow more texture to show. In areas of shadow, mix a few colors that are a little darker and brush lightly to apply them over the top. Be careful not to completely cover the texture underneath.

I continued to add touches of grainy pastel using the media to add color and texture interest on the breaking waves and on the beach in the foreground. I also added grainy strokes of light golden yellow to the clouds to carry the sunny warm color theme into the sky.

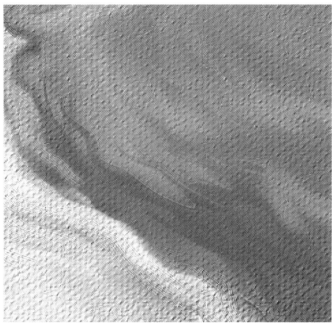

Using the Distorto Impasto brush to pull paint at the water's edge

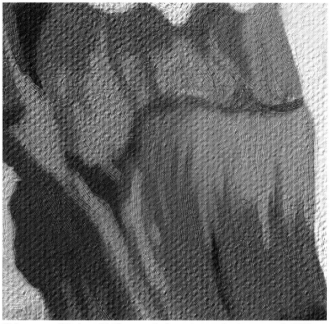

Using a small Palette Knife to work the paint on the foreground cliff face

5 Adding expressive details with thicker paint. Make a new layer to hold the thicker Impasto paint, and then choose the Impasto category and the Thick Bristle variant. As you rotate your hand and tilt the stylus toward you, the bristles of this brush spread out on the far side of the brushstroke. The width of the brushstroke and the opacity of the paint also changes based on the pressure you apply. As you work over an area, the paint builds up more thickly. To scrape back into an impastoed area, use the Palette Knife (Impasto), and use heavier pressure to carve into existing Impasto paint. I recommend reducing the size of the Palette Knife to 5–10 pixels and using the brush to move smaller areas of paint. To push and pull paint with a more pointed tool, try the Distorto Impasto. I used this brush to add a swirly look to the waves. When you're using your stylus and the Distorto Impasto to push and pull paint, the paint moves like wet oily paint. To finish, I added a few more touches of thick paint to the cliffs and water. You can see the entire completed painting on page 186.

 **Impasto appearance.** Two features control the height and depth of Impasto: the Depth setting of individual brushstrokes (located in the Impasto panel of Brush Controls) and the Canvas > Surface Lighting dialog box, which controls the global appearance of Impasto.

The Impasto panel of Brush Controls with Depth set to 20% for an individual brush

The Surface Lighting dialog box includes settings for the appearance of the Impasto for the entire document.

In this project, you've learned ideas for mixing media with your images. The next spread features ideas for adding more texture to your images.

Embossing Texture on an Image

For *Distribudor,* I painted, layering oil and chalk brushwork, using a similar process to *Downstream Path, Summer.* You can use the Grain Emboss variant of the Impasto brush to "paint" three-dimensional textures on your images. I used two images and applied a single texture emboss to each one. This technique looks best if you do not paint texture equally over the entire image. The idea is to fool the eye.

Embossing a paper texture. Here you'll use a brush to paint a three-dimensional paper texture effect. Open an image you've painted using the Chalk, Pastels, or Oils Pastels brushes. (My image was about 1500 pixels wide.) Begin by choosing the Grain Emboss variant of Impasto in the Brush Selector. For a subtle look, reduce the opacity of the brush to 30–50% in the Property Bar. To apply the paper texture effect like the image at the top right, choose Basic Paper in the Paper Selector. For more realism, keep the paper scale size (in the Papers panel) the same scale that you used when you painted the image. (I used 100%.) Apply gentle pressure as you emboss the texture. (I added it to a few of the foreground walls on the stucco buildings.)

Before using the Grain Emboss brush

After using Grain Emboss with paper texture

Before using the Grain Emboss brush

After using Grain Emboss with canvas texture

Embossing a canvas texture. This time, open an image that you have painted with the Oils or Acrylics brushes. (I used an earlier version of *Distribudor* painted with the Soft Oils brush. Choose a canvas texture in the Paper Selector. Using your low-opacity Grain Emboss brush and gentle pressure, have fun applying the canvas texture to your image. I added canvas texture to a few of the foreground areas on the right side of the image. You can view the completed painting in the gallery near the end of the book.

Distortion ...urface ...xture

You can use Painter's powerful Glass Distortion effect to bend an image, and use its versatile Apply Surface Texture effect to add realistic highlights and shadows to the image.

The completed *Distribudor* painting is featured in the gallery near the end of the book.

Before applying the two effects

After applying the distortion and surface texture

1 **Distorting the image.** Open an image that you've painted with an Acrylic, Gouache, or Oils brush. First, you'll "bend" the image based on its luminance by choosing Effects > Focus > Glass Distortion. Experiment with the values. You need higher settings for larger images. (My image measured about 1500 pixels wide.) I set the Using menu to Image Luminance, the Map

 Using paper texture. You can use the Glass Distortion and Apply Surface Texture filters to apply Paper textures in addition to the Image Luminance effect that I've demonstrated here. In the Using menu of both dialog boxes, choose Paper, leaving the other settings the same. Have fun experimenting!

menu to Refraction, and chose Good Quality. I set the Amount to .25 and left the other settings at their defaults.

The Glass Distortion dialog box

The image after applying Glass Distortion

2 **Applying texture.** Now choose Effects, Surface Control, Apply Surface Texture. In the dialog box, set the Using menu to Image Luminance, Amount to 15–20% (for a subtle look), Shine to 0% (for a matte finish), and experiment with the Light Direction. (I chose the lower-left button.)

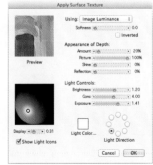

The Apply Surface Texture dialog box

Like magic, you have thick paint! Now you're ready to move on to working with photographs in Chapter 13, "Retouching, Tinting, and Painting."

Wanda, 1945

13

RETOUCHING, TINTING, AND PAINTING

This chapter has two parts. In the first section, you'll use the Clone Stamp tool in Photoshop and your stylus to eliminate scratches and other problems from a photo. Next, you'll add a few subtle tints to the image and create a vignette border. In addition, you'll learn how to make a custom History brush preset in Photoshop so that you can use your photo as a source for a painted study.

In the second section, you'll create a rich paper surface in Painter and use Painter's powerful cloning features to add painterly interest to the image using brushwork that complements the forms. In addition, you'll use luscious Oils brushes with Artists' Oils capabilities to paint a portrait based on a photo.

A vintage photo of my mother, Wanda, provided me with inspiration for Wanda, 1945. *I liked the warm, aged sepia look of the photograph, so I worked to preserve this color throughout the development of the image. I used Photoshop's efficient Clone Stamp, brushes, and selection tools, and my Wacom tablet and stylus to retouch the photo and add a vignette. For* Wanda 1945, Study *on page 210, I wanted a more textured look, so I built a light-colored paper surface in Painter and used that program's cloning features and brushes to paint over the clothes, hair, and background, taking care to preserve the important features in my subject's face. For the photo-painting* Afternoon Self Portrait *on page 218, I wanted to create the look of an oil painting. Oils brushes with Artists' Oils capabilities and small Palette Knives allowed me to apply colored paint, and blend the paint with imagery from the photograph.*

ouching and
g a Vignette

The scan of the vintage photo

Airbrush Soft Round, 65 pixels, Normal and Color modes

ARTIST'S MATERIALS

Tablet: Medium pressure

Program: Photoshop

Paint: Sampled information from the image and colors from the Color Picker

Brushes:
- Clone Stamp Pressure: ideal for subtle retouching; opacity is controlled by pressure on the stylus
- Airbrush Soft Round, various sizes: flow of paint is based on pressure on the stylus

Inspired by the warm, aged sepia look of the photograph of Wanda, I wanted to preserve the color throughout the development of the image. Using favorite Photoshop features, I retouched the photo, brightened the subject's eyes and teeth, and added a few subtle color tints to the image. To complete the look, I added a soft vignette.

1 Selecting a subject. Choose a black-and-white or color portrait photo without a cluttered background, and with good detail. Your digital photo or scan should be in RGB mode and should measure about 1800 × 2500 pixels.* Before you start the retouching process, save a new version of the image to work with and preserve the original just in case you want to start over.

Retouching in Painter. If you do not have Photoshop, you can follow the retouching process in Painter. The Lasso tool, Select, Feather command, and layers operate similar to the functions in Photoshop. You can perform point-to-point clone repairs in Painter using the Cloner tool in much the same way that you can in Photoshop with the Clone Stamp. In addition, Painter offers useful retouching tools in the Photo brush category, such as the Scratch Remover brush and the Saturation Add brush, in addition to the Dodge and Burn brushes. All of these brushes are already set up to work well with a pressure-sensitive tablet and stylus.

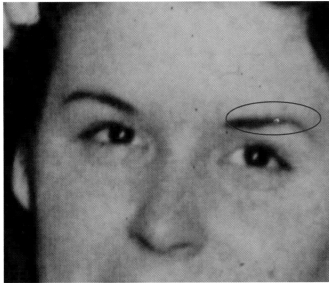

The scratch on the right eyebrow

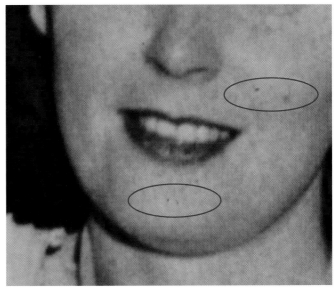

The dirt spots on the cheeks and chin

2 Analyzing the subject and setting up. To begin, use the Zoom tool to magnify your image, and analyze the areas that need repair. If you've chosen a vintage photo, your subject might have scratches and spots of dirt. To repair these areas, I recommend using a custom Clone Stamp that changes opacity based on the pressure you apply to the stylus. (You can also use the Healing Brush, but the Clone Stamp was a better choice for my subject with freckles.) The directions for building this custom Clone Stamp are described in the "Retouching using pressure" sidebar on this page. After you've built the brush, I recommend using it with the Normal Painting mode.

Before beginning, it's a good idea to copy your photo to a new layer so that you can control the opacity of the retouching edits if needed. Simply drag the Background layer over the Create a New Layer button on the Layers panel, and a new layer will appear in the layers list.

LEARN MORE ABOUT. . .

★ scanning. . . pages 124–125

Retouching using pressure. Using this special Clone Stamp, you can repair images with more finesse and control because the opacity of the tool is based on the pressure you apply to your stylus. Begin by choosing the Clone Stamp tool. From the Brush Presets panel, choose the Soft Round preset and scale it to 45 pixels. In the Options bar, enable the Airbrush Style Build Up Effects button. In the Brush panel enable the Transfer check box in the left side of the Brush panel, and in the Transfer window, set the Control menu under Opacity Jitter to Pen Pressure. Then save your new Clone Stamp tool preset by choosing New Tool Preset from the Tool Preset Picker menu in the Options Bar.

Setting Opacity to Pen Pressure in the Transfer window

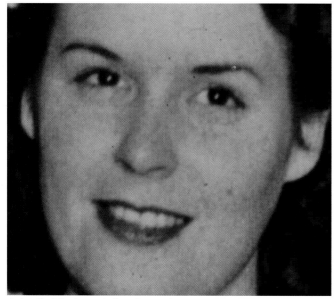

A detail of the image before the repair

3 **Sampling and repairing.** To repair a dirt spot or a scratch, you'll want to use the Clone Stamp to sample a similar but clean area near the area you want to repair, and then apply the sample information to cover the spot. Carefully choose an area that is the same tonal value and color of the area surrounding the problem area so that the repair will be "seamless." Press Alt/Option. (You'll see a cross-hair cursor appear.) Now, click to sample from the clean area, and release. Then click on the area you want to repair. (You might need to adjust the size of your brush tip as you work.) Be careful not to scrub the area as

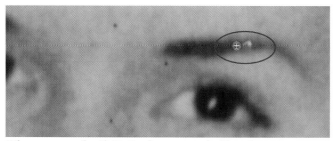

When you press the Alt/Option key, you see the Clone Stamp cursor. Here, I am sampling information from the eyebrow.

You can see the retouched eyebrow, cheeks, and chin.

you apply the new information, but click with the stylus. If you drag or scrub with the Clone Stamp, you will build up an undesirable repeated pattern.

To repair my subject's eyebrow, I scaled the brush tip smaller. To ensure that I would build up paint gradually, I set the Opacity slider in the Options Bar to about 30%. Then I used gentle pressure and a steady hand to apply the sampled pixels to repair the scratch on the eyebrow. I repeated the process to repair the dust spots on the face, while being careful not to completely paint over the freckles on the woman's face.

More useful retouching tools. In addition to the tools used in this project, Photoshop offers more retouching tools that work well with a pressure-sensitive tablet, such as the Dodge, Burn, and Sponge tools, and the Healing Brush. You can create your own pressure-sensitive presets for each of these tools, in much the same way that you created the pressure-sensitive Clone Stamp on page 203.

The soft-edged selection for the eyes

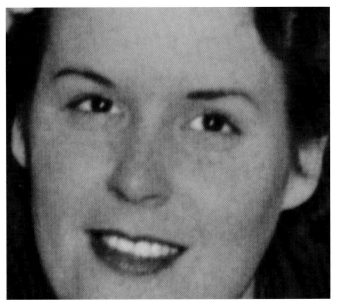

The eyes and teeth are brighter in this example.

4 **Brightening the eyes and teeth.** Now that you've repaired the scratches and dirt, you might want to focus more attention on the eyes and teeth by lightening them. First, analyze your image. If the photo is sepia or gray, do the whites of the eyes and the teeth look muddy or have too much tone? I recommend brightening them subtly so that your correction will not stand out too much. I used the Levels dialog box to adjust the light areas of the eyes and teeth.

Begin by making a freehand selection of the whites of the eyes using the Lasso tool and your stylus. Draw a selection for the left eye, press the Shift key to add to your selection, and draw the selection for the right eye. Now give your selection a soft edge by choosing Select > Feather and typing a value in the field. (For my 1800-pixel-wide image, I used a 5-pixel feather.) Just in case you might need it later, save your selection as an alpha channel in the Channels panel by choosing Select > Save Selection. (I named my alpha channel "eyes.") To make the tonal adjustment, choose Image > Adjust > Levels, and in the dialog box, drag the Input Levels Highlights slider a little

bit to the left. This will take some of the tone out of the lighter areas of the eyes, while preserving the highlights and shadows on the forms. If the effect is too strong, you can always choose Edit, Undo and try again.

When you're happy with the eyes, use your stylus and the Lasso tool to draw a freehand selection for the teeth, and follow the same process you used for the eyes to save the selection and to brighten the teeth. (I named this alpha channel "teeth.") I made these adjustments separately because the eyes and teeth in my image needed different highlight adjustments.

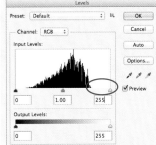

The Levels dialog box before the adjustment

Moving the Highlights slider to the left to lighten the teeth and eyes

You can see the active freehand selection in this image.

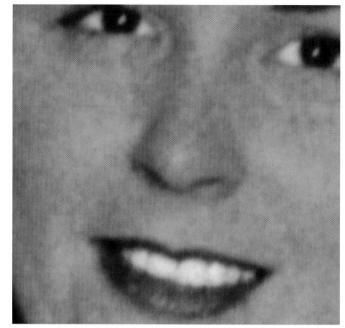

Painting the color tint on the lips, with the selection marquee hidden

5 Coloring the lips and details on the clothes. If your subject is a woman, you might want to add a color tint to her lips. Begin by making a copy of the retouching layer for editing flexibility. (I named my new layer "color tints.") Then make a selection to constrain the paint. Using the Lasso tool and your stylus, draw a selection border around the outside edge of the lips. You can use the selection you saved for the teeth to protect them during the tinting process as follows. With the new selection for the lips active, choose Select > Load Selection, and when the dialog box appears, choose the "teeth" channel from the Channel menu, click the Subtract from

Setting up the Load Selection dialog box so that I could protect the teeth while painting the lips

Selection button, and click OK. Your selection should look similar to the above left image.

When the selection is as you want it, hide the selection marquee so that you can focus on the painting. (Press Ctrl/Cmd-H to hide your selection marquee.) Now choose the Brush tool and the Soft Round preset. In the Options bar, enable the Airbrush Style Build Up Effects button. Choose a color that will complement your image—make sure that it is not too bright or saturated—so that you will achieve a subtle result. In the Options bar, set the Painting Mode menu to Color, and choose a reduced opacity for the brush. (I used 30% opacity.) Then use your stylus to gradually build up color on the lips.

For your image, you might choose to add colored tints to all of the clothes, or to color just a few details, as I did. I added subtle yellow tints to the flower and to the blouse, following the same selecting and tinting process used for the lips. After your tinting is complete, save a new version of your image before moving on to the next step.

A detail of the image with the tints

The oval selection on the image

The vintage portrait with the soft vignette

6 Adding a vignette to the image. A soft vignette adds elegant style to your portrait. Begin by making a copy of your "color tints" layer, and name your new layer "vignette." Next, make an oval selection around the subject using the Elliptical Marquee tool. For a soft edge, choose Select > Feather. (I used a value of 30 pixels for my 1800-pixel-wide image.) Save your vignette selection in the Channels panel in case you need to use it later. With the feather in place, choose Select > Inverse to select the area outside the original oval boundary, and then clear this area by pressing Backspace/Delete. Next, make a new layer and fill it with white to help show off the vignette, and drag this layer directly below the vignette layer. Good work! You have retouched and tinted your image, and you've created a beautiful vignette on your photo.

Now save the image in Photoshop format, which preserves the layers and alpha channels, in case you want to make changes to one of the layers later. Now that the retouching, tinting, and vignette steps are complete, you are ready to move on to the next phase of the project.

The Layers panel shows the retouch, color tints, vignette, and white fill layers.

Painting with History in Photoshop

Y ou can use your stylus with the History brush tool in Photoshop to create paintings from your photos. Although the process is not as intuitive as painting from a photo in Painter, you can achieve some pleasing results.

The vintage portrait with the soft vignette

The Background copy layer at 30% opacity

1 Setting up layers. To begin, open the portrait you retouched earlier in this chapter in Photoshop and make a copy by choosing Image > Duplicate. Merge the layers with the Background by choosing Flatten Image from the Layers menu. Save the new file in TIFF format. (You can begin with a layered file for this technique, but to make the process easier to follow, it's best to start with a flat file.)

Now you'll make the layers for the technique to give you editing flexibility. Make a copy of the background layer by dragging it over the Create a New Layer button on the Layers panel. Set the opacity of the Background copy layer to about 30%. Then add an empty new layer directly below it and fill

this new layer with white. This layer "hides" the original on the Background. Finally, add an empty new layer, and give it a unique name. (I named mine "chalk.")

The Layers panel is set up for using the Background copy layer as a low-opacity reference while painting.

2 Painting with history. Select the Background layer, and open the History panel (Window > History). Choose New Snapshot from the History panel menu. In the New Snapshot dialog box, choose Current Layer from the pop-up menu.

Next, choose the "chalk" layer. Then choose the History Brush tool, and in the Brush Presets panel, choose the Chalk preset with the 36-pixel tip from the default brush preset list. Save your new tool preset for later use by choosing New Tool Preset from the Tool Preset Picker on the Options Bar. (I named my new preset "History Brush Chalk.")

Using the Background copy layer as a guide while painting with the History Brush Chalk

The final study with the Background copy layer hidden

You can see the chalky texture in this detail.

Next, in the History panel, set the source for the History Brush to Snapshot 1, which allows you to paint using information from this snapshot.

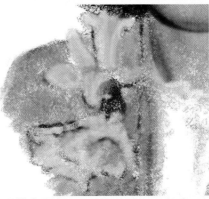

The source is set to Snapshot 1 in the History panel.

Using your stylus and the History Brush Chalk preset, begin to lay in brushstrokes. Concentrate on making strokes that follow the direction of the forms, rather than scrubbing with your stylus or making the brushstrokes in just one direction. Imagine that you are sculpting the forms, as you did when you worked through the modeling exercises in Chapter 6, "The Illusion of Volume," even though you are working from a photo. The opacity of the "History Brush Chalk" is controlled by the pressure that you apply to your stylus. You'll also notice the appearance of more grain if you apply less pressure. I painted the face at nearly full opacity to showcase the portrait. For a casual vignette look, you might want to make looser strokes and apply less pressure to vary the opacity of the strokes on the edges of the hair and clothing, as I did. In areas where I wanted brighter color than the source image provided, I switched to the Brush tool. Using the default Chalk preset, I painted deeper yellow strokes on the flower, varying the size of the brush as I worked. To brighten the eyes and teeth, I used the Brush tool and a tiny Chalk brush to carefully paint lighter color on the teeth and the eyes.

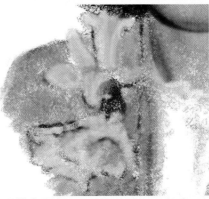

I added more warm yellow colors to the flower corsage.

Wanda, 1945, Study

Working Over a Portrait with Chalk

Soft Cloner

Square Chalk, *varied sizes and opacities*

Square Chalk Cloner, *varied sizes and opacities*

Square Chalk, *smudged with* **Grainy Water**

The portrait retouched in Photoshop

1 Setting up. Painter offers realistic natural-media brushes and textures, which you can use with your photo images, and when painting "from scratch." To begin, open the portrait you retouched in Photoshop earlier in this chapter—in Painter—and flatten it by dropping the layers. Save the flat file in TIFF format. (You can open a layered Photoshop file in Painter, but to make the technique easier, I recommend starting with a flat file.)

To add brushwork to the image, you'll use cloning in Painter. Make a clone of the TIFF file by choosing File > Clone, save the clone image in RIFF format, and name it to help you keep your files organized. In this technique, you'll clear the clone canvas, create a paper surface, and then paint the photo back into the clone image. This process is useful when you want to achieve an irregular edge on a portrait. Now delete the contents of the clone canvas by choosing Select > All and Backspace/Delete. On the next spread, you'll see a sidebar that describes how to build a rich paper surface in Painter.

 Powerful, intuitive cloning. Painter offers easy-to-use cloning features that allow you to sample source imagery and apply it from the source image to a destination image or from one point to another on a single image. You can use most brushes in Painter as cloning brushes by enabling the Clone Color button on the Color panel.

Building a Rich Paper Surface

Working with rich textures is one of Painter's most exciting features. You can create a colored paper surface to sketch and paint on or to clone imagery into. For the most realistic look, it's important to keep the texture at the same scale when applying the effects and brushwork.

The image with Color Overlay texture applied

Choosing a texture. Rather than clone the image into an empty white Canvas, you can set up a paper surface and then paint in more interest and background color using brushstrokes. Simply choose a texture from the Paper Selector. (I used Basic Paper texture because its versatile medium grain works well with Painter's chalk and pastel brushes.) For this effect, you might want to increase the size of the paper texture, based on the size of your image. For my 1800-pixel-wide image, I scaled Basic Paper to 150% in

the Papers panel. If the Papers panel is not open, choose, Window > Paper Panels > Papers.

Scaling the paper in the Papers panel

Applying a colored texture. Next, add a subtle colored texture to the background. Choose Effects > Surface Control > Color Overlay. In the Color Overlay dialog box, choose Paper from the Using menu. (I settled on an amount of 40% and clicked the Dye Concentration button.) Dye Concentration produces a more transparent result, whereas Hiding Power is semi-opaque. I recommend experimenting with both options.

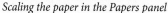

Applying Color Overlay using Paper

LEARN MORE ABOUT. . .

* making a new layer. . . page 68

The image with Apply Surface texture added

Applying chalk strokes over the rich paper surface

Adding highlights and shadows. Now that you have the colored texture in place, it's time to give your paper surface realistic highlights and shadows. Choose Effects > Surface Control > Apply Surface Texture, and in the dialog box, set the Using menu to Paper. I recommend using a subtle Amount

Adding subtle surface texture

setting between 10–30% for a more realistic look. (I used an Amount of 12%.) For this technique, you'll want a matte surface, so reduce the Shine setting. I set Shine at 0%, and left other settings at their defaults. It's fun to experiment with the Light Direction buttons to see which one best complements your image.

Surface effects on a layer. The texture you applied with the Color Overlay and Apply Surface Texture effects can be covered over by paint or edited with an eraser. Because of this, I often paint or clone imagery onto a layer above the surface. You can also blend the texture layer with transparent composite methods (blending modes) such as Multiply or Gel.

Adding brushstrokes. If you'd like to add more interest to your image background, consider applying background brushwork before you begin to clone or paint. I recommend adding a new layer to your image for these background brushstrokes.*

Textures work well on layers as well as on the image Canvas in version Painter 8 and later. I wanted to add a more casual, textured look to my image, so I used the Dropper tool to sample a light brown color from the vignette image. Then I chose a large Square Chalk variant of Chalk & Crayons and painted loose strokes over much of the background. To maintain realistic texture, keep the scaling of the Paper texture the same size that you used when applying the effects.

Cloning the image with Tracing Paper enabled

The image with Tracing Paper turned off

The cloned image, ready for the paint strokes

2 Painting the photo into the image. Before you begin to clone the photo into your image, add a new layer to your file.* Then choose the Soft Cloner variant of Cloners in the Brush Selector. The opacity of the Soft Cloner changes based on the pressure that you apply to the stylus. You might need to increase the size of

the Soft Cloner and reduce its opacity to about 10% to cover a large area smoothly. I set my brush size to 380 pixels in the Property Bar for this 1800-pixel-wide image. Enable Tracing Paper (Canvas > Tracing Paper) so that you can see your subject as you import it into the file. Beginning with light pressure, I carefully painted

the subject's face solidly into the clone, and then added softer, lower-opacity edges around the subject. I did not follow the oval vignette in the example, but created an irregular edge that showcased the hair, hat, and shoulders. It's a good idea to toggle Tracing Paper off and on as you work, so you can see how much of the actual image is coming in. With Tracing Paper enabled, it can be challenging to see the true tone and color.

 Saving a file with a clone source. When you choose File, Clone in Painter, Painter makes a copy of the file, with a link to the original file. To embed the original file as a clone source in the working image, save the file in RIFF format. The clone source will be visible in the Clone Source panel. To open the Clone Source panel, choose Window > Clone Source.

LEARN MORE ABOUT. . .

★ adding a layer . . page 60
★ building a paper surface. . . page 213
★ cloning in Painter . . page 159

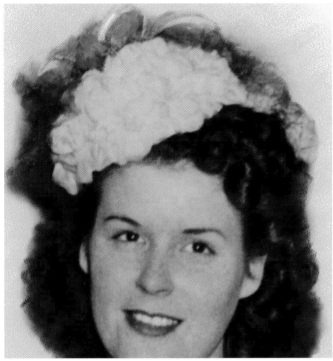

The first textured strokes on the hat feathers and hair

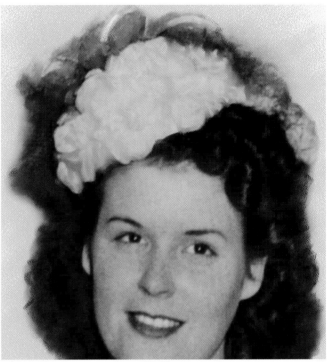

The simplified forms on the crinkled hat material

3 **Adding textured brushwork.** Now that you've painted the focal point of the portrait into your clone image, it's time to add textured brush work. For more realistic texture, you'll want to keep Basic Paper chosen in the Paper Selector, and use the same scale you used when building the paper surface.* In this step, you'll paint brushstrokes on the hair, clothes, and background using color imported from the clone source photo. Make a new version of the Square Chalk variant that you can use for cloning using the instructions in the "Making a grainy chalk cloning brush" sidebar.

As you use the Square Chalk Cloner, pay careful attention to the direction of the forms. Take care not to scrub or paint strokes in only one direction. My subject had curly hair, and this inspired me to paint short, curved strokes using my stylus. The feathers and the crinkled material on the hat provided more opportunities I painted short, dabbing strokes with my stylus, focusing on

the more important planes to simplify the shapes in the crinkled hat material.

Making a grainy chalk cloning brush. You can set up the Square Chalk to sample color from a clone source while you paint. Choose the Square Chalk variant of Chalk & Crayons from the Brush Selector. In the Color panel, click the Clone Color button (the Stamp). Using Clone Color allows you to paint with the Square Chalk and import color from the source image. Save your new brush by choosing Save Variant from the Brushes menu, and give it a unique name. I named my brush "Square Chalk Cloner." Finally, for good Painter housekeeping, return the original Square Chalk variant to its default settings by choosing Restore Default variant from the Brushes menu.

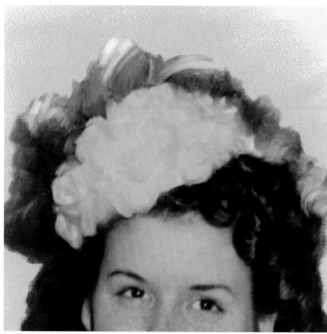

More highlights added on the hair and hat

Refining the dark shapes on the hair

4 **Blending areas on the hair, hat, and clothes.** In areas where detail is not important, you can use the Grainy Water variant of Blenders to simplify and smooth areas of the cloned photo and to subdue the chalk texture if you feel it is too strong. Making these kinds of judgements helps the design of the portrait and makes it more unique. For instance, simplifying the shapes in the hat focuses more attention on the woman's face.

The opacity and grain of the Grainy Water are affected by the pressure you apply to the stylus. If you apply less pressure to the stylus, you will reveal more texture; if you apply heavier pressure, you'll notice the blending will be smoother, with less texture. To refine overall shape and texture of the hair, I used the Grainy Water to blend the edges of the hair.

LEARN MORE ABOUT. . .

⋆ form and volume. . . pages 93–103

5 **Painting more grainy strokes.** After blending, I switched to the Square Chalk Cloner brush. Using gentle pressure, I applied grainy strokes to the edges of the hair and to the highlights on the curls. In areas where I wanted brighter highlights, I switched to the Square Chalk and used a lighter color to brighten them. I did not apply a lot of expressive brushstrokes to the face because I wanted to preserve the integrity of the portrait. When painting over the forms on your subject, imagine that you are sculpting the forms. Let your stylus and brushstrokes follow the direction of the forms.

The final brushwork on the hair and hat

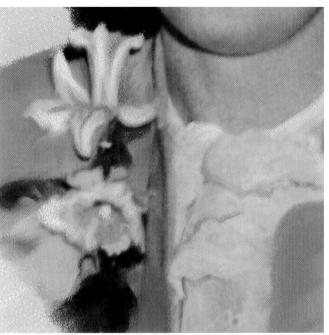

Adding yellow brushstrokes to the flowers with the Square Chalk and the blended ruffles on the blouse

6 **Adding final touches.** Take a careful look at your image. What details need to be refined? To finish, I used the Square Chalk to apply yellow color to the flower and lighter colors to the blouse. Then, using the Grainy Water, I blended a few areas on the blouse to simplify the ruffles and focus more attention on her face. I also added more light brown brushstrokes to the "paint" layer using the Square Chalk.

Blending edges on the hat

Congratulations! You've learned how to use Painter's powerful cloning features, how to make a cloning brush, and more! Now you're ready to move on to the next technique.

The final Layers panel

Afternoon Self Portrait

Painting an Expressive Oil Portrait

Wet Oily Brush brushstrokes

Oily Bristle brushstroke

Oily Bristle strokes with *Palette Knife* strokes used to blend, using various sizes

ARTIST'S MATERIALS

Tablet: Medium-soft pressure

Program: Painter

Paper: Artists' Canvas

Paint: Colors sampled from the photo or from the Color panel

Brushes:

• Wet Oily Brush: size varies with pressure

• Oily Bristle: size varies with pressure; grain varies subtly with pressure

• Oil Palette Knife: size varies with pressure, blends paint

• Tiny Smeary Knife: opacity varies with pressure, applies paint and blends

To create *Afternoon Self Portrait*, I used the Oils including brushes with Artists' Oils capabilities and Palette Knives—to paint over a reference photo. Using a different work flow than earlier in the chapter, I laid in large areas of wet paint directly over a clone of the photo. To improve the composition, I simplified the background and added colors that would focus on the face. For more interest in the background, I modulated the background color and used interesting curves and angles in the brushwork. For smoother brushwork on the face and for details in the hair, I used tiny palette knives.

The scanned portrait photo

1 **Selecting a photo, scanning, and cloning.** Choose a photo with good lighting and contrast to use as a reference for your portrait painting. My subject had dramatic side lighting that would add interest to the portrait. My original photo measured 1200 × 1600 pixels. Adjust the tonal range* of your photo in Photoshop or Painter, if needed.

In Painter, make a clone of your image* and name it. I named my clone Portrait Retouch to keep my version files organized.

LEARN MORE ABOUT. . .

* adjusting tonal range. . . page 125
* making a clone. . . page 159

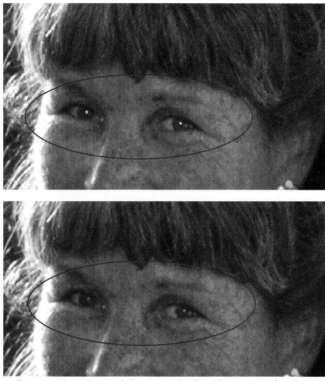

Before retouching the overly bright catchlights (above) and after (below)

Strokes painted with the Oily Bristle, Wet Oily Brush, and Palette Knife

2 **Retouching the image.** Take a good look at your image. Are there areas that you would like to improve by retouching? You can do the retouching in Photoshop or Painter, as described earlier in this chapter. Working on the clone image, I used a tiny airbrush to subdue the overly bright catchlights in the eye. I wanted a natural look, so I left the rest of the image as it was. To retouch, zoom in, and use the Dropper to sample color from a nearby not-so-bright highlight. Then use a tiny Fine Detail Airbrush (Airbrushes) to paint over the highlights. Save your retouched image, and then make a clone of it, save and name the new clone version. (I named mine Portrait Study 1.)

LEARN MORE ABOUT. . .

* Artists' Oils. . . pages 164, 222

3 **Painting and blending.** Oils brushes with Artists' Oils* capabilities let you apply wet oily paint and blend pigment just like traditional wet oil paint. These Oils are ideal for painting from scratch or for working over photos because of the medium's unique blending capabilities. Choose the Oils in the Brush Selector, and the Oily Bristle variant. Use your stylus to paint a brush-stroke. You'll notice that the brush run out of paint like a conventional brush. To apply new color with each brush-stroke, lift the stylus and then replace it on the tablet when you make a new stroke. Now try painting with the Wet Oily Brush variant of Oils. To blend existing color (or the existing pixels in your reference), do not lift the stylus, but continue to brush back and forth. For more blending options, experiment with the Palette Knives such as the Palette Knife, and Smeary Palette Knife variants.

Painting over the background with the Oily Bristle

Adding brushwork with the Oily Bristle and Palette Knife

4 **Simplifying the background.** You can focus more attention on the face and improve the composition of a portrait photo by reducing the clutter in the background. Working directly on the image canvas, I used the Oily Bristle and Wet Oily Brush variants Oils to apply oily paint and smear it over the background. Laying in the background first also helps to refine the design and brings the subject forward in the composition.

You can turn on Clone Color in the Color panel to paint with color from your retouched photo, or you can sample color from the working image using the Dropper and paint freehand strokes.

I chose to paint on the canvas to take advantage of the Artists' Oils feature that the entire canvas is covered with oil. The oily feeling is less noticeable when painting on a layer. For more information, see the sidebar on page 222.

5 **Painting the hair.** For this image, I used an additional reference photo as inspiration for the hair. The bangs were thick in the original photo, and I wanted to paint the front of the hair differently. I used the second photo as a reference to look at, but did not clone with it.

 Using a reference image. You can open an image to refer to as you paint. Choose Window > Reference Image to open the panel. Painter can open 8-bit PSD or RIFF files with layers, TIFF and JPEG files. The panel features an eyedropper for sampling color from the reference, a magnifier button and a grabber hand for panning an enlarged image. The size of the panel can be enlarged for easy viewing.

The Reference Image panel with photo

The broader strokes painted with the Oily Bristle brush on the highlights

The thinner brushstrokes painted with a small Palette Knife

Now that the background is laid in, paint brushstrokes that follow the general shapes in the hair using a small Oily Bristle brush. Then use a smaller Oily Bristle brush or a small Palette Knife (Palette Knives) to repaint the area. To paint thinner strands of hair or to smooth over the skin, you can also use the Tiny Smeary Knife variant of Palette Knives. Applying strokes using a light pressure allows you to apply low-opacity paint and blend. Let your brushstrokes follow the growing pattern in the hair.

If you overwork an area and want to start over, you can switch to

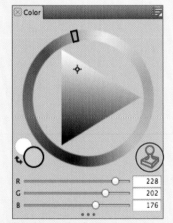

The Clone Color button is enabled in the Color panel.

the Soft Cloner variant of Cloners temporarily to bring the details back.

 Painting on a layer with Artists' Oils. If you prefer painting on a layer instead of directly over the cloned photo, you can do so using Oils brushes with Artists' Oils capabilities, but the paint will have less of an oily feel. Make a new layer, and in the Layers panel, enable the Pick Up Underlying Color button. Using Pick Up Underlying Color allows you to pull color from any layers and the Canvas below and mix it with new color you paint on the layer. When you apply Artists' Oils brushstrokes to the layer, oil is applied within the Artists' Oils brushstrokes.

The Layers panel with Pick Up Underlying Color enabled

The image before the sunlit strands of hair were painted.

Loosely painting the sunlit hair in the left side of the image

As you can see, I used a small Oily Bristle brush to paint broader strokes to lay in the shapes and values on the hair (and to cover the photo pixels). Then, using the Tiny Smeary Knife (Palette Knives) with varied pressure on my stylus, I layered sensitive, thinner strokes over the top that would suggest the individual strands of hair.

 Painting the pixels. Leaving unpainted, stray pixels from the photo can make your portrait look untidy. As you use your photo for a template, be careful to paint over all of the photo pixels. You can zoom in to 200–300% and use the Grabber Hand to pan around as you examine your image and then touch up the unpainted pixels with a small brush.

6 **Painting the shirt.** Carefully study the folds in the fabric and forms of the subject. Use the Oily Bristle variant of Oils (with color sampled from your image) to paint the shirt. To sample color from your image as you paint, use the Dropper tool. Paint expressively and loosely, as you sculpt the forms. Carefully study the forms on the figure. The highlights and shadows, and the transitions in between the lights and darks will give you important clues as to how to paint the forms.

For my image, I used the Oily Bristle to paint the shirt, and shoulders. Much of this area was in shadow and not in the center of interest. My subject was wearing a print shirt. To focus more attention on the face by simplifying the shirt, I loosely painted the shirt using varied blues.

Using a low-opacity Oily Bristle brush the sculpt the face

The in-progress sculpted and smoothed face

7 Modeling the face and painting details. As you examine the forms and planes of the face, remember the form and value studies that you painted in Chapters 5, 6, and 7. The human form can be simplified into cylinders, spheres, and cubes, and so on. Pay careful attention to the highlights and shadows on the facial forms, because these lighting transitions reveal the forms.

To work out the skin tone colors, you can sample color from the working image and paint freehand brushstrokes as I did, or sample color from the retouched photo by enabling Clone Color for a particular brush and then painting. I recommend using the Oily Bristle brush or Wet Oily Brush (Oils) and a small Oil Palette Knife or Smeary Palette Knife (Palette Knives) to paint over most of the skin. To preserve the freckled skin, I lowered the opacity of the brushes to about 20% in the Property Bar. As you paint, let your brushstrokes follow the direction of the forms and planes of the face. While carefully paying attention to the lighting, I sculpted the rounded forms and planes of the face* using the Oily Bristle brush (Oils), the Oil Palette Knife and a low opacity Smeary Palette Knife (Palette Knives).

To add activity and interest to the portrait, I used looser brushwork on the hair and clothing, but I painted the face more realistically because it is the center of interest. To emphasize the nose highlight, I used a small Oily Bristle brush and my stylus to paint a fairly straight brushstroke down the nose to widen the highlight. Then I strengthened the highlight on the side of the face using this brush.

LEARN MORE ABOUT. . .

* modeling form. . . page 111

The more refined highlights along the side of the face and brighter teeth

Adding a few more highlights to the hair with a small Oily Bristle

For smoother details on the skin, I recommend using the Tiny Smeary Knife. Zoom in and use this tiny brush to touch up areas on the face. To preserve the natural freckled skin, I lowered the opacity of the Tiny Smeary Knife to about 20% in the Property Bar.

For the teeth, I began by sampling color from a light area on the teeth. Then I lightened it a bit more in the Color panel, and applied the lighter color using a low-opacity Tiny Smeary Knife. I also used this technique to brighten the whites of the eyes. To finish, I modulated color in the shadows and blended the shirt collar. To finish, I used a small Oily Bristle to paint a few warmer colored highlights on the sunlit areas of the hair. You can see the final image on page 218.

Good work! Now that you've completed this photo-painting technique, you're ready to move on to the next chapter.

The brushwork on the face and hair are nearly complete in this detail.

Live Aloha

14
COMPOSING FROM THE IMAGINATION

This chapter reviews some of the techniques taught in earlier chapters, such as enhancing the center of interest. It carries these concepts further to build compositions with multiple elements. The first project begins with a digital sketch that is composed in Adobe Photoshop Touch; this part of the process is featured in Chapter 2. After the layered sketch is opened in Photoshop and adjustments are made, it is saved and opened in Painter. Brushwork is applied in Painter to complete the collage. The second project has three parts. In the first section, you'll use Photoshop to lay out a composition using Painter sketches and scanned drawings. In the second section, you'll open the composition in Painter and add rich brushwork (including painting wet-into-wet) with Digital Watercolor and more. In the final section, you'll take the image back into Photoshop, where you'll build a layer mask that will hide areas of the light layer, including painting on the layer mask with your stylus and large brushes.

 Live Aloha was inspired by my love of Hawaii, its people, and its culture, and was created using imagery from my time spent in Hawaii. After sketching the collage in Adobe Photoshop Touch, I imported the layered sketch into Photoshop, where I made adjustments. To finish, I opened the working collage file in Painter and added brushwork to the sky, mountains, and ocean.

Where All Creativity Comes From was inspired by a wonderful dream. When I searched my library of sketchbooks for ideas, I came across the drawing of lilies, which gave me a concrete direction. To depict the scene of an angel bringing inspiration to the artist, I used a stylized approach that incorporates drawings and rich, colored washes. To guide the eye around the illustration and tell the story, I designed a circular composition.

CP

Collage and Retouching

The Live Aloha *collage sketch created in Adobe Photoshop Touch*

Clone Stamp Pressure, *various sizes*

The iPad gives me freedom to sketch with various materials when I'm away from my studio. For the *Live Aloha* collage, I began by making a photo collage sketch on my iPad using Adobe Photoshop Touch; then I used Photoshop and Painter to complete the work.

The collage sketch with layers in Adobe Photoshop Touch

1 Opening the layered file. Launch Photoshop and open the PSD file that you exported from Adobe Photoshop Touch. In Photoshop, the layers will appear in the Layers panel. Save a new version of your file so that you can leave your sketch file untouched in case you need it later.

The Layers panel in Photoshop showing the layers in the collage file

Using Free Transform to scale the surfer layer

Retouching the background with the Clone Stamp tool. The surfer layer is hidden in this example.

2 Finessing the composition.

Carefully examine your image. Will your composition have more impact if you change the size of one of the elements? Do the individual elements need refinement?

For more interest in my collage, and to enhance its focal point, I subtly increased the size of the surfer layer, and I retouched the layer with the mountain and ocean.

In the Layers panel, click on the name of the layer that you want to work with. To edit its size, choose Edit > Free Transform > Scale.* Press the Shift key and drag on a corner handle to scale the element. When

LEARN MORE ABOUT. . .

* Free Transform. . . page 127
* Clone Stamp tool. . . pages 202–204

you are satisfied with the size, press the Enter/Return key to accept.

Target the next layer that you want to edit. (For my image, I chose the lower layer with the ocean.) Choose the Clone Stamp tool and the Clone Stamp Pressure preset.* Use cloning to simplify the water. In my image, I removed some of people from the water behind the surfer. I retouched carefully, as I wanted to preserve the shimmering light on the water. If you see distracting artifacts in your image, simplify them by retouching the areas.

When your image is as you like it, save a new version of your file in PSD format. Good work! You have completed this section of the project.

In the next spread, we will open the working collage in Painter and add brushwork to the collage.

Exporting a sketch from Photoshop Touch.

You can export an Adobe Photoshop Touch file with layers using File Sharing between the iPad and your computer. The layered file can then be opened in Photoshop. Connect the iPad to your computer, launch iTunes, and choose Apps. On your iPad, launch Photoshop Touch and select Share. When the dialog box appears, select the file and the PSD file format. On your computer, launch iTunes, select File Sharing, and select the Adobe Photoshop Touch app. The file you shared will appear in the window on the right. Select the name of your file and click the Save To button to save the file to your computer. Launch Photoshop, navigate to the file, and open it.

Adding Painter Brushwork to the Collage

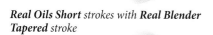

Real Oils Short *strokes with* ***Real Blender Tapered*** *stroke*

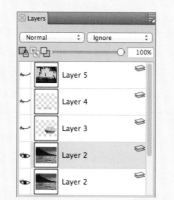

Soft Diffused Brush *stroke with* ***Round Water Blender*** *strokes*

The retouched mountain and water is shown in this detail.

The in-progress painting on the sky with the brighter color painted with the Real Oils Short

ARTIST'S MATERIALS

Tablet: Medium-soft pressure

Program: Painter

Paper: French Watercolor Paper: a medium-grain texture

Paint: Mix color using the Mixer

Brushes:
- Real Oils Short: opacity, size and blending vary with pressure
- Real Blender Tapered: opacity, size and blending vary with pressure
- Soft Diffused Brush: opacity, size, and grain vary with pressure
- Round Water Blender: opacity, size, and grain vary with pressure

1 Setting up in Painter. Launch Painter and open the layered file that you saved in Photoshop and save a new version of the file in RIFF format. (I named mine Live Aloha paint.psd). For more flexibility, make a copy of the layer you want to paint by choosing Layers > Duplicate Layer. (For my image, I chose Layer 2 with the mountains, sky, and ocean.)

The duplicate of Layer 2 is selected in the Layers panel.

2 Painting with Oils. Prior to painting, the visibility for the above layers is turned off for fewer distractions while painting. To paint over the sky and mountain, I used an Oils brush and a blender. Using loose, expressive strokes, I painted brighter colors onto the sky.

The Real Oils Short variant of Oils works nicely for painting clouds. Using the Real Oils Short, paint loosely over the sky in your image. I also used the Real Oils Short to paint over the mountain and water. To blend and smooth areas, use the Real Blender Tapered variant of Blenders.

The painted oil brushwork on the sky and water, prior to the clear painted glazes

Painting clear transparent washes of Digital Watercolor onto the water

A detail of the final collage is shown in this example.

3 **Painting colored glazes.** Next, I used Digital Watercolor brushes on a new layer to paint transparent washes of color onto the water. In the examples above, the surfer layer, palm trees layer, and title layer are hidden.

For control and flexibility, add a new layer to your file. I renamed this layer "washes." Set the Composite Method for the new layer to Gel in the Layers panel. Choose the Soft Diffused Brush variant of Digital Watercolor,* and paint loose brushstrokes over the water in your image.

To blend areas, I suggest using the Round Water Blender* variant of Digital Watercolor. I painted washes of tropical turquoise and aqua colors over the water in my image. The transparent washes of color enlivened the water with a beautiful glow.

4 **Finessing final details.** Now that the painting of the mountains, sky, and water is complete, turn on the layers above the painted layer. Step back and take a careful look at your collage. Are there areas that need adjustment? Are you pleased with the color and contrast in your image? If your composition calls for it, add brushwork to other layers. For my image, I chose to leave the palm trees layer and surfer layer as edited photos, and leave the title layer as is. The final *Live Aloha* collage can be seen on page 192.

Good work! You have completed the collage project. In the following project, you will work with scanned drawings, digital sketches, and paint to create an imaginative composition that incorporates several elements.

LEARN MORE ABOUT. . .

* Round Water Blender. . . pages 204, 206
* Digital Watercolor. . . pages 144, 145, 177

The washes layer is selected in the Layers panel.

The sketch composition for Where All Creativity Comes From

Compositing Sketches and Scans in Photoshop

The drawing of the artist created in Painter

The scanned drawing of the white lilies

You can perform this stage of the project in Photoshop or Painter. I'm using Photoshop for this stage to demonstrate the portability between the two programs.

I wanted to combine traditional drawings that were scanned and touched up in Photoshop with a drawing created in Painter. I sketched the drawing of the artist in Painter using the Croquil Pen variant of Pens.

LEARN MORE ABOUT. . .

* scanning. . . pages 124–125
* the Clone Stamp. . . pages 202–204

1 **Assembling elements.** In the previous spread, you sketched in Painter. Now choose a sketch from your conventional sketchbook that you'd like to combine with your drawing done in Painter, or use pencils and paper to create a new drawing to scan.*

If you'd like to preserve the paper grain in your scan, use the Rubber Stamp to retouch the scan. I recommend using the pressure-sensitive Clone Stamp preset described in Chapter 13.*

I drew the pen sketch of the lilies from life in my 9 × 12-inch sketchbook. After scanning the drawing into Photoshop at 300 pixels per inch at actual size in grayscale mode,* I retouched the scan using my stylus and the Clone Stamp Pressure preset described in Chapter 13. I wanted

The retouched drawing

The drawing of the angel

Using Free Transform to scale the lilies

to preserve the paper texture (rather than clean up the drawing using the Eraser). Using the Clone Stamp Pressure, I retouched the handwriting from the lower portion of the sketch.

Next, I opened the drawing of the artist at her easel (the working composite file) in Photoshop. I also opened the scanned drawing of the lilies and a third pen drawing of an angel that was drawn in Painter.

Choose the Move tool, and drag and drop each element into your working composite file. You can also copy and paste the elements into the working file. Take time to enjoy positioning elements in your composition.

2 Transforming for more drama. Take a good look at your composition. Will your composition have more impact if you transform one of the elements?

To create a surreal juxtaposition of elements, I increased the size of the lilies, making them larger in proportion to the artist. I also made a duplicate of the lilies layer and transformed this image to be small enough

to fit onto the painting on the easel. I linked the artist and easel layers and merged them into one layer.

To transform an element that is on its own layer, select the layer in the Layers panel. Next, choose Edit > Free Transform,* and while pressing the Shift key (to constrain the proportions if you'd like), drag on a corner handle to change the size. (I increased the size of the lilies

 Using a layer mask. For the utmost in flexibility, use a layer mask to hide a portion of a layer rather than removing the area using an Eraser, which is much more destructive. To add a layer mask to a layer in Photoshop, select the layer and then click the Add Layer Mask button on the Layers panel. A mask filled with white appears to the right of the layer thumbnail. To hide a portion of the layer, paint with black on the mask; to reveal, paint with white. Layer masks work in a similar way in Painter. For more information, see page 207 later in this chapter.

Transforming the lily copy

The small lilies shown using Multiply mode

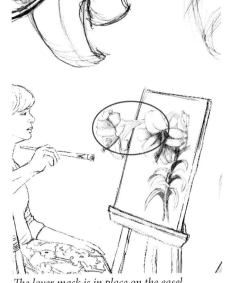
The layer mask is in place on the easel

by pulling on the handles.) When you've adjusted the Free Transform handles as you like them, double-click inside the marquee (or press the Return or Enter key) to accept the transform.

To make the white areas in the scanned sketch appear to be transparent, change the blend mode for this layer to Multiply in the Layers panel. I used this blend mode with the small lily and the lilies layers.

LEARN MORE ABOUT. . .

∗ Free Transform. . . page 127

∗ layers. . . page 127

3 **Masking an element.** To make a portion of an element appear in front of another, you can hide part of the layer underneath using a layer mask.∗ So the lily would extend past the edge, I selected the artist at easel layer and added a layer mask. I

The Layers panel showing the artist at easel layer with its mask

painted on the mask with black to hide the portion of the easel. The effect can be seen in the illustration above.

Now you've completed the assembly of your sketch images. Save the file in Photoshop format. Then save a new copy of the working file in Photoshop format. To make it easier to work with the image in Painter on the next spread, merge all of your drawing layers into one layer.∗

The Layers panel with the drawing layers merged

Adding Colored Brushwork in Painter

Broad Water Brush strokes

New Simple Water stroke

Soft Diffused Brush stroke with Pointed Wet Eraser and Round Water Blender strokes

ARTIST'S MATERIALS

Tablet: Medium-soft pressure

Program: Painter

Paper: French Watercolor Paper: a medium-grain texture

Paint: Mix color using the Mixer

Brushes:

- Broad Water Brush: opacity, grain, and blending vary with pressure

- New Simple Water: opacity and size vary with pressure

- Soft Diffused Brush: opacity, size, and grain vary with pressure

- Pointed Wet Eraser: opacity and size vary with pressure

- Round Water Blender: opacity, size, and grain vary with pressure

The composite drawing

Sampling color from the Mixer

1 Mixing colors. Experiment with color for your image by applying color to the Mixer. My illustration uses a palette of warm golds with accents of a varied orange, salmon, blue, and green.

The Mixer with colors. The Mix Color tool is chosen.

2 Applying colored washes. Open the composite sketch file you built in Photoshop, and add a new layer (in Gel mode) to hold the colored paint. In the Mixer panel, click on the Sample Color tool so that you can go to the Mixer and automatically pick up color with your brush and

The Layers panel with the new colored washes layer in Gel mode

The short dabs of color on the clouds

In this detail, you can see the modulated color on the background behind the lily stem.

stylus as you work. To add color in the order I did, begin with the background. I recommend using Digital Watercolor for the washes because this medium performs faster when

 A sensitive brush. The Broad Water Brush allows you to create beautiful transparent paint effects that are much like traditional watercolor. The opacity of the Broad Water Brush changes based on the pressure you apply, and the way it reacts to paper grain varies based on pressure. I love this brush because you can also control how it blends and bleeds into existing paint, by the pressure you apply to the stylus.

you have a large file with several layers. (Experiment with the Watercolor brushes and Watercolor media layers also, because the Watercolor brushes can achieve richer texture.) To paint loose transparent washes, choose the Digital Watercolor category and the Broad Water Brush variant. For an interesting background, paint shorter brushstrokes of varied color to give the area an active but subtle modulated look. Use varied pressure and angle on the stylus for more varied, natural brushstrokes. You can see this brushwork in the large detail of the painting above. I applied washes of varied blues, purples, and greens to the background. Then I added warmer gold tones to the focal point area (around the angel

in the sky) and varied blue-green and light yellow-green washes to the foreground grass.

The background washes are nearly complete.

Adding light-colored washes to the lilies

Adding color to the stamens

The washes in-progress on the painting

3 Painting form with wet washes.
If you want the foreground colors to mix with the background colors (as in traditional "wet-into-wet" watercolor), paint all of the colored elements on the same layer. If you don't want the colors to run into one another when you blend, paint the foreground elements on a new layer. I painted the foreground elements on their own layer, so I could control the washes and clean up the edges of elements with the Pointed Wet Eraser if needed. Because I wanted the colors to mix on the large flowers and the leaves and stem, I painted them on this same layer. Later, I planned to paint the artist, easel, and chair on this layer as well.

To paint form and detailed areas (the angel, artist, and flowers, for instance), you can reduce the size of the Broad Water Brush, or if you'd like crisper edges, try using the New Simple Water brush. To blend, experiment with the Round Water Blender.* I used the New Simple Water Brush to paint the central elements on the flowers. Then to soften the transitions in color on the petals, I used a low-opacity Round Water Blender.

You can paint a darker colored wash, and then use a small Broad

Water Brush to paint into the original wet Digital Watercolor* paint with a lighter color and achieve subtle watery blends (as I did, for the angel). Because I wanted to have

LEARN MORE ABOUT. . .

* Round Water Blender. . . pages 230, 231, 236, 238, 240
* Digital Watercolor. . . pages 144, 145, 177

The Layers panel showing the foreground washes layer selected

Using a small Broad Water Brush to lay in the first color on the angel's robe

Going over the area with a lighter color, with a little more pressure to blend the shoulder

Adding touches of golden yellow to the shoulders with the small Broad Water Brush

control on the edges on the angel, I added a new layer for the angel's color. When laying in the lighter color to blend, use a light pressure on your

The Layers panel showing the angel color layer selected

stylus and dab the lighter color on. Then gently pull into the darker color with the brush.

For the angel's robe, I used a small Broad Water Brush to paint loose washes of blue-green on the robe, leaving white areas for the highlights. Then I chose a lighter version of the color and used more pressure to sculpt the folds in the clothing and to blend areas. To warm up the highlights, I added touches of golden yellow to the angel's shoulders and back.

Throughout the process of adding new layers for the washes, I kept the BW drawing layer on top. This allows you to add opaque paint on a lower layer if needed, while keeping the drawing intact on top.

Using a small New Simple Water brush to add color to the angel's flower wand, ribbon sash, and feet

The loose, light washes on the figure and the back of the chair on the foreground washes layer

Adding more vibrant color to the flower petals and stamen on the foreground washes layer

Painting loose brushwork on the stem and leaves on the foreground washes layer

Next, using a similar brushing technique that I used for the angel, I laid in light washes to suggest the forms in the artist's face and folds in the clothing. Because the artist is a secondary element in the composition, I used less saturated colors.

 A custom colorless Round Water Blender. If you'd like to use the Round Water Blender to blend without applying new color, open the Brush Controls (Window > Brush Controls > Well). In the Well panel reduce the Resat value of the Blender to 0%. Save your new variant for use later.

4 **Adding details and texture.** Now that you have the overall washes painted, it's a good time to step back and look at your composition. Are there areas that need more contrast? Would it help to subdue color in areas, or to add brighter color in an area? Where do you want to add more details?

For more flexibility, add a new layer for the details. To paint crisp-edged details, use a small New Simple Water brush (about 5 pixels).

Using a low-opacity New Simple Water brush, I painted darker tones on the easel where it was in shadow, and added deeper color to the interior of the large lilies. To make the foreground elements stand out more

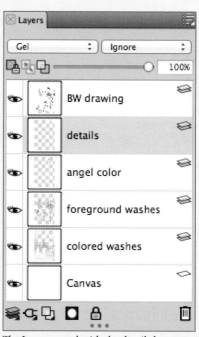

The Layers panel with the details layer selected

Adding vivid color to the small lilies

Using light pressure to apply medium-toned washes "wet-into-wet" on the clothing and chair

and the background have a subtle, rich texture, I used the default Broad Water Brush to modulate deeper blue and purple washes onto the background. You can see this color

in the area behind the easel in the illustrations above. For the small lily growing out of the artist's canvas, I used more vibrant, saturated colors and applied them with the New Simple Water brush. To complete

the artist, chair, and easel, I selected the foreground washes layer again and loosely applied medium-toned browns and blues, allowing the watery colors to overlay and to mix on the layer.

 Preserving "wet" paint. To keep the Digital Watercolor (or Watercolor layer) paint "wet," save your working file in RIFF format to preserve the native layer effects and Painter's native media. "Wet" paint allows fluid blending, similar to conventional watercolor paint.

 Selectively softening and touching up. In traditional watercolor, you can use pure water with a brush to soften an edge on existing paint. In Painter, try the Soft Diffused Brush variant of Digital Watercolor (sized to about 5–10 pixels) and choose white in the Color panel. (White is analogous to clear water.) Gently brush the area with your stylus, pulling from the edge into the area of paint. To remove paint from an area, use the Wet Eraser or the Pointed Wet Eraser variant of Digital Watercolor. The Wet Erasers are also useful for brightening highlights.

| The image before the lighting effect | The light effect applied to the filled layer | The light layer is now set to Multiply. |

5 Adding to the mood. You can use the Apply Lighting effect to add mood and color to your image, to focus more attention on your center of interest, and to unify the composition. For the most flexibility, make a new layer to hold your light. You'll need to fill the layer with a color for the lighting effect to work because the filter cannot operate on a layer without pixel information. (I filled my new layer with a rich golden color.) Now, choose Effects > Surface Control > Apply Lighting, and choose the Splashy Colors light. This light has two light sources: gold and blue. The gold will warm the lower part of the image, and the blue will neutralize color in the upper area. For an effect like mine, make these changes: Click on the large circle on the gold light and drag it up toward the right corner, with the small end pointing up. Then click on the large circle on the blue light and drag it down toward the lower left. When you have your settings as you like them, save and name your custom light.

To blend the colors in the light layer with the image, change its Composite Method to Multiply in the Layers panel. I liked this effect, but I decided to keep the original clearer color in the focal point and

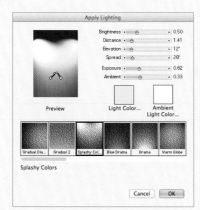

The Apply Lighting dialog box with settings for the Splashy Colors light

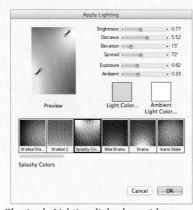

The Apply Lighting dialog box with settings for the custom light

Detail showing light around the angel

Enhancing Lighting Using a Gradient Layer Mask

Y ou can create a layer mask in Painter, but I chose to use Photoshop for this layer mask because Photoshop allows more control if you want to use multiple gradients in a layer mask. I used the layer mask to hide areas of the light layer that I did not want to use.

The light areas that the mask will hide

around the artist, and use the light layer at full strength in other areas. A layer mask is the ideal way to (non-destructively) hide part of a layer that you don't want to use.

With the lighting on a layer you can control the strength of the light using both the opacity of the layer, and the area of the light using a layer mask. Building the layer mask is described in the following sidebar. Make sure to save your working Painter file in RIFF format. On a second copy of your file, drop the color paint layers to the canvas, leaving only the line drawing and the lighting layers above the canvas. To drop specific layers, Shift-select them and choose Drop from the Layers panel menu. Then save this copy in Photoshop format.

1 Opening the file in Photoshop. Open the image with the drawing and light layers, and colored brush-work on the canvas that you created in Painter and saved in Photoshop format. You will see the layers in the Layers panel in Photoshop.

The Layers panel showing the light layer selected, with the Blend mode set to Multiply, and opacity lowered. The BW drawing layer is also set to Multiply.

2 Setting up for the layer mask. Decide what portion of your light layer you want to hide with the mask. I wanted to enhance the mood of my illustration by neutralizing colors in some areas, while highlighting the center of interest. To achieve this, I needed to make a layer mask with two gradient areas. This process requires a few steps because the Gradient tool overwrites itself if you try to apply it twice.

To add the layer mask, click the Add Layer Mask icon at the bottom of the Layers panel. An empty mask filled with white appears to the right of the layer thumbnail.

Return Photoshop's foreground and background color swatches to the default of black and white by pressing "D."

Pulling the gradient on the layer mask. You can see the lighter area created by the mask.

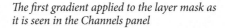

The first gradient applied to the layer mask as it is seen in the Channels panel

The selection loaded from the layer mask. You can also see the lighter area under the mask.

3 Applying the first gradient. To set up a layer mask like mine, choose the Gradient tool from the Toolbox, and in the Options Bar choose the Radial Gradient. (Again, set your Foreground color to black and your Background color to white in the Toolbox.) From the Gradient Picker, choose the Foreground to Background gradient. Position the tool and pull the gradient out with the stylus. A long line

Choosing the Radial gradient from the Options Bar. Select the Foreground to Background gradient.

creates a larger, more gradual gradient, and a short one creates a steeper, smaller gradient. To create the gradient at the top, I pulled about one-third of the way down the image, at an angle. You should have a white background in your mask, and a dark area where you added the gradient. This dark area hides part of the light layer. Apply the gradient carefully. It might take a few times to achieve the effect that you want. I wanted to create a soft glow, a lighter area around the angel that had no hard edges, so the soft gradient was the ideal tool to use.

By default, Photoshop overwrites the first gradient when you apply a second one. Here's a great workaround: You can load the layer mask as a selection by Ctrl/Cmd-clicking the layer mask thumbnail in the Layers panel. With this selection active, you can protect the original gradient and pull the second gradient in the lower part of the image.

Pulling the second gradient across the artist and easel, with the selection active above

The two gradients in the layer mask, viewed in the Channels panel

You can see the soft light areas on the angel, artist, and easel.

Now that the selection is active, use the Gradient tool to pull the second gradient. If you don't get it the way you want it, choose Edit > Undo. If you continually reapply the second gradient, it can begin to erode the original one because of the soft-edged selection. The illustration above shows my layer mask with the two gradients. In the illustration on the top right, you can see the two lighter glow areas that help to accentuate the center of interest. I was close to the effect that I wanted, but the image needed a little more emphasis on the angel. To accomplish this, I painted on the layer mask right over the angel. In the next step, you'll brighten areas of your image even more by editing the layer mask using your stylus and a large, soft-edged brush.

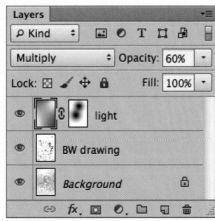

The light layer mask with its two gradients, as seen in the Layers panel

Editing the layer mask with a soft brush

The layer mask with brushwork, as seen in the Channels panel

Detail of the final image showing the enhanced lighting and final details

4 Painting on the layer mask. You can use a big soft brush and your stylus to paint on the layer mask and add to the gradient areas. I used this technique to hide areas of the light layer so that more of the original color on the angel and the clouds underneath would be revealed. I also used this technique in a more subtle way on the artist and easel.

Choose the Brush tool and the Soft Round preset from the Brush Preset picker. Size the brush to 300 pixels. Set the Opacity to about 30% and Flow to 50% in the Options Bar. Make sure black is still chosen for the Foreground Color, and that the layer mask thumbnail is still selected. Use a light touch on your stylus and brush onto the area of the light layer (mask) that you want to edit. For larger areas, increase the size of the brush. (I used the brush up to a size of 960 pixels.)

It's helpful to view the illustration while you edit the mask. When you have the layer mask the way you want it, you might want to experiment by

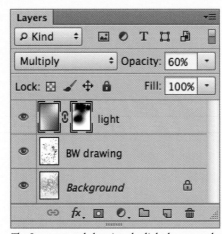

The Layers panel showing the light layer mask with the brushwork selected

adjusting the opacity of the light layer. (I settled on 60%.)

Remember to save your working file in Photoshop format to preserve the layers.

If you want to take your image back into Painter to add more brushwork, Painter will open the Photoshop file and recognize the layer mask that you built in Photoshop.

I opened my file again in Painter and used the Runny Wash Bristle variant of Watercolor on a new Watercolor layer to add a few darker hues and more texture to the background behind the flower and figure.

Congratulations! You have completed the project. On the next page you'll find information about masked layer sets in Photoshop.

Masking using a nested layer set in Photoshop. The introduction of masked folders in Photoshop 7 allowed users to apply masks not only to layers, but also to layer sets. With Photoshop CS and later versions, Photoshop allows the nesting of folders, each with its own mask. Although the steps I've outlined in this chapter work with each version of Photoshop that supports layer masking, current versions of the program allow far more editing flexibility. In this example, I began by applying a layer mask (the first gradient) to the light layer. Then I added a layer set (folder), put the light layer into the set, and assigned a mask to the set (the second gradient). Finally, I placed the layer set into a second layer set and added a mask to it. On this mask, I painted with the large soft brush. If I needed to edit one of the masks, I could do so without disturbing the other masks.

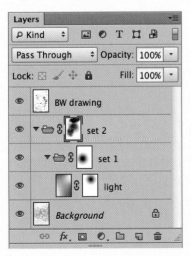

Where All Creativity Comes From

In this project, you learned about portability between Painter and Photoshop using your own drawings and sketches. You practiced sketching in Painter and then, in Photoshop, you incorporated scanned images with the Painter drawings to build a composite drawing. Next, you took the image back into Painter, where you added rich Digital Watercolor washes and a lighting effect on a layer. After saving a new copy of the file, you dropped the colored wash layers to the Canvas to get the image ready to open in Photoshop again, where you edited the lighting layer using layer masks. I enjoy this workflow because it demonstrates the strengths of both programs.

In the next several pages, you'll find a gallery of my favorite paintings that span nearly two decades of working with Painter, Photoshop, the pressure-sensitive tablet, and the predecessors of these tools. I hope you enjoy walking down this memory lane of digital painting with me.

Gallery

This gallery of digital paintings spans more than two decades of painting on the computer, and focuses on paintings that I've created for my own personal expression.

I painted the first black-and-white images using a mouse and Image Studio before I owned a color Macintosh and a pressure-sensitive tablet. (Image Studio is a grayscale program that was written by Mark Zimmer and Tom Hedges, who later created Painter.) Then, beginning with an early black-and-white painting, I created *Tranquil Beach, Color* using Photoshop 1.0. After this color image, I used Painter (or a combination of Painter and Photoshop) and a Wacom pressure-sensitive to create the later paintings.

Jake and Maria, *painted from the imagination using a mouse and Image Studio, 1987. This study demonstrates the use of early digital pencil and smudge tools.*

Tranquil Beach, Color, *painted using a mouse and Photoshop 1.0, 1990. Beginning with the gray version, I created selections and channels in Photoshop 1.0 that would limit the paint. Then I set the brushes to use transparent paint modes that preserved the luminosity of the image. I used the Smudge tool to blend paint.*

Agave Meadow, *painted using a Wacom pressure-sensitive tablet and Painter 6.0, 1999. For this painting, I referred to drawings made on location. I also painted from my memory of the sparkling morning light and moisture in the air. To achieve a sense of atmosphere and sparkling light, I used a coarse canvas texture that would work well with the loose hatching strokes made with the Chalk and Pastel brushes.*

Agaves on the Edge, Summer. *For this painting, I referred to color studies made on location, and painted from my memory using a Wacom pressure-sensitive tablet and Oils brushes in Painter IX, 2004.*

Blue Nude, *painted using a Wacom pressure-sensitive tablet and Painter 6.1, 2000. This study was painted from the imagination using the expressive Opaque Bristle and Round Camelhair brushes.*

View From Point Loma, *painted using a Wacom pressure-sensitive tablet and Painter 7.1, 2002. While referring to drawings made on location, I also painted from my memory of the sparkling morning light at dawn and the atmosphere across the bay. To apply paint, I used custom oil brushes and the Opaque Bristle and Round Camelhair brushes. To finish, I blended areas using the Grainy Water.*

In the Barrel, *painted using a Wacom pressure-sensitive tablet and Painter 8.0, 2003. While referring to drawings of waves and my memories of surfing, I used custom oil brushes and the Round Camelhair brush. To finish, I blended areas using the Grainy Water, and then added more brushstrokes using Impasto brushes: the Distorto Impasto, and the Thick Bristle.*

For Light and Shadow Play, *I painted the live, blooming orchid plant from observation using a Wacom pressure-sensitive tablet and a variety of Oils brushes in Painter X, 2007.*

Lennox Twilight, *painted using a Wacom pressure-sensitive tablet and Oils brushes in Painter 12, 2011. For this painting, I referred to traditional watercolor studies painted on location in Australia. I also painted from my memory of the beautiful morning light on the clouds.*

A study for The Fetch. *Beginning with a color study painted with traditional opaque watercolor paint, I scanned my study and painted more brushwork using a Wacom pressure-sensitive tablet and Oils brushes in Painter X3. 2013.*

Appendix A
Vendor Information

HARDWARE

Apple Computer, Inc.
apple.com

Epson America / *Desktop color printers*
P.O. Box 2854
Torrance, CA 90509
epson.com

Wacom Technology Corp. / *Intuos and Bamboo tablets*
1311 SE Cardinal Court
Vancouver, WA 98683
wacom.com

INKS AND SUBSTRATES

Digital Art Supplies / *Substrates and Inks*
digitalartsupplies.com

Epson / *Substrates and Inks*
epson.com

InkjetMall / *Substrates and Inks*
inkjetmall.com

SOFTWARE

Adobe Systems / *Photoshop*
345 Park Avenue
San Jose, CA 95110
adobe.com

Corel / *Painter X3*
1600 Carling Avenue
Ottawa, ON
Canada K1Z 8R7
corel.com

Appendix B
Reference Materials

Here's a sampling of recommended references for both traditional and digital art forms.

ART BOOKS

Art Through the Ages
Fifth Edition
Revised by Horst de la Croix and Richard G. Tansey
Harcourt, Brace and World, Inc.
New York, Chicago, San Francisco, and Atlanta

The Art of Color
Johannes Itten
Van Nostrand Reinhold
New York

Drawing Lessons from the Great Masters
Robert Beverly Hale
Watson-Guptill Publications
New York

Mainstreams of Modern Art
John Canaday
Holt, Reinhart and Winston
New York

The Natural Way to Draw
Kimon Nicolaïdes
Houghton Mifflin Company
Boston

COMPUTER IMAGERY BOOKS

**Digital Art Studio
Techniques for Combining Inkjet
Printing with Tradional Art Materials**
*Karin Schminke, Dorothy Simpson Krause,
Bonny Pierce Lhotka*
Watson-Guptill Publications
New York

**Photoshop Restoration and
Retouching**
Katrin Eismann and Doug Nelson
New Riders
Berkeley, CA

Photoshop Studio with Bert Monroy
Bert Monroy
New Riders
Berkeley, CA

The Painter Wow! Book
Cher Threinen-Pendarvis
Peachpit Press
Berkeley, CA

The Photoshop CS3/CS4 Wow! Book
Linnea Dayton and Cristen Gillespie
Peachpit Press
Berkeley, CA

PUBLICATIONS

Communication Arts
Coyne & Blanchard, Inc.
110 Constitution Drive
Menlo Park, CA 94025
commarts.com

Plein Air Magazine
Streamline Publishing, Inc.
1901 South Congress Avenue
Suite 118
Boynton Beach, FL 33426
pleinairmagazine.com
outdoorpainter.com

Appendix C
Fine Art Output Suppliers

*My colleagues and I have worked
with these bureaus that specialize in
making large format prints for fine
artists.*

Cone Editions Press / *Fine Art Prints*
East Topsham, VT
coneeditions.com

Green Flash Photography / *Fine Art
Prints*
San Diego, CA
greenflashphotography.com

Nash Editions / *Fine Art Prints*
Manhattan Beach, CA
nasheditions.com

Salon Iris / *Fine Art Prints*
Vienna, Austria
salon-iris.com

Trillium Press / *Fine art prints; Monotypes;
Silk Screen*
Brisbane, CA
trillium-graphics.com

Urban Digital Color / *Fine art prints*
San Francisco, CA
urbandigitalcolor.com

Index

A

Acrylics brushes (Painter), 164, 198
    Real Dry Flat, 82–83
    Thick Acrylic Round, 52
Adjustments tool (Adobe Photoshop Touch), 38
Adobe Ideas
    coloring, 36–37
    overview, 13
    sketching, 34–35
Adobe Illustrator, 7
Adobe Photoshop. *See* Photoshop
Adobe Photoshop Touch
    collage sketch, 38–41
    exporting files to Photoshop, 13, 228–229
    File Sharing with computers, 229
    overview, 13
Adobe Systems, 258
Advanced Brush Controls (Painter), 67
Afternoon Self Portrait, 218
Agave Meadow, 250
Agaves on the Edge, Summer, vii, 251
Airbrush Hard Round brush (Photoshop), 54
Airbrush Soft High Density Grainy brush
    (Photoshop), 75–77
Airbrush Soft Round brush (Photoshop), 55,
    202–203, 206
Airbrush stylus (Painter), 3
Airbrushes brushes (Painter)
    Coarse Spray Airbrush, 55, 83
    Digital Airbrush, 3, 55
    Fine Detail Airbrush, 220
    Fine Spray Airbrush, 55, 82–83
    Soft Airbrush, 82
    Tapered Detail Air, 82
Along Tomales Bay, 9
Alt/Opt Modifier key (Intuos tablet), 45
Apple Computers, Inc., 258
Apply Color tool (Painter), 80, 120
Apply Surface Texture effect (Painter)
    Appearance of Depth
        Amount, 213
        Shine, 213
    Light Direction, 213
    Using menu, Paper, 213
Art History Brush (Photoshop), 58, 61
The Art of Color, 258
Art Through the Ages, 258
Artists' Oils brushes (Painter), 163–164, 166,
    168, 219–222
    Impressionist, 57

ArtStudio
    overview, 12
    painting
        color study, 20–23
        with wet paint, 24–25
    pencil sketching, 18–19
artwork (examples). *See* drawings/sketches/
    paintings
At work in the studio, xviii
atmosphere, building with hatching, 114–121,
    138, 141–143, 250
Autodesk's Sketchbook. *See* Sketchbook

B

Bamboo Solo stylus, 13
Basic Paper (Painter), 86, 94, 96, 106–107, 136
Bird of Paradise, 12, 25
Blend modes, 60
    Color Burn, 63, 182
    Dissolve, 115, 153
    Multiply, 63, 129, 146–147, 235, 243
    Normal, 114–115, 155
    Overlay, 38–40, 63, 182–183
    Soft Light, 63, 182–183, 185
    transparent, 38, 40, 182
Blender Bristle brush (Painter), 165–166
Blender Palette Knife brush (Painter), 164
Blenders brushes (Painter), 164
    Blender Bristle, 165–166
    Grainy Water, 106, 108, 211, 216–217
    Just Add Water, 162, 166
    Pointed Stump, 108
    Real Blender Tapered, 230
    Soft Blender Stump, 106, 108, 111
Blue Nude, 252
Bluetooth and PogoConnect stylus, 13
Blunt Chalk brush (Painter), 70
Blur tool
    Adobe Photoshop Touch, 38
    Photoshop, 58, 61
Broad Water Brush (Painter), 236–239, 241
Brush Controls (Painter)
    Angle Expression
        Bearing, 57
        Rotation, 57
    Color Expression, Rotation, 56
    Color Variability, Hue and Value, 70
    Dab Preview, 70
    Depth, 197
    Expression options, 71
    General, Cover method, 173
    Impasto panel, 190, 197
    Size, Expression
        Pressure, 70, 194
        Wheel, 55

Size, Min Size, 70
Spacing, 194
Stroke Jitter, Expression, Rotation, 57
Stroke Preview, 70
Brush Editor
    Sketchbook Express, 26
    Sketchbook Pro, 28–29
Brush Ghost (Painter), 73, 87
Brush panel (Brushes 3), 16
Brush panel (Photoshop)
    Brush Tip Shape, 61, 77, 153
    Color Dynamics
        Brightness Jitter, 64
        Control options, 64
        Foreground/Background Color Jitter, 64
        Hue Jitter, 64
        Purity, 64
        Saturation Jitter, 64
    Erodible Square tip, 102–103
    New Tool Preset, 179
    Scatter, Count Jitter Control, Rotation, 57
    Shape Dynamics
        Angle Jitter Control, Rotation, 56
        Size Jitter Control, Pen Pressure, 62, 77,
            152
        Size Jitter Control, Stylus Wheel, 55
    Smoothing, 65
    Softness slider, 103
    Texture
        consistency of, 156
        Fine Grain, 152, 182, 184
        Wrinkles, 157
    Transfer
        Flow Jitter Control, Stylus Wheel, 55
        Opacity Jitter Control, Pen Pressure, 63,
            99, 203
Brush panel (Procreate), 30–32
Brush Presets/Brush Preset Picker (Photoshop),
    90–91, 128
    Brush Size slider, 98, 102, 116, 155
    loading new libraries, 64, 73, 78
    options, 61
    Small List, 62, 77, 152
Brush Properties Puck
    Sketchbook Express, 26–27
    Sketchbook Pro, 28
Brush Selector (Painter)
    Brush Library, 69
        loading Painter 11 Artists' Oils, 164
    categories
        displaying as list, 69
        exporting/saving, 71
        naming new, 71
        opening/selecting, 47, 67, 87
    Recent Brushes, 69
Brush Size and Brush Opacity (ArtStudio), 18